W9-DFV-657

Problems of the Self

BD450
.W499

Problems of the Self

Philosophical Papers 1956—1972

BERNARD WILLIAMS
Knightbridge Professor of Philosophy in the University of Cambridge

CAMBRIDGE
At the University Press
1973

Published by the Syndics of the Cambridge University Press
Bentley House, 200 Euston Road, London NW1 2DB
American Branch: 32 East 57th Street, New York, N.Y.10022

© Cambridge University Press 1973

Library of Congress Catalogue Card Number: 72–97881

ISBN: 0 521 20225 6

Printed in Great Britain by
Western Printing Services Ltd, Bristol

Contents

For
Rebecca

Preface

This is a selection of the philosophical papers I have published, together with two new pieces and a couple of additional notes to older material. I have left some papers out on grounds of subject matter (what is here all relates to two or three themes), some on grounds of what I now think of them, and some for both reasons. The ones included I have tried so far as possible to leave as they were, but I have made one or two minor revisions, put in one or two footnotes of cross-reference, and done a limited amount of stylistic tinkering.

After some hesitation I have decided to include two critical notices of books, one of Strawson's *Individuals*, one of Shoemaker's *Self-Knowledge and Self-Identity*, even though the first, particularly, has very much the form of a book review. I have done this because both these books very much retain their interest, and because points raised in the notices relate closely to material in other papers. I have more or less cut down the notices to their argumentative content; if some expressions of praise have disappeared in the process, this is not because I have retracted them. The Shoemaker notice has also lost its first section, which now seems to me to make a lot of fuss about not much.

References to papers which have not been included will be found in a list at the end of the book, together with the original sources of those that are here. I am grateful to the original publishers for permission to reprint.

B.W.

Cambridge November 1972

1

Personal identity and individuation

There is a special problem about personal identity for two reasons. The first is self-consciousness – the fact that there seems to be a peculiar sense in which a man is conscious of his own identity. This I shall consider in Section 3 of this paper. The second reason is that a question of personal identity is evidently not answered merely by deciding the identity of a certain physical body. If I am asked whether the person in front of me is the same person as one uniquely present at place *a* at time *t*, I shall not necessarily be justified in answering 'yes' merely because I am justified in saying that this human body is the same as that present at *a* at *t*. Identity of body is at least not a sufficient condition of personal identity, and other considerations, of personal characteristics and, above all, memory, must be invoked.

Some have held, further, that bodily identity is not a necessary condition of personal identity. This, however, is ambiguous, and yields either a weak or a strong thesis, depending on one's view of the necessity and sufficiency of the other conditions. The weaker thesis asserts merely that at least one case can be consistently constructed in which bodily identity fails, but in which the other conditions will be sufficient for an assertion of personal identity; even though there may be some other imaginable case in which, some other condition failing, bodily identity *is* a necessary condition of personal identity. The stronger thesis asserts that there is no conceivable situation in which bodily identity would be necessary, some other conditions being always both necessary and sufficient. I take it that Locke's theory[1] is an example of this latter type.

I shall try to show that bodily identity is always a necessary condition of personal identity, and hence that both theses fail. In this connexion I shall discuss in detail a case apparently favourable to the weaker thesis (Section 1). I shall also be concerned with the stronger thesis, or rather with something that follows from it – the idea that we can give a sense to the concept of *a particular personality* without reference to a body. This I shall consider chiefly in Section 4, where the individuation of personalities will be discussed; the notion occurs, however, at various other places in the paper. The criterion of bodily

[1] *Essay Concerning Human Understanding*, II, 27.

identity itself I take for granted. I assume that it includes the notion of spatio-temporal continuity, however that notion is to be explained.

In discussions of this subject, it is easy to fall into ways of speaking that suggest that 'bodily' and other considerations are easily divorced. I have regrettably succumbed to this at some points, but I certainly do not believe that this easy divorce is possible; I hope that both the general tenor of my thesis and some more direct remarks on the subject (Section 2) will show why.

1 *Deciding another's identity*. Suppose someone undergoes a sudden and violent change of character. Formerly quiet, deferential, church-going and home-loving, he wakes up one morning and has become, and continues to be, loud-mouthed, blasphemous and bullying. Here we might ask the question

(*a*) Is he the same person as he used to be?

There seem to be two troubles with the formulation of this question, at least as an *identity* question. The first is a doubt about the reference of the second 'he': if asked the question 'as *who* used to be?', we may well want to say 'this person', which answers the original question (*a*) for us. This is not a serious difficulty, and we can easily avoid it by rephrasing the question in some such way as

(*b*) Is this person the same as the person who went to sleep here last night?

We do not, however, *have* to rephrase the question in any such way; we can understand (*a*) perfectly well, and avoid paradox, because our use of personal pronouns and people's names is malleable. It is a reflection of our concept of 'a person' that some references to *him* cannot be understood as references to *his body* or to parts of it, and that others can; and that these two sorts of reference can readily occur in one statement ('He was embarrassed and went red.') In the case of (*a*), the continuity of reference for 'he' can be supplied by the admitted continuity of reference of 'his body', and the more fundamental identity question can be discussed in these terms without any serious puzzlement.

The second difficulty with (*a*) is that it is too readily translated into

(*c*) Is he the same sort of person as he used to be? or possibly

(*d*) Has he the same personality as he used to have? But (*c*) and (*d*) are not identity questions in the required sense. For on any interpretation, 'sort of person', and on one interpretation, 'personality', are quality-terms, and we are merely asking whether the same subject now has different qualities, which is too easy to answer.

But this is only one interpretation of 'personality'. It corresponds interestingly to a loose sense of 'identity', which is found for instance in Nigel Dennis' novel *Cards of Identity*. There 'identity' is often used to mean 'a set of characteristics', and 'giving someone an identity' means 'convincing someone that he is a certain sort of person'. It does not, however, only mean this; for Dennis' Identity Club do not stop at giving someone a new character – they give him a new background as well, and a local sponger is made by their persuasive methods not just into a submissive old-style butler, but into such a butler who used to be at sea and has deserted his wife.

We might feel that this was the point at which something specially uncanny was beginning to happen, and that this was the kind of anomalous example we were really looking for – the uncanniness of someone's acquiring a new past is connected with our increasing reluctance to describe the situation as one in which the same man has acquired a new set of qualities. Here we have one powerful motive for the introduction of memory. It can be put by saying that there are, or we can imagine, cases where we want to use some term like 'personality' in such a way that it is not a type-expression, meaning 'set of characteristics', but is a particular term meaning something like *individual* personality. It may seem that this particularity is attained by reference to memory – the possession of a particular past. Thus we are concerned here with cases more drastic than those in which for instance people say 'it has made a new man of him', or even 'he is not the same person as he used to be' in the sense suggested by a change of character; these cases we can too readily redescribe. Thus we may put our question in the barbarous form

(*e*) Is the (particular) personality he has now the same as the one he had before?

We must now see whether we can make sense, in terms of memory, of the idea of a particular personality; and whether there can be personal identity without bodily identity.

In doing this, two obvious but important features of memory have to be borne in mind.

(I) To say 'A remembers x', without irony or inverted commas, is to imply that x really happened; in this respect 'remember' is parallel to 'know'.

(II) It does not follow from this, nor is it true, that all claims to remember, any more than all claims to know, are veridical; or, not everything one seems to remember is something one really remembers.

So much is obvious, although Locke[2] was forced to invoke the

[2] *loc. cit.* § 13. He is speaking, however, only of the memories of actions.

providence of God to deny the latter. These points have been emphasised by Flew in his discussion of Locke's views on personal identity.[3] In formulating Locke's thesis, however, Flew makes a mistake; for he offers Locke's thesis in the form 'if X can remember Y's doing such-and-such, then X and Y are the same person'. But this obviously will not do, even for Locke, for we constantly say things like 'I remember my brother joining the army' without implying that I and my brother are the same person. So if we are to formulate such a criterion, it looks as though we have to say something like 'if X remembers doing such-and-such, then he is the person who did that thing'. But since 'remembers doing' means 'remembers himself doing', this is trivially tautologous, and moreover lends colour to Butler's famous objection that memory, so far from constituting personal identity, presupposed it. Hence the criterion should rather run: 'if X claims to remember doing such-and-such. . .' We must now ask how such a criterion might be used.

Suppose the man who underwent the radical change of character – let us call him Charles – claimed, when he woke up, to remember witnessing certain events and doing certain actions which earlier he did not claim to remember; and that under questioning he could not remember witnessing other events and doing other actions which earlier he did remember. Would this give us grounds for saying that he now was or had, in some particular sense, a different personality? An argument to show that it did give us such grounds might be constructed on the following lines.

Any token event *E*, and any token action *A*, are by definition particulars. Moreover, the description 'the man who did the action *A*' necessarily individuates some one person; for it is logically impossible that two persons should do the same *token* action.[4] In the case of events, it is possible that two persons should witness the same token event; but nevertheless the description 'the man who witnessed *E*' may happen to individuate some one person, and 'the man who witnessed $E_1, E_2 \ldots E_n$' has a proportionately greater chance of so doing. Thus if our subject Charles now claims to re-

[3] *Philosophy*, xxvi (1951) pp. 53 *seq.*

[4] This is to ignore the case of joint or co-operative actions. Thus when three persons A, B and C jointly fell a tree, it might be said that each of them has done the same action, that of felling the particular tree. But this would not be quite accurate. They have *all* felled the tree; what *each* of them has done is to share in the felling of the tree, or to have felled the tree with the help of the other two. When the variables implicit in this last expression are replaced with names, we obtain descriptions of token actions which indeed individuate; thus it is true of A, but not of B or C, that he is the man who felled the tree *with the help of B and C*.

member doing certain actions A_1, A_2, etc., and witnessing certain events E_1, E_2, etc., which are themselves suitably identified, we have good grounds for saying that he is some particular person or has some particular personality.

Now by principle (II), we have no reason without corroborative evidence of some kind to believe Charles when he now claims to remember A or E; so we must set about checking. How are we to do this in the present case? Ordinarily if some person X claims to have witnessed E, and we wish to check this, we must find out whether there is any record, or anyone has any memory, of X's witnessing E. This is evidently inapplicable to the present case. For either the evidence shows that Charles was *bodily* present at E, or it does not. If it does, then Charles is remembering in the ordinary way, which is contrary to the hypothesis. If it does not, then there is no corroboration. Here we have a first important step. We are trying to prise apart 'bodily' and 'mental' criteria; but we find that the normal operation of one 'mental' criterion involves the 'bodily' one.

However, the situation may not be quite as desperate as this makes it appear. We can examine Charles' putative memories, and we may find that he can offer detailed information which there is no reason to believe he would ordinarily have known, and which strongly suggests the reports of an eye-witness of some particular events. What we can do with this information in the present case depends on a number of considerations. I shall now examine these, first in connexion with events, and then with actions. Events can in principle be witnessed by any number of persons, or by none. Some of the events which Charles claims to remember witnessing may be events of which we have other eye-witness accounts; others may be events which we believe to have occurred, though we do not know whether or not anyone witnessed them; others again may be events which we believe to have occurred, but which we believe no-one to have witnessed.

For all these, there is an hypothesis about – or, perhaps, description of – Charles' present condition which has nothing to do with a change of personality: the hypothesis of clairvoyance (together, of course, with the loss of his real memories). To describe Charles as clairvoyant is certainly not to advance very far towards an *explanation* of his condition; it amounts to little more than saying that he has come to know, by no means, what other people know by evidence. But so long as Charles claimed to remember events which were supposedly or certainly unwitnessed, such a description might be the best we could offer. We might do better than this, however, if the events Charles claimed to remember were witnessed; in this case we could begin to advance to the idea that Charles had a new identity, because we would have the chance of finding someone for him to be identical *with*. Thus if the events were witnessed, we might say that Charles was (now) identical with a witness of these events. This is ambiguous; it might mean that he was identical with anyone who witnessed the events, or with some particular person who witnessed the events. The former of these is no advance, since it comes to a roundabout way of saying that he claims to have witnessed the events, i.e. is possibly clairvoyant. The situation is different, however, if we can identify some one person who, it is plausible to suppose, witnessed all the events that Charles now claims to remember. That this should be possible is, indeed, a necessary condition of describing what has happened to Charles as *a change of identity*; I shall return to this point a little later.

If we now turn to actions, it looks as though we can find even better grounds for describing the case in terms of a change of identity. While there can be unwitnessed token events, there can be no unwitnessed token actions; moreover, as we noticed above, each token action can be performed by only one person. So if we can find out who performed the actions that Charles now claims to remember performing, it looks as if we can find out who he now is. These supposed advantages, however, are largely illusory. We may say, crudely, that there are many features of actions in which they are just like events – which, from another point of view, they indeed are. What differentiates actions from events are rather certain features of the agent, such as his intentions. In a particular case, some of these latter features may be known to, or inferred by, observers, while others may remain private to the agent. In neither case, however, do these special features of actions much help our investigation of Charles' identity. In so far as these special features may be known to observers, they are still, for the purposes of the investigation, in the class of events, and Charles' claim to remember them may still be plausibly described as clairvoyance; and in so far as these features remain private to the performer of the actions in question, we can have no ground for saying whether Charles' claims to remember them are even correct.

Again, the logical truth that a description of the form 'the person who did the (token) action A' individuates some one person, does not give unfailing help. How much help it gives depends on how effectively, and by what means, we can identify the action in question. Suppose that several men at a certain time and place are each sharpening a pencil. In these circumstances the description 'the man sharpening a pencil' fails to individuate: the action of sharpening a pencil is common to them all. If, however, the pencils were of different colours, I might be able to identify a particular pencil, and through this a token action of sharpening; thus 'the man sharpening the red pencil' may individuate. But such methods of identifying token actions are not always available. In particular, there are some cases in which a token action can be effectively identified only through a reference to the agent. Thus if several men were all dancing the czardas, I might be able to identify a token dancing only as e.g. '*Josef's* dancing of the czardas'. In such a case reference to a token action cannot help in identifying its agent, since I must identify him in order to identify it.

However, we often can effectively identify actions without actually identifying the agents, and so have a use for descriptions like 'the person who murdered the Duchess, whoever it was'. It is obvious that such descriptions can play a peculiarly useful rôle in an enquiry into identity; and this rôle may, for several reasons, be more useful than that played by descriptions like 'the man who witnessed the event E'. For, first, granted that I have identified *an action*, the description cannot fail of reference because there is no such agent; while the mere fact that I have identified a certain event E of course does not guarantee the description 'the man who *witnessed* the event E' against failure of reference. Secondly, it is inherently less likely that the description referring to an action should fail of unique reference because of multiplicity, than it is that the description referring to an event should so fail. For it is in general less probable that a certain action should have been co-operatively undertaken than that a certain event should have been multiply witnessed; and, as we noticed above, for every description of a co-operative action, we can produce a series of descriptions of constituent actions which have progressively greater chance of unique reference. Last, knowledge of a particular action can give one knowledge not only of the location, but of the character, of its agent, but knowledge of a particular event will standardly give one knowledge only of the location of its witnesses.

Let us now go back to the case of Charles. We may suppose that our enquiry has turned out in the most favourable possible way, and that all the events he claims to have witnessed and all the actions he claims to have done point unanimously to the life-history of some one person in the past – for instance, Guy Fawkes. Not only do all Charles' memory-claims that can be checked fit the pattern of Fawkes' life as known to historians, but others that cannot be checked are plausible, provide explanations of unexplained facts, and so on. Are we to say that Charles is now Guy Fawkes, that Guy Fawkes has come to life again in Charles' body, or some such thing?

Certainly the temptation to say something on this pattern is very strong. It is difficult to insist that we *couldn't* say that Charles (or sometime Charles) had become Guy Fawkes; this is certainly what the newspapers would say if they heard of it. But newspapers are prone to exaggeration, and this might be an exaggeration. For why shouldn't we say that Charles had, except for his body, become just like Guy Fawkes used to be; or perhaps that Charles clairvoyantly – i.e. mysteriously – knows all about Guy Fawkes and his *ambiance*? In answer to this, it will be argued that this is just what memory was introduced to rule out; granted that we need similar personal characteristics, skills, and so on as necessary conditions of the identification, the final – and, granted these others, sufficient – condition is provided by memories of seeing just *this*, and doing just *that*, and it is these that pick out a particular man. But perhaps this point is fundamentally a logical trick. Granted that in a certain context the expressions 'the man who did A', 'the man who saw E', do effectively individuate, it is logically impossible that two different persons should (correctly) remember being the man who did A or saw E; but it is not logically impossible that two different persons should *claim* to remember being this man, and this is the most we can get.

This last argument is meant to show only that we are not forced to accept the description of Charles' condition as his being identical with Guy Fawkes. I shall now put forward an argument to strengthen this contention and to suggest that we should not be justified in accepting this description. If it is logically possible that Charles should undergo the changes described, then it is logically possible that some other man should simultaneously undergo the same changes; e.g. that both Charles and his brother Robert should be found in this condition. What should we say in that case? They cannot both be Guy Fawkes; if they were, Guy Fawkes would be in two places at once, which is absurd. Moreover, if they were both identical with Guy Fawkes, they would be identical with each other, which is also absurd. Hence we could not say that they were both identical with Guy Fawkes. We might instead say that one of them was identical with Guy Fawkes, and that the other was just like him; but this would be an utterly vacuous manoeuvre, since there would be *ex hypothesi* no principle determining which description was to apply to which. So it would be best, if anything, to say that both had mysteriously become like Guy Fawkes, clairvoyantly knew about him, or something like this. If this would be the best description of each of the two, why would it not be the best description of Charles if Charles alone were changed?

Perhaps this last rhetorical question too readily invites an answer. It might be said that there is a relevant difference between the case in which two persons are changed and the case in which only one is changed, the difference being just this difference in numbers; and that there is no guarantee that what we would say in one of these situations would be the same as what we would say in the other. In the more complicated situation our linguistic and conceptual resources would be taxed even more severely than in the simpler one, and we might not react to the demands in the same way. Moreover, there is a reason why we should not react in the same way. The standard form of an identity question is 'Is this *x* the same *x* as that *x* which . . .?', and in the simpler situation we are at least presented with just the materials for constructing such a question; but in the more complicated situation we are baffled even in asking the question, since both the transformed persons are equally good candidates for being its subject, and the question 'Are these two *x*'s the same (*x*?) as the *x* which...?' is not a recognisable form of identity question. Thus, it might be argued, the fact that we could not speak of identity in the latter situation is no kind of proof that we could not do so in the former.

Certainly it is not a proof. Yet the argument does indicate that to speak of identity in the simpler case would be at least quite vacuous. The point can be made clearer in the following way. In the case of material objects, we can draw a distinction between identity and exact similarity; it is clearly not the same to say that two men live in the same house, and that they live in exactly similar houses. This notion of identity is given to us primarily, though not completely, by the notion of spatio-temporal continuity. In the case of character, however, this distinction cannot be drawn, for to say that A and B have the same character is just to say that A's character is exactly similar to B's. Nor can this distinction be drawn in the case of memories – if you could say that two men had the same memories, this would be to say that their memories were exactly similar. There is, however, an extreme difficulty in saying these things about memories at all; it is unclear what it would mean to say that there were two men who had exactly similar, or the same, memories, since to call them real memories is to imply their correctness. Thus if we are to describe Charles' relations to Guy Fawkes in terms of *exact similarity* of everything except the body, we are going to have difficulty in finding a suitable description in these terms of his memory claims. We cannot say that he has the same memories as Guy Fawkes, as this is to imply, what we want to deny, that he really is Guy Fawkes; nor can we say that the memory claims he makes are the same as those made by Guy Fawkes, as we have little idea of what memory claims Fawkes in fact made, or indeed of how much he at various times remembered. All we actually know is that Charles' claims fit Fawkes' life.

These difficulties, in applying the concept of exact similarity in the matter of the supposed memories, are (I suspect) a motive for the thought that we *must* describe the situation in terms of identity. This is where the reduplicated situation of Charles and Robert gives some help. In that situation it is quite obvious that the idea of identity cannot be applied, and that we must fall back on similarity; and that one respect in which the trio are similar is – however we are to express it – that of 'memory'. (If the situation sometimes occurred, we might find an expression; we might speak of 'similarity of one's supposed past'.) This eases the way for doing the same thing in the case of Charles alone, whose relation to Fawkes in his unique case is exactly the same as both his and Robert's in the reduplicated one. We can then say that Charles has the same character, and the same supposed past, as Fawkes; which is just the same as to say that they are in these respects exactly similar. This is not to say that they are identical at all. The only case in which identity and exact similarity could be distinguished, as we have just seen, is that of the body – 'same body' and 'exactly similar body' really do mark a difference. Thus I should claim that the omission of the body takes away all content from the idea of personal *identity*.

I should like to make one last point about this example. This turns on the fact, mentioned before, that in order to describe Charles' change of identity, we must be able to identify some one person who might plausibly be supposed to have seen and done all the things that Charles now claims to remember having seen and done; otherwise there would be nothing to pin down Charles' memory claims as other than random feats of clairvoyance. We succeeded in doing this, just by discovering that Charles' memory claims fitted Fawkes' life. This could be done only by knowing what Fawkes did, and what Fawkes did could be known only by reference to witnesses of Fawkes' activities, and these witnesses must have seen Fawkes' *body*. In order for their accounts to be connected into the history of one person, it is necessary to rely on the continuity of this body.

Now the fact that Fawkes is in this sense identified through his body does not rule out the possibility that Charles should later be identified with Fawkes without reference to a body; i.e. this fact does not rule out the weaker thesis about the non-necessity of bodies. To illustrate this, one might compare the case of someone's going to a crowded party, where he sees a girl who is very like all the other girls at the party except that she has red hair. This girl sings various songs and quarrels with the band; she is easily identified on each occasion by the colour of her hair. The man later meets a platinum blonde who recalls singing songs at a party and quarrelling with the band. He can identify her as the red-haired girl at the party, even though she has changed the colour of her hair in the meantime. There is an important difference, however, between this case and that of Fawkes. If the girl had remarkably changed the colour of her hair between songs and before the quarrel, identifying her at the various stages of the party would have been more difficult, but not in principle impossible; but if the Fawkes-personality changed bodies frequently, identification would become not just difficult but impossible. For the only other resource would be the memory criterion, and the operation of this would once more make exactly the same requirements. Hence it is a necessary condition of making the supposed identification on non-bodily grounds that at some stage identifications should be made on bodily grounds. Hence any claim that bodily considerations can be absolutely omitted from the criteria of personal identity must fail; i.e. these facts do rule out the stronger thesis.

2 *Some remarks on bodily interchange.* Anyone who believed that personalities could be identified without reference to bodies might be expected to make sense of the idea of bodily interchange; and anyone who thought that they might always be identified in this way would presumably require that for any two contemporaneous persons we should be able to make sense of the idea that their bodies should be interchanged. It is worth considering how far we can make sense of it, if we look at it closely.

Suppose a magician is hired to perform the old trick of making the emperor and the peasant become each other. He gets the emperor and the peasant in one room, with the emperor on his throne and the peasant in the corner, and then casts the spell. What will count as success? Clearly not that after the smoke has cleared the old emperor should be in the corner and the old peasant on the throne. That would be a rather boring trick. The requirement is presumably that the emperor's body, with the peasant's personality, should be on the throne, and the peasant's body with the emperor's personality, in the corner. What does this mean? In particular, what has happened to the voices? The voice presumably ought to count as a bodily function; yet how would the peasant's gruff blasphemies be uttered in the emperor's cultivated tones, or the emperor's witticisms in the peasant's growl? A similar point holds for the features; the emperor's body might include the sort of face that just *could not* express the peasant's morose suspiciousness, the peasant's a face no expression of which could be taken for one of fastidious arrogance. These 'could's are not just empirical – such expressions on these features might be unthinkable.

The point need not be elaborated; I hope I have said enough to suggest that the concept of bodily interchange cannot be taken for granted, and that there are even logical limits to what we should be prepared to say in this direction. What these limits are, cannot be foreseen – one has to consider the cases, and for this one has to see the cases. The converse is also true, that it is difficult to tell in advance how far certain features may suddenly seem to express something quite unexpected. But there are limits, and when this is recognised, the idea of the interchange of personalities seems very odd. There might be something like a logical impossibility of the magician's trick's succeeding. However much of the emperor's past the sometime peasant now claimed to remember, the trick would not have succeeded if he could not satisfy the simpler requirement of being the same *sort* of person as the sometime emperor. Could he do this, if he could not smile royally? Still less, could he be the same person, if he could not smile the characteristic smile of the emperor?

These considerations are relevant to the present question in two ways. First, the stronger view about the identification implies that an interchange is always conceivable; but there are many cases in which it does not seem to be conceivable at all. Secondly, there is connected with this the deeper point, that when we are asked to distinguish a man's personality from his body, we do not really know what to distinguish from what. I take it that this was part of what Wittgenstein meant when he said that the best picture of the human soul was the human body.[5]

3 *A criterion for oneself?* I now turn to a different supposed use of a criterion of identity for persons. It may be objected that I have been discussing all the time the use of memory and other criteria of personal identity as applied to one man by others; but that the real rôle of memory is to be seen in the way it reveals a man *to himself*.

[5] *Philosophical Investigations*, II, iv.

Thus Locke speaks of 'consciousness' (and by this he means here memory) as 'what makes a man be himself to himself'.[6]

It is difficult to see what this can mean. If we take it to mean that a man could use memory as a criterion in deciding whether he was the same person, in the particular sense, as he used to be, the suggestion is demonstrably absurd. I hope that a short and schematised argument will be enough to show this point. Suppose a man to have had previously some set of memories S, and now a different set S_1. This should presumably be the situation in which he should set about using the criterion to decide the question of his identity. But this cannot be so, for when he has memories S, and again when he has memories S_1, he is in no doubt about his identity, and so the question does not even occur to him. For it to occur to him, he would have to have S and S_1 at the same time, and so S would be included in S_1, which is contrary to the hypothesis that they are, in the relevant sense, different.

Alternatively, let S_1 include a general memory to the effect that he used to remember things that he no longer remembers. This would again present no question to him, for it is the condition of most of us. So let us strengthen this into the requirement that S_1 include a general memory Σ to the effect that he used to remember things empirically incompatible with memories in S_1. In this situation he might set about trying to find out what kind of illusion he was under. His most economical hypothesis would be that Σ itself was an illusion. If he were not satisfied with this, or if some parts of S *were* left over in S_1, so that he seemed to have definitely incompatible 'memories', there would be nothing he could do with the help of his own memory; he would have to ask others about his past. In doing this, he would be relying on other people's memories of his past; but this is certainly not what was meant by the suggestion of memory as a criterion for the man himself. It is just a reversion to the case of such a criterion being used by some persons about another. Thus there is no way in which memory could be used by a man as a criterion of his own identity.

A criterion, however, must be used by someone. This is a point that has been notably and unhappily neglected by theorists of personal identity. Thus Hume, for instance, in the course of his account revealingly says[7] 'Suppose we could see clearly into the breast of another, and observe that succession of perceptions, which constitutes his mind or thinking principle, and suppose that he always preserves the memory of a considerable part of past perceptions...' Others, in criticising or expanding Hume's account, have

[6] *loc. cit.*, § 10.   [7] Hume, *Treatise of Human Nature*, Bk. I, Pt. IV, Sec. VI.

written in terms that similarly require an externalised view of the contents of a man's mind, a view obtainable from no conceivable vantage-point. Theorising which is in this sense abstract must be vacuous, because this privileged but positionless point of view can mean nothing to us.

At this point it might be objected that if what has been said is true about a criterion of identity, then it was not a *criterion* that memory was supposed uniquely to provide. 'You have argued', it might be said, 'that no man can use memory as a criterion of his own identity. But this is just what shows that memory is the essence of personal identity; figuratively speaking, memory is so much what makes him a certain person that when provided with certain memories, he cannot doubt who he is. This is just the heart of the thesis.' Or the objection might be put by saying that a man might conceivably have occasion to look into a mirror and say 'this is not my body', but could never have occasion to say 'these are not my memories'. Or, again, a man who has lost his memory cannot say who he is.

If this is what the thesis asserts, however, it comes to little. A man who has lost his memory cannot say who anyone else is, either, nor whether any object is the same as one previously presented, since he will not remember the previous presentation. So the last argument shows nothing about personal identity as such; it just shows that identifying anything is a process that involves memory. Nor is the first argument more illuminating. It comes really to no more than the trivialities that in order to remember, you have to have something you can remember, and that if you are remembering everything you can remember, there is nothing else you can remember. Again, the example of the man looking into the mirror does not do what is required. In order to sustain the objection it would be necessary to show not just that a man might say 'this is not my body', but that if he said it, he would necessarily be right; or at least that the question whether he was right or not did not involve any reference to other people's memories. It is obvious that neither is the case, because the situation of the example *might* be best described by saying that this was a man who misremembered what he looked like, and the question whether this was the best description of the situation would have to be decided by other people conducting the kind of enquiry into identity that was earlier discussed at length.

It is not part of my aim to discuss in general consciousness of self. I have tried in this section to show in a limited way that although we may have the feeling that, by consideration of it alone, we may be given the clue to personal identity, this is in fact an illusion. That it is an illusion is disguised by those theories of personal identity which, by assuming no particular point of view, try to get the best of both worlds, the inner and the outer. If we abandon this for a more realistic approach, the facts of self-consciousness prove incapable of yielding the secret of personal identity, and we are forced back into the world of public criteria.

If we accept these conclusions, together with the earlier ones, it may seem that the attempt to give a sense to 'particular personality' that omits reference to the body has failed. However, there is another and familiar class of cases that seems to provide strong independent grounds for the view that such a sense can be given: these are the cases in which more than one personality is associated with one body. I shall end by discussing this type of case and some related questions.

4 *Multiple personality and individuation.* Examples of multiple personality, such as the notorious case of Miss Beauchamp,[8] raise identity questions interestingly different from those that arose in the case of Charles. In that case, we identified, by means that turned out to involve the body, what would normally, if tendentiously, be called a different person, and asked whether the person in front of us was identical with him. In the cases of multiple personality, we are in a sense more directly confronted with personalities, and naturally make direct reference to them in order to ask our identity questions at all. The standard type of identity question about Miss Beachamp is whether the personality that is now being manifested in her behaviour (or some such description) is the same as that which was being manifested two hours ago. In asking a question of this type, we may in fact feel a doubt about the reference of descriptions like 'the personality now manifesting itself', because the principal question here just is what personalities there are to be referred to – how many personalities there are, and how the subject's behaviour is to be 'sorted out' into the manifestations of different personalities.

For this reason, there is a strong motive for not putting our questions about Miss Beauchamp in the form of identity questions at all. Instead of asking something of the form 'Is this personality the same as that?' we may prefer to ask, 'Do these two pieces of behaviour belong to one personality or to two?'; that is, instead of referring to personalities *through* their manifestations and asking whether they are identical, we may refer *to* manifestations and ask how they are to be allocated to personalities. A parallel to this would be the case of a tangled skein of wool, where, catching hold of a piece at each end, we might ask either 'Is this thread the same as that?' or 'Are these pieces parts of

[8] See Morton Prince, *The Dissociation of a Personality* (New York: Longmans, 1906).

one thread?' The second formulation in each case might seem to be strictly preferable to the first, because the references that are being made are more determinate; I can tell you exactly which *part* or which *manifestation* I am referring to in the second formulation, but can tell you much less exactly which *thread* or which *personality* I am referring to in the first. It is useful to distinguish these sorts of questions, and I shall call the first, questions of identity, and the second, questions of individuation. I shall also in this section speak of our having individuated a personality when, roughly, we have answered enough questions of this type for us to have picked out a certain personality from the pattern of manifestations. I shall not here examine the complexities involved in a proper formulation of these concepts.

We have just seen that it might be preferable to put our questions about Miss Beauchamp in the form of individuation, and not of identity, questions. It might seem, indeed, that it is essential to do this. Because asking an identity question about personalities involves referring to personalities, and this involves knowing what personalities one is referring to, it is tempting to think that we could not use the identity form in a case where our problem was just what, and how many, personalities there were. This, however, would be an exaggeration. I do not have to be able to answer the question 'which personality are you referring to?' in the thorough-going way suggested by this argument. I may do enough to establish the reference by saying 'I just mean the personality now being manifested, whichever that is', without committing myself thereby to more than the belief that there is at least one personality to be referred to, and possibly more. I should be *debarred* from using the identity form only in a situation where I was in doubt whether there was even one personality to be referred to.

The case of Miss Beauchamp is more relevant to the discussion of the rôle of the body in the individuation of personalities than it is to the straightforward question whether bodily identity is a necessary condition of personal identity; since bodily identity is granted, this case can have no tendency to show that bodily identity is not a necessary condition (though it will of course tend to show that it is not a sufficient condition). It will, however, lend colour to the idea that we can individuate particular personalities, and not through bodies; if there are here four different particular personalities, and only one body, it is clear that there can be some principle for distinguishing personalities without at least *distinguishing* bodies. There is such a principle; but it does not yield as exciting a result from this case as might be hoped.

Miss Beauchamp's striking different personalities were individuated in the first place by reference to personal characteristics, in which they were largely opposed; also by tastes and preferences (*B*1 and *B*4 hated smoking, for instance, and *B*3 loved it); and by skills (*B*3, unlike the others, knew no French or shorthand). Memory did not serve straightforwardly to individuate them, because their memories were asymmetrical. *B*1 and *B*4, for instance, knew only what they were told by the investigator about the others, but *B*3 knew, without being told, everything that *B*4 did, and in the case of *B*1 knew all her thoughts as well; she referred to them both in the third person.[9] These remarkable and systematic discontinuities in Miss Beauchamp's behaviour, together with the violent and active conflict between her various selves, who abused and tricked each other, make the reference to different particular personalities completely natural. Thus we have individuated various personalities by reference to character, attainments and (up to a point) memories, and without reference to bodies.

This claim, however, is liable to serious misinterpretation. There has been no reference to bodies only in the sense that no such reference came into the principles used; but it does not follow from this that there was no reference to a body in starting to individuate at all. Obviously there was, because too many and too various things were going on in connexion with one body; if Miss Beauchamp had been four sisters, there would have been no problem. Thus the individuation by reference to character and so on alone, was individuation in the context of the continuity of a certain body; and the fact that these principles were successful in individuating in this case does not show that they would be successful in so doing generally. The point may be put by saying that what we have succeeded in doing on these principles is individuating particular personalities *of Miss Beauchamp*, who is bodily identified; this is not to say that they provide us with a principle for individuating particular personalities without any reference to bodies at all.

This is quite obvious if we look at the principles themselves. Leaving aside memory, which only partially applies to the case, character and attainments are quite clearly general things. *Jones'* character is, in a sense, a particular; just because 'Jones' character' refers to the instantiation of certain properties by a particular (and bodily) man.[10] Even so, the sense in which it is a particular is

[9] Prince, *Dissociation of a Personality*, p. 181. The extent of memory discontinuity in such cases varies cf., e.g., William James, *Principles of Psychology*, I (London: Macmillan, 1890), pp. 379 *seq.*

[10] Cf. P. F. Strawson, Particular and General', PAS LIV (1953–4), pp. 250 *seq.*

peculiar and limited. This can be seen from the odd workings of its criterion of identity. Consider the statement

(i) He has the same character as his father (*or* he has his father's character)

and compare the two statements

(ii) He wears the same clothes as his father

(iii) He has his father's watch.

Of these, (ii) is ambiguous, the expression, 'the same clothes' see-sawing over the line between particular and general (though its companion 'he wears his father's clothes' seems to allow only the particular interpretation). Neither (i) nor (iii) is ambiguous in this way; and in (iii) 'his father's watch' obviously refers to a particular. But (i) is quite different from (iii). If (iii) is true, then if the watch he has is going to be pawned tomorrow, his father's watch is going to be pawned; but it does not similarly follow from (i) that if his character is going to be ruined by the Army, his father's character is going to be ruined. This illustrates how little weight can be laid on the idea of Jones' character being a particular, and throws us back on the familiar point that to talk of Jones' character is a way of talking about what Jones is like.

Miss Beauchamp's various personalities are particulars only in the weak sense that Jones' character is a particular, a sense which is grounded in the particular body. In using character and attainments to individuate them, I am telling the difference between them in just the sense that I tell the difference between sets of characteristics; Miss Beauchamp was peculiar in having more than one set of characteristics. Her personalities, like more normal people's, each had *peculiarities*, the combination of which might well have been, as a matter of fact, uniquely instantiated; but this does not affect the fundamental logical issue. About her memories, it need only be said that if different personalities have the same memories, memory is not being used to individuate; if they have different memories, the bodily identity connecting the various remembered occasions makes it easy to describe the situation as one of Miss Beauchamp's sometimes being able to remember what at other times she could not.

When Miss Beauchamp was nearly cured, and only occasionally lapsed into dissociation, she spoke freely of herself as having been $B1$ or $B4$. 'These different states seem to her very largely differences of moods. She regrets them, but does not attempt to excuse them, because, as she says, "After all, it is always myself."'[11]

[11] Prince, *Dissociation of a Personality*, p. 525.

2

Bodily continuity and personal identity

Note 1972. This was a reply to criticisms made by Robert C. Coburn (*Analysis*, 20.5, 1960) of an argument which I used in 'Personal identity and individuation' to try to show that bodily continuity was a necessary condition of personal identity, and more particularly that similarity of memory claims and personal characteristics could not be a sufficient condition of it. There is some more about the 'reduplication' argument discussed here, in 'Are persons bodies?', on pp. 77 *seq* of this book.

The argument which Coburn criticises runs like this. Suppose a person A to undergo a sudden change, and to acquire a character exactly like that of some person known to have lived in the past, B. Suppose him further to make sincere memory claims which entirely fit the life of B. We might think these conditions sufficient for us to identify A (as he now is) with B. But they are not. For another contemporary person, C, might undergo an exactly similar change at the same time as A, and if the conditions were sufficient to say that A=B, they would be sufficient to say that C=B as well. But it cannot be the case both that A=B and C=B, for, were it so, it would follow that A=C, which is absurd. One can avoid this absurdity by abandoning one or both of the assertions A=B and C=B. But it would be vacuous to assert one of these and abandon the other, since there is nothing to choose between them; hence the rational course is to abandon both. Therefore, I argued, it would be just as vacuous to make the identification with B even if only one contemporary person were involved.

Coburn claims that this argument can be applied just as well to another case in which it gives unacceptable results. He supposes the case of a man George who suddenly disappears; 'a moment later an individual begins to exist who is in all discernible respects exactly similar to George (say, George*)'.[1] Coburn argues that to this case, too, my argument would apply, with the result that it would be vacuous to identify George* with George. But this, he argues, is unacceptable: such an identification would certainly not be vacuous, since much would depend on it (concerning e.g. punishment for George's crimes). Moreover it is an identification that we should justifiably accept. Hence my argument is called into doubt.

[1] *Analysis* 20.5, p. 118.

First, a point about 'vacuity'. In saying that an identification of *A* with *B* in the imagined circumstances was 'vacuous', I did not mean that no consequences would follow from it. If the identification were taken seriously, consequences of the kind Coburn mentions could as well follow in my sort of case as in his. My use of the term 'vacuous' concerned not the consequences, but the grounds, of such an identification, my argument being meant to show that there would be in principle for such a case no grounds to justify a judgement of identity as against a judgement of exact similarity. I agree that the term 'vacuous' is misleading, in that it suggests that there would be no difference at all between the two judgements, and this, in terms of consequences, is false.

My argument can be put in another way to incorporate this point. Where there is a difference in the consequences, in this sense, of two judgements, there should all the more be a difference in their grounds, for it is unreasonable that there should be no more grounds for applying one of a pair of judgements to a situation rather than the other, and yet one judgement carry consequences not carried by the other. On the thesis that similarity of character and of memory claims is a sufficient condition of personal identity, there would be no difference in the grounds of two judgements, that of identity and that of exact similarity, one of which does carry consequences not carried by the other. Hence that thesis is to be rejected. (What is meant by 'exact similarity' here is '*mere* exact similarity', an assertion of which would entail the denial of identity.)

More important than this point about vacuity is the conclusion which Coburn states, or rather implies, that we should in fact in a case such as he describes identify George* with George, and be justified in so doing. If this conclusion is correct, and it is also correct that my reduplication argument would apply as well to this case, my argument must be defective. Now Coburn does not make entirely clear the circumstances of his imagined case. He does not say whether George* appears in the same place as that from which George disappeared; and while he says that George* appears 'a moment later', he does not say whether he regards the shortness of the interval as essential to his example or not. If Coburn allows distant places and long intervals of time for the appearance of George*, his case would in fact approximate to my original one, with physical resemblance added to the resemblances of character and memory claims. If, on the other hand, a short interval of time and reappearance in the same place are essential to Coburn's example, it is worth asking why this should be so.

I shall argue that if Coburn's example is to provide a case of identity, it must be restricted in this way; but that when it is restricted in this way, it is not a counter-example to my argument. The principle of my argument is, very roughly put, that identity is a one–one relation, and that no principle can be a criterion of identity for things of type *T* if it relies only on what is logically a one–many or many–many relation between things of type *T*. What is wrong with the supposed criterion of identity for persons which relies only on memory claims is just that '. . . being disposed to make sincere memory claims which exactly fit the life of . . .' is not a one–one, but a many–one, relation, and hence cannot possibly be adequate in logic to constitute a criterion of identity. (There are well-known difficulties about speaking of identity as a relation at all. The point being made here can be expressed more rigorously in terms of the sense and reference of uniquely referring expressions, but I hope it is clear enough in this rough, and shorter, form.)

This principle states a necessary condition of anything's serving as a criterion of identity. It clearly does not state a sufficient condition; still less does it state a sufficient condition of anything's being, for a given type of thing *T*, a philosophically satisfactory criterion of identity for *T*s. In particular (and this was the basis of the later part of my original argument), no principle *P* will be a philosophically satisfactory criterion of identity for *T*s if the only thing that saves *P* from admitting many–one relations among *T*s is a quite arbitrary provision.

Returning now to Coburn's example, it can be seen that if it is taken as quite unrestricted, the criterion of identity suggested by it will not pass the test just stated, any more than the bare memory and character criteria do; for the relation '. . . being in all respects similar to, and appearing somewhere at some time after the disappearance of, the individual. . .' is many–one, and could not suffice to do what a criterion of identity is required to do, viz. enable us to identify uniquely the thing that is identical with the thing in question. However, if the principle is restricted in certain ways, this difficulty can be avoided. If, for instance, it is modified to: '. . . being in all respects similar to, and appearing as the first subsequent occupant of the place vacated by the disappearance of, the individual . . .', it will pass the test, so long at least as two, slightly different, conditions are satisfied about the application of the expression 'the place vacated by . . .': first, that it should be so restricted that it will not be possible for two persons simultaneously to occupy that place, and, second, that it should be sufficiently determinate not to leave it in doubt which of two or more places, so restricted, is the place in question.

It is perhaps this latter condition, among others, that introduces the consideration, not mentioned in the criteria as so far stated, but mentioned in Coburn's example, of the length of the lapse of time between disappearance and appearance. One reason at least why one might be moved to introduce a very brief lapse of time into Coburn's example is this: that if the lapse of time is very short, it is very much clearer what 'the same place' will be. Granted a longer time, in which various changes can take place, it may become less clear and determinate what 'the same place' will be. For instance, if George had been in bed in his bedroom when he disappeared, and the bed, before George* appears, is moved into another room or another house, where must George* appear in order to appear in the place vacated by George? Difficulties of this kind could be multiplied indefinitely. One motive for the introduction of a brief lapse of time is, then, perhaps this: that it makes the application of 'same place' more determinate than it might otherwise be.

However, there is perhaps another motive for thinking in terms of a brief lapse of time: that it is only this that makes a criterion of identity in terms of 'same place' plausible *at all*. For if the appearance of George* happens some substantial time after the disappearance of George, why should his appearance in precisely the place vacated by George be privileged in giving an answer to the identity question? Here we have a dilemma: on the one hand some such restriction is needed, to make the principle implied in the example into a criterion of identity at all; on the other hand, it seems equally to be in these circumstances quite arbitrary.

One reason for the latter is that in thinking about the imagined case we are in fact using a model drawn from the real world and our normal identification of persons: a model in which the disappeared George, though 'immaterial', in some sense goes on existing, and in particular can move from one place to another. This model contains an illusion, no doubt; but to see that there is an illusion should lead one, not to stick unthinkingly to a criterion of identity to which identity of place is essential, but to conclude that the application of criteria of personal identity to these imagined cases of disappearance is a far less certain and indisputable buisiness than may at first sight appear.

Now Coburn himself cannot consistently have in mind a restricted principle as the criterion of identity presupposed in his example, since he says that in his example reduplication would be possible. If the criterion presupposed in his example were restricted in the ways I have been discussing, no reduplication would be possible, since it could not be the case that two persons could both be the first subsequent occupants of the place (in the required sense) vacated by the disappearance of George.

It seems, then, that Coburn has in mind as suggested by his example a principle unrestricted in space and time. If so, I do not see how it can satisfy the logical requirements of being a criterion of identity. If, on the other hand, the principle were restricted in space and time, it would be a possible criterion of identity, in the sense at least that it satisfied the logical requirements of such a criterion; but in that case, the possibility of reduplication could not exist, and his case would not be a counter-example to my argument, which was directed against supposed criteria of identity which did not satisfy the requirements. If, again, the principle were restricted in space but not in time, it might still satisfy the logical requirements (though there would be systematic doubts about its application), but it would scarcely seem a plausible or philosophically satisfactory sort of criterion. Whether, granted this point, the fully restricted criterion would be plausible or satisfactory, is a question I shall not pursue here, though I think the answer is in fact 'no'.

It may be objected to this argument that I have set too high the standard for a principle's serving as a criterion of identity, by requiring that it guard against the logical possibility of reduplication such as I have discussed. No criterion can guard against this, it may be said; and this can be seen from the fact that even a criterion of identity in terms of spatio-temporal continuity, on which I lay the weight for personal identity, is itself not immune to this possibility. It is possible to imagine a man splitting, amoeba-like, into two simulacra of himself. If this happened, it must of course follow from my original argument that it would not be reasonable to say that either of the resultant men was identical with the original one: they could not both be, because they are not identical with each other, and it would not be reasonable to choose one rather than the other to be identical with the original. Hence it would seem that by my requirements, not even spatio-temporal continuity would serve as a criterion of identity: hence the requirements are too high.[2]

I do not think, however, that this case upsets the principle of my

[2] This sort of case has been discussed in his contribution to this topic by C. B. Martin (*Analysis* 18.4, March 1958). Martin's own criticism, however, seems merely to confuse identity with the quite different concept of 'having the same life-history as', where this is defined to suit the amoeba-like case. To say that (putatively) two amoebae are identical is to say that *pro tanto* I have only one amoeba; to say that they share the same life-history is not. Cf. G. C. Nerlich, *Analysis* 18.6, June 1958, on this point.

argument. There is a vital difference between this sort of reduplication, with the criterion of spatio-temporal continuity, and the other sorts of case. This emerges when one considers what it is to apply the criterion of spatio-temporal continuity. To apply this criterion – for instance, in trying to answer the question whether a certain billiard ball now in my hand is the billiard ball that was at a certain position at the start of the game – is to engage in a certain sort of historical enquiry. The identity-question contains two expressions each of which picks out an object of a certain type under a description containing, in each case, a different time-reference; to answer the question is to chart an historical course which starts from the situation given by one of the descriptions, in order to see whether this course does or does not lead to the situation given by the other. This procedure, ideally carried out, will give the entire history in question; and in particular, if there were any reduplication of the kind under discussion, *it would inevitably reveal it*. This consideration puts the spatio-temporal continuity criterion into a different situation from the others discussed; for in this case, but evidently not in others, a thorough application of the criterion would itself reveal the existence of the reduplication situation, and so enable us to answer (negatively) the original identity question. To enable us to answer such questions is the point of a criterion of identity. Thus, in this case, but not in the others, the logical possibility of reduplication fails to impugn the status of the criterion of identity.

I think that these considerations perhaps suffice for us to say that in a case of fission, such as that of an amoeba, the resultant items are not, in the strict sense, spatio-temporally continuous with the original. The justification for saying this would be that the normal application of the concept of continuity is interfered with by the fact of fission, a fact which would itself be discovered by the verification procedure tied to the application of the concept. There would be a motive for saying this, moreover, in that we might want to insist that spatio-temporal continuity, in the strict sense, was transitive. But for the present issue, nothing immediately turns on our decision on this point.

It may be said that for most sorts of objects to which spatio-temporal continuity applies, we do not in fact pursue our identity enquiries in this thorough-going historical way. This is true, but nothing to the point; because, for most sorts of objects, we have the strongest empirical reasons for disbelieving in reduplication. Where we have not such reasons – for instance with amoebae – one would indeed (in the unlikely event of one's wanting to answer an identity question) have to watch out for reduplication, by constant observation or otherwise.

I conclude, then, that this sort of case, because of its special nature, does not tell against my general position; which is that in order to serve as a criterion of identity, a principle must provide what I have called a one–one relation and not a one–many relation. Unless there is some such requirement, I cannot see how one is to preserve and explain the evident truth that the concepts of identity and of exact similarity are different concepts.

3
Imagination and the self

I start with a notorious argument of Berkeley's.

Phil. But (to pass by all that hath been hitherto said, and reckon it for nothing, if you will have it so) I am content to put the whole upon this issue. If you can conceive it possible for any mixture or combination of qualities, or any sensible object whatever, to exist without the mind, then I will grant it actually to be so.

Hyl. If it comes to that, the point will soon be decided. What more easy than to conceive a tree or house existing by itself, independent of, and unperceived by any mind whatsoever? I do at this present time conceive them existing after that manner.

Phil. How say you, Hylas, can you see a thing which is at the same time unseen?

Hyl. No, that were a contradiction.

Phil. Is it not a contradiction to talk of *conceiving* a thing which is *unconceived*?

Hyl. It is.

Phil. The tree or house therefore which you think of, is conceived by you.

Hyl. How should it be otherwise?

Phil. And what is conceived is surely in the mind.

Hyl. Without question, that which is conceived is in the mind.

Phil. How then came you to say, you conceived a house or tree existing independent and out of all minds whatsoever?

Hyl. That was, I own, an oversight; but stay, let me consider what led me into it – it is a pleasant mistake enough. As I was thinking of a tree in a solitary place, where no one was present to see it, methought that was to conceive a tree as existing unperceived or unthought of, not considering that I myself conceived it all the while. But now I plainly see, that all I can do is to frame ideas in my own mind. I may indeed conceive in my own thoughts the idea of a tree, or a house, or a mountain, but that is all. And this is far from proving, that I can conceive them *existing out of the minds of all spirits.*

Phil. You acknowledge then that you cannot possibly conceive how any one corporeal sensible thing should exist otherwise than in a mind.

Hyl. I do.

First Dialogue between Hylas and Philonous

It is not very difficult to refute this argument. I shall not rehearse a number of the considerations that might be brought against it. Yet it seems to have something in it which is not utterly implausible; the difficulty is to pin this down. A first step to doing this is to recall the familiar Berkelian insistence on the connexion of thinking and images, and to take him to mean by 'conceiving' a thing, having an image of it or – to concentrate on the leading case – visualising it. Not, of course, that this interpretation will save the argument for the very ambitious purpose to which, as I suppose, Berkeley assigned it, that of showing that an unperceived object is logically impossible. For one thing, in the sense of 'conceive' in which what is conceivable is logically possible, and what is not conceivable is not logically possible, conceiving and visualising are clearly different things; as Descartes explicitly and correctly remarked. Indeed, Berkeley himself had to concede this for the case of minds, and in particular of God, but then they were not the sorts of things that could be perceived at all; for things of such a sort that they could be perceived, to think of them is for him (roughly) to visualise them. This is a mistake, and inasmuch as the argument rests on it, it fails. But if we jump over that mistake, and inspect the ground on the further side of it, we meet a much more interesting question: whether we can visualise something that is not seen. At least here, it might seem that Berkeley has a good point – not indeed to establish his idealism, but a good point nevertheless. For it is plausible to say that if I visualise something, then I think of myself seeing it; and that I could think of myself seeing something which was not seen does look as though it involved a contradiction. Does it indeed do so?

There is one sense, certainly, in which it does not, and this must be got out of the way first. This is the sense in which the relative clause, 'which is not seen', is taken in a purely extensional manner: that is to say, that in which the statement 'A thinks of himself seeing *x*, which is not seen' is equivalent to the bare conjunction, with external quantification, 'A thinks of himself seeing *x*, and *x* is not seen'. Such a conjunction can obviously be true: the fact that someone in the nineteenth century visualised the South Pole had no tendency to anticipate the feat of those who first saw that place. This rather blank consideration is enough to dispose of Berkeley's argument for his idealist purpose, I think, even with respect to visualisation; if at least he really wants to 'put the whole upon this issue'. It would only be if we had already accepted his earlier arguments about the status of the objects of sense that we might find the considerations drawn from visualisation persuasive for idealism.

This extensional sense, however, constitutes only one way of taking a relative clause of this type and it is of limited application. The question of taking the statement in this way would seem to arise only in those cases in which what I visualise is something that actually exists; only in this case can we quantify over the statement 'A thinks of himself seeing *x*' and conjoin it with the statement '*x* is not seen'. But the fact that what is visualised is an actual object, while it may allow the extensional interpretation, certainly does not demand it. For – to change the example for the moment – the statement 'He thought of himself seeing the Queen, who was riding a bicycle' admits, as well as the extensional interpretation, an intensional interpretation by which it means the same as 'he visualised the Queen riding a bicycle'; under this latter interpretation the statement is not equivalent to a conjunction of the previous type, and not falsified by its being the case that the Queen was not at that time, or indeed at any other time, riding a bicycle.

I said just now that it was only with the visualisation of actual objects that the extensional interpretation could even present itself; if that is true, with imaginary objects only an intensional one is available. I gave as a reason for this claim the consideration that only with actual objects could one make the quantification required for the bare conjunction which is the mark of the extensional interpretation. I think that this is right, but there is a complication about it that I shall explore a little since it will be relevant to the argument later on.

The complication emerges if we consider the following case. A man is invited to visualise an ideal girl friend; and he visualises a girl who turns out to be exactly like Claudia Cardinale. We might report this state of affairs by saying, 'Asked to visualise his ideal girl, he visualised a girl like Claudia Cardinale.' At first glance we may be inclined to take the expression 'just like Claudia Cardinale' here in the same way that we took the expression 'riding a bicycle' in the earlier example 'he visualised the Queen riding a bicycle'. But this could be misleading. For in that former example, the phrase 'riding a bicycle' represents an essential element of what he visualised: if he were to give as exact an account as he could of his thought he would tell a story in which the Queen was described as riding a bicycle. Now this *could* be the case with the man who visualised a girl just like Claudia Cardinale; Claudia Cardinale might occur essentially in his account of what he visualised – if he constructed his ideal girl to the specification of Claudia Cardinale, as it were. But this does not have to be so. It might merely be that he visualised a girl, and that that girl happened to be just like Claudia Cardinale – he may, indeed, never have heard of Claudia Cardinale, and no reference to her would appear in his description of the girl he visualised. Since, in these circumstances, the description 'just like Claudia Cardinale' does not occur essentially in the characterisation of what he visualised, it is tempting to revert to the bare conjunction analysis and represent the state of affairs by saying, 'He thought of himself seeing a certain girl; and that girl was just like Claudia Cardinale.' But this of course will not do, since it keeps the description 'just like Claudia Cardinale' out of the content of his thought only if we read it fully extensionally, with a quantifier external to the whole thing, so that it comes to saying that there is a certain girl of whom it is true both that he thought of himself seeing her, and that she is just like Claudia Cardinale: which is of course false. Recoiling from this, we may seem to be left with no option but to put the description 'just like Claudia Cardinale' straightforwardly into the account of his thought; which obscures the fact that this was not in the present case an element of his thought, but an *ex post facto* comment on it.

I think that in this present case a solution might be achieved on the lines of representing the statement 'He visualised a girl just like Claudia Cardinale' as 'He visualised a girl of a certain sort; and Claudia Cardinale is a girl of that sort' – that is to say, as indeed a conjunction, but a conjunction that does not rest on quantifying over individuals. However, even if such a solution might do here, I think that there will prove to be a wider range of problems of a similar kind, which may well require other sorts of treatment. They concern more generally the rôle that a man's knowledge and beliefs may play in relation to what he visualises, imagines, and so forth; and if we take a further look at this we shall see that the complication introduced by the present example goes deeper than this example by itself reveals. I have discussed this example in terms of a contrast between what is essential to what the man visualised, as he visualised it, and what comes into a description of it only via an *ex post facto* comment – an external fact, as we might say. But if we now take a case that introduces not merely ignorance (in the sense that the previous man had not heard of Claudia Cardinale), but false belief, we shall see that the phrase 'essential to what he visualised' is not merely vague (as it evidently is) but also in an important way ambiguous.

Suppose a man imagines assassinating the Prime Minister; and that his imagining this takes the form of visualisation. Suppose, further, that being rather radically misinformed about political developments, he supposes Lord Salisbury to be the Prime Minister. What is it in fact that this man imagines? It seems difficult to deny that he does imagine assassinating the Prime Minister, since that is the act – let us suppose him to be a violent anarchist – which he sets himself to imagine. Yet it would be very misleading just to say without qualification that he imagined assassinating the Prime Minister: it would naturally imply that in giving the name of the actual Prime Minister, we would be giving the name of the person that he imagined assassinating. (That it would be misleading in this way illustrates the difficulty of keeping intensional contexts pure.) However that may be, if his mistaken belief was operative in this piece of imagining, he will certainly have imagined assassinating Lord Salisbury. Elements drawn from Lord Salisbury will occur in his visualising; his image of the fallen Prime Minister will be an image of Lord Salisbury.

Another way of putting the situation here, which will be useful to us later on, is to introduce the notion of the story that the man would ideally tell if telling what he imagined. I do not mean by this a genuinely autobiographical story, rehearsing for instance the sequence of his images, but rather the story, as full as possible, of what, as he imagined it, happened – a piece of fiction, which in this case might start off 'I was standing in front of 10 Downing Street, the gun in my pocket . . .' Such a story I shall call – merely using the term as a label and no more – the *narration*. In this present case, if indeed the man's mistake about the Prime Minister's identity was operative in his imagining, the narration will introduce Lord Salisbury – very possibly by name. In this sense, the introduction of Lord Salisbury is essential to the account of what the man on this occasion imagined, in a way in which the introduction of Claudia Cardinale was not essential to the account of what the man in our first example imagined; in that case, we made an addition for him in telling the tale, in this case not. Yet, while Lord Salisbury is in this way essential to the account of what the man imagined, it may not be that Lord Salisbury is essential to what he was really trying to imagine – and if it at all depends on false belief, as we are supposing, he is probably not essential in this second sense. For it may be that precisely what this man wants to do is to imagine assassinating the Prime Minister *whoever he may be*; and when his mistake is pointed out to him, he regards the Salisbury elements in his previous act of imagining as at best an irrelevance, at worst an embarrassment.

In this sense of 'essential' – the sense in which an element is not merely essential to the account of what I do imagine, but is essential to my particular imaginative *project* – the Salisbury element will be essential, not to a man who is imagining the assassination of the Prime Minister and merely believes that Lord Salisbury is the Prime Minister, but rather to a man who is imagining the assassination of the Prime Minister and also *imagining Salisbury as the Prime Minister*. For such a man, it will be a misunderstanding to point out, with respect to his narration, that Salisbury is not the Prime Minister; it is part of the point of his imaginative tale that Salisbury should occur in it in this rôle.

The point about the different nature of the project in the two cases seems not merely to *emerge* in the difference of the treatments which would be appropriate to the narrations, but in some more basic way to be characterised by that difference. For if we take the two men I have described, one of whom merely thinks that Salisbury is the Prime Minister, the other of whom is, as part of his imagining, imagining Salisbury as the Prime Minister, it is surely obvious that there need be no difference at all in the *content* of their respective narrations. Exactly the same story could come from either; similarly, on the purely psychological level, the same visualisings, the same images, could surely occur in both cases. The difference lies rather in how the story is meant.

Let us now go back to the problem of whether one can visualise an unseen object. We saw earlier on that if what is in question is a real object, together with a purely extensional interpretation of the statement that it is not seen, there is evidently no difficulty at all. We then broached an intensional interpretation, and have been pursuing a complication that attended getting clearer about what was involved in intensional interpretations. Using a distinction we have made in the course of that, we may now consider the case of visualising an object – let us say a tree – where the idea that it is not seen by anyone is intensionally contained and is essential in the strongest sense: that is to say, the idea that it is not seen is essential to the imaginative project (it was such a project that Hylas was invited to undertake, presumably, in the original Berkeley argument).

Consider now two possible narrations. One goes roughly: 'A tree stands on an utterly deserted island; no one has ever seen it or will see it. It is a green deciduous tree, flowers on one side of it, etc., etc.' The second goes: 'I see in the middle distance a tree. As I get nearer I see it is green. Moving round, on the far side I glimpse some flowers. This tree has never been seen by anyone and never will be.'

The first of these two narrations would surely be that of a man whose project it was to *imagine an unseen tree*. If that was his project, his narration reveals him as having succeeded in it. Notice that the narration does not contain any incoherence; nor does any incoherence arise from the fact that he is able to give this narration. A difficulty of this latter kind *would* arise if what we were considering were not an imaginative narration, but a description which claimed to be factually true of the world; for in that case, one could of course ask, 'If what you are saying is true, how do you or anyone else know that it is?' But since it does not claim to be factually true, but is a product of imagination, no such question can arise. It is *his* story. So we can coherently *imagine* an unseen tree: but, remember, we knew that already. Our question is about visualisation.

The second narration would seem to be that of a man whose project it was to *imagine himself seeing a tree*. And in his narration, surely, there is something incoherent. For the last element in it, that the tree was not seen by anyone, really does clash with the rest of the narration, which is precisely a narration of his seeing it. Thus there does seem to be some incoherence in imagining oneself seeing an unseen tree, unless – boringly – this merely meant that one imagined oneself seeing a tree never seen by anyone else.

Now how are we to take the claim that it is impossible to *visualise* an unseen tree? One way of taking it would perhaps be this: that a man who was a visualiser, who did his imagining by way of visual images, would be bound in honesty to give the second type of narration and not the first. If he visualised this tree, he would by that fact be *imagining himself seeing a tree*; and that, as we have seen, does appear incoherent with an element in what he imagines being that the tree is unseen. Hence a visualiser, on this view, cannot imagine an unseen tree; he can only imagine himself seeing a tree, and that tree cannot be unseen. But if this is what the claim about visualisation means, it is patently absurd. For if, as has been said, there is a coherent project of imagining an unseen tree, how can the fact that a man is a visualiser debar him from carrying it out? The narration – which is the fullest account of what he imagined – makes no reference to anything being seen, and is coherent. How could such a narration be in some way impugned by the discovery that the man was a visualiser?

Well, it may be said, what this shows is that the correct thesis about the relations of imagination, visualisation, and the unseen is not *that* thesis, namely that one who does his imagining by way of visualising is incapable of imagining an unseen tree. The correct thesis will rather be this: that although a man may imagine an unseen tree, and do it by visualising, he cannot do it by *visualising an unseen tree*. For visualising, it was suggested earlier, means 'thinking of oneself seeing': and to think of oneself seeing an unseen tree is (the thesis claims) a nonsense, in much the same way as (we have already seen) imagining oneself seeing an unseen tree is. So we cannot visualise an unseen tree; though we can imagine one, and possibly by way of visualising.

If this is the thesis, what now is the relation between what I imagine and what I visualise? It is tempting to say that if I imagine by visualising, then what I visualise is what I imagine, or at least part of it; but clearly this temptation must be resisted, if the present thesis is to stand up. But perhaps there is a way of doing this, in terms of the distinctions I made earlier. We recall the man who imagined assassinating the Prime Minister, and who suffered at the time from a false belief that Lord Salisbury held that office. There were Lord Salisbury elements in his visualising which, I suggested, were not essential to his imaginative project. Now it might be the case that a man who visualised found himself visualising various elements which he realised were unsuitable to his imaginative project, and correspondingly left them out of his narration.

Thus suppose a man to be imagining a bath, and that he indeed visualises a bath. Having been recently much at the Bonnard exhibition, he finds himself unable to visualise a bath without a woman in it. However, the woman being irrelevant to his imaginative project, he leaves her out of the narration. If, moreover, his imaginative project positively demanded the absence of the woman – if he were required to imagine an empty bath, for instance – he would *have* to leave her out. – But, it may be objected, the narration was said to be the fullest account of what he imagined; and if he leaves out these elements in what he visualises, surely it is not the fullest account? – Yes, it can still be the fullest account of what he *imagined*; what it is not, is the fullest account of what he *visualised*. What this means is that, for certain purposes at least, and for certain applications of 'imagine', we can properly make the determinant of *what he imagined* his imaginative project, and not what he visualised, if he visualised anything. There seems to be a strong case for this in the example of the man and the bath; for it seems insane to say that this man could not imagine an empty bath, while it is perfectly true that in his present state he cannot visualise one.

Thus even when we imagine by way of visualising, we can properly be said to imagine something lacking an element which is present in what we visualise. The suggestion I am now considering is that this is how things are with imagining and visualising the unseen; it is like the bath example, with the man precisely setting out to imagine an empty bath, but with this difference: that the inseparability of the woman from the bath is a contingent fact about this man's present visualisings, whereas the inseparability of *being seen* from the objects of visualisation is a necessary and ubiquitous feature of them. Thus on this account, a man can imagine an unseen tree, and by way of visualising a tree; but he does not, and cannot, visualise an unseen tree, and the reason why what he visualises is different from what he imagines is that he is allowed to discard elements from his visualisation incompatible with the essentials of his imaginative project.

One merit of this cumbrous proposal is that it at least seems to leave a place for something like the visual in visualising, without jeopardising the truth that visualisers are not debarred from imagining the unseen. Moreover, the idea which it introduces of a man constructing his narration to suit his imaginative project fits well what I take to be a fact, that a man who vividly visualises may be incautiously drawn on into a narration which actually does not suit his imaginative project. Thus the bath man, narrating a scene supposedly with an empty bath, might make a lunge in his narration into suggestions of the presence of the woman. Rather similarly, the man who was a visualiser giving the narration of the tree, while he is unlikely to move off into talking about his own perceptual activities, as in the second narration I considered before, might very well find himself saying things like this: 'A tree stands on a deserted island. On this side there are green leaves, round towards the back some flowers. To the right, a cactus plant . . .' – a narration not incoherent like the one before, but which, as a narration of an unseen tree, gives grounds, let us say, for disquiet.

But not for ultimate disquiet; and we shall now see that the cumbrous account I have just been considering made too many concessions. The fact that the narration just given introduces something like a perceptual point of view may well reveal something familiar about visualisation; visualisation is (at least usually, and if vivid) visualisation of an object as seen from a point of view. The object may well be as though seen from one side rather than another. But this does not in fact mean that any imagined seeing is going on *in* the visualised scene. Even if we accept the description of visualising as *thinking of oneself seeing* – and we shall come back to that later – this still does not mean that an element or feature of what I visualise is that it is being seen; as it was an element or feature of the visualised bath that it contained a woman. I as perceiver do not necessarily belong inside the world that I visualise, any more than I necessarily do so in the world that I imagine; or the painter in the scene that he paints; or the audience in the world of the stage. The cumbrous account I have been considering was wrong in treating the 'seeing' element in visualising as an element in what is visualised. Let us then abandon that account – though not, I hope, everything that was said in the course of formulating it – and see what sense we can make of what is surely nearer the truth here, that we can in fact even visualise the unseen, because the fact that in visualisation I am as it were seeing is not itself necessarily an element of what is visualised.

We may start with the analogy of the stage; and I shall consider, begging a large number of interesting questions which revolve around this point, only what may be called very vaguely the illusionist stage, problems of alienation and so forth being left on one side. The audience at such a play are spectators of a world they are not in. They see what they may well describe as, say, Othello in front of a certain palace in Venice; and they see that from a certain point of view – not meaning by that that they see it from a certain seat in the theatre, but rather that what they are presented with is a certain view of that palace, e.g. a view of its front. But they are not themselves at any specifiable distance from that palace; unlike Othello, who may be (thus he may be just about to enter it).

They are, of course, at a certain specifiable distance from certain pieces of scenery, as is Sir Laurence Olivier, and they again at a certain distance from him. It is also true that they would not be seeing Othello unless they were seeing Sir Laurence or another real man moving around in such an area, nor would they be seeing the palace, unless they saw some such scenery. But we must not say that the reason why, in seeing Sir Laurence, they see Othello, is that Sir Laurence *is* Othello: at least if that 'is' is the 'is' of identity. For if Sir Laurence *is* Othello, then Miss Maggie Smith, or whoever, *is* Desdemona, and since Othello strangles Desdemona, it would follow that Sir Laurence strangles Miss Smith, which is false. What Sir Laurence does to Miss Smith is (something like) pretending to strangle her: but Othello does not pretend to strangle Desdemona, and it would be a very different play if he did. This lack of formal identity between actor and character holds also, of course, for the relations of scenery and setting: when in a play someone sets fire to the palace, they do not, hopefully, set fire to the scenery. It is just because of these failures of identity that we can sensibly say that we are, as spectators, at a certain distance from the scenery and the actors, but not from the palace or from Othello; if identity held, we should, in being 150 feet from Sir Laurence, be just that distance from Othello.

Although this is, of course, only the crudest gesture towards a complex and fascinating subject, it is enough perhaps to contribute some of the content to saying that we as spectators are not *in* the world of the play itself; we – in a sense – see what is happening in that world, but not in the same sense as that in which we see the actors, nor as that in which the characters see one another or events in the play. For if I see Othello and Desdemona, then I see Othello strangle Desdemona; but that will not entail that I, as part of my biography, have ever seen anyone strangle anyone. Nor need the actress who plays Emilia ever see a dead body; but Emilia does, for she sees the dead body of Desdemona. These points suggest a particular consideration relevant to our argument, that things can happen in the play unseen; not just in the sense, obvious enough, in which things can happen on the stage unseen (as when an actor skilfully conceals from us a prop left over from the last act), but in that sense in which the playwright can provide the direction, 'Enter First Murderer unobserved', and yet still consistently hope that his piece will have an audience, an audience who will indeed see this unobserved murderer.

The cinema provides more complex considerations of the same sort. Here the point of view from which things are seen moves. This point of view, relative to the actors and to the set, is in fact that of the camera. What is done artistically with this point of view can, of course, vary very greatly. It can in some rather unusual films be itself, in the film, the point of view of a camera: that is to say, when the scene presents straight on the front of a mirror, what we see in it is the lens of a camera. In many films for some of the time, and in at least one film for all of the time, it is the point of view of a character: when it is directed to a mirror, we see the face of that character, and when that character is struck, a fist grows larger until it fills the screen, and so on. In most conventional films most of the time, it is neither of these things. What then is it? We cannot say, at least without great care, that it is *our* point of view; for we are not, in the usual case, invited to have the feeling that we are near to this castle, floating towards its top, or stealing around these lovers, peering minutely at them. This effect *can* be created, sometimes unintentionally – but in the general run, it is not. One thing, in the general run, is certain: *we* are not *there*. Nor, again, can we say in any simple way that this point of view is the director's, though this suggestion does not entirely fail to make a point. We cannot quite simply say it, since we are no more invited to think of Griffith or of Antonioni floating up towers or creeping around lovers. It is his point of view only in the derivative sense that he is directing our attention to this and that by showing it to us as it appears from that point of view. In the standard case, it is not anyone's point of view. Yet we see the characters and action from that point of view, in that sense, or near it, in which we saw Othello. Thus once more, and very obviously, we can see in this way what in terms of the action is unseen.

That there are clues to be found in the dramatic and visual arts to the problems of visualisation is, I suppose, obvious and unsurprising. If, however, what we are concerned with is the *nature* of visualisation, these clues notoriously run out at the crucial stage. One reason that they run out is that in both theatre and cinema we really see *something* – something which we might say (coming out into the open a bit more than I have done so far) *represents* the characters and action. But in visualisation nothing is really seen – and this is a big difference. It is a big enough difference to defeat, I think, Sartre, who seems to hope (in *L'Imaginaire*) that he has acquired enough impetus from the representational cases to convey him through the air to visualisation, where our 'intention', in his terminology, is not sustained by any matter at all. But the impetus does not seem sufficient.

Yet even if these analogies leave us baffled, as they certainly leave me baffled, about the nature of visualisation, they seem to provide sufficient clues to relieve us of puzzlement at least about visualising the unseen. For even if visualising is in some sense thinking of myself seeing, and what is visualised is presented as it were from a perceptual point of view, there can be no reason at all for insisting that that point of view is of one *within* the word of what is visualised; any more than our view of Othello is a view had by one in Othello's context, or the cinematic point of view is necessarily that of one stealing around the characters. We can, then, even visualise the unseen.

But now – if we are impressed at all by these analogies, and in particular by the cinematic analogy, should we remain satisfied with this formula: visualising is thinking of myself seeing? Why does it have to be *myself*? The cinematic point of view, I suggested, did not have to be anyone's point of view; what is the ground for insisting that the point of view in visualisation must be mine? Berkeley perhaps – to revert to him for the last time – was struck by a consideration that this point of view did not need to be distinctively mine. This may help to explain an extraordinary feature of his argument, that Hylas is not supposed to conclude from his thought-experiment, as one might suppose, that he cannot conceive an object unperceived by himself; he is supposed to conclude that he cannot conceive an object unperceived by any mind.

At this point we must distinguish some different kinds of visual imagery in relation to myself; something that we have so far not needed to do. The first is that which we have just been discussing at some length, that in which I merely visualise something, without myself being in the visualised world at all. The second is contrasted with this: that in which I visualise a world in which I am acting, moving around, seeing things, and so forth – a form of imagery involving, very often, kinaesthetic imagery of various sorts. This second sort is, of course, possible and frequent; in what I said earlier, I was not denying that I *could* be in my imagined scene, I was merely denying that I had to be. In terms of imagining, it is natural (though not inevitable) to associate the first sort of imagery with imagining a certain thing, the second with imagining (myself) doing, seeing, etc., certain things.

But the expression 'imagining myself doing, etc.' could cover also a third possibility for imagery, which constitutes not really a distinct third kind, but a special application of the first: namely that of visualising from the outside a figure who is myself doing the things in question. This sort is capable of alternating quite happily with the second – as we might say, *participation* – type: thus, if I am prone to fantasies of being a world champion racing driver, this could involve kinaesthetic imagery of tension, hands clasped on the steering-wheel, and visualisation of wet tarmac as seen through an oil-spattered windscreen, and so forth; and, also at some different point, some visual image of myself, as though in a newspaper photograph, having a garland hung around my neck.

All these types of imagery are familiar, of course, from dreams, as well as from fantasy in waking life. Dreams present also further possibilities, less common perhaps in waking life; notably that of an uncomfortable half-way house between the first type, in which I am not in the scene, and the second or participation type; that in which I am there, in the same space as the happenings, but am, for no apparent reason, a transfixed and impotent observer of them. Still more painful is that case in which all this is compounded with the third type of imagery, and the happenings of which I am a transfixed observer are happenings which I can see happening to me. The complexities of dream-dissociation, however, we may leave.

Now in a great deal of fantasy and imagination of the second, participation, type, there is no great problem concerning the *me* that the fantasy is about: it is the actual empirical me, or more or less so. This does not mean, of course, that in order to entertain this fantasy of myself as a champion racing driver I have to engage in an elaborate work of intercalating racing-driving activities hypothetically into my past career, or extending hypothetically my future career so as to embrace them; I do not have to join the imagined activities in any determinate way on to my actual history. Nevertheless, I am, very often, putting quite a lot of my actual self into it, and where not consciously doing this, am prepared, as it were, to accept a lot of my actual self in the fantasied scene. It is, for instance, relative to my real wants, ambitions, and character that the imagined happenings are, to me in them, satisfying or upsetting.

Again, in the third type, very often, there is no problem about the figure that I visualise being me; at least no more problem than there is anyway about any imaged figure being someone in particular: the problem, for instance, that it looks as though an image I have of someone can be an image of that person only because I *mean* it to be so, and yet at the same time there is such a thing as *recognising* an imaged figure. These problems I shall not pursue. The present point is that there is no special problem about the visualised figure being myself; he looks, for instance, like me (or at least like what I think I look like).

In the sense in which these types of imagining involve myself, simple visualising – type one – does not involve myself, except as the person who, as a matter of simple biographical fact, does the visualising. I indeed, at a certain point in my empirical history, visualise, say, a tree; but I do not occur in this operation again, as that person concerning whom, when I visualise a tree, I think that *he* sees a tree. So, bearing in mind those other relatively straightforward cases, it is misleading to say that straight visualising is thinking of myself seeing something. It may indeed have actually misled people; for instance, Schlick. Schlick famously claimed that survival after death must be a contingent matter, because he could imagine watching his own funeral. In order to make good this claim, Schlick would have had to give a coherent account of how, as a participant at his own funeral, he could be himself, Schlick; all the problems of continuity, personal identity, and so forth are called up. It is no good trying to rest the case for this logical possibility merely on the alleged possibility of imagining oneself watching one's own funeral. In default of an independent argument that this is a coherent description of anything, we have only too readily to hand another account of the experience which, I suspect, was the one that Schlick reported in this way: namely, that he was not imagining himself watching his own funeral, he was *visualising his own funeral*. And what that proves in the way of logical possibility, if it proves anything, is only the logical possibility *of his funeral*, which is not in dispute.

However, it is obviously not enough merely to eliminate from the discussion at this stage any reference to a 'myself' which is not the actual, empirical myself. I have said only that a *lot* of imagery about myself is recognisably about my actual self as – roughly – I am. But it looks as though some imagery, and in particular participation imagery, can be about myself, and yet precisely involve the elimination of my actual characteristics. I can imagine, in particular, being somebody else. It is with some remarks about this sort of possibility, which involves perhaps the most intimate relations between the imagination and the self, that I shall end.

'I might have been somebody else' is a very primitive and very real thought; and it tends to carry with it an idea that one knows what it would be like for this 'I' to look out on a different world, from a different body, and still be the same 'I'. To start at the easiest place, we know perfectly well that a great deal of what we are, in terms of memory, character, and bodily development, is the product of accidental factors which we can readily conceive to have been otherwise: 'if my parents had, as they considered doing, emigrated when I was two . . .' – yet it would still have been me. Suppose, further, that I had had different parents, who had borne me in a different year, a different century, even. . . . Such speculations can retain a grip on the imagination only up to a certain point, perhaps; and it is a significant fact that the point at which the grip slips, as it were, will differ with different people. For instance, it may well be the case that many people would find the first line of speculation I just imagined, about the emigration of one's parents, much more compelling than the second, concerning one's parents' identity; and I suppose this to be not because of some beliefs about the overwhelming importance of heredity in the formation of character (which may well be false, and are dubiously relevant), but because in our form of society parents play such a large part in one's early history, one is emotionally involved with them, and so forth. In the Guardian class of Plato's Republic the difficult supposition would not have been that one might have had different parents (since one was not to know who they were, anyway), nor yet that one might have been born years earlier (since the state was supposed to go on without historical social change), but rather that one might have been born somewhere else, and not be a Platonic Guardian at all. One's sense of identity involves one's identifications.

Nevertheless, it is an important fact that, whatever the limits, one seems to be able to carry on these speculations about *oneself* in a way in which one cannot about other people. 'I might have been . . .' is a form of thought that holds up much longer than 'he might have been . . .', although the latter, too, does better if there is identification, in the sense for instance of a close emotional attachment. In general, if we carry speculations about him very far, there soon comes a point where it is vacuous to say that we are talking about *him* at all – we are just imagining some arbitrary historical figure. In thinking that I might have been . . ., it is not like this; or not so soon.

If we press this hard enough, we readily get the idea that it is not necessary to being *me* that I should have any of the individuating properties that I do have, this body, these memories, etc. And for some of them, such as the body, we may think that it is not necessary to have one at all; and, quite readily, we might not have any memories. The limiting state of this progress is the Cartesian consciousness: an 'I' without body, past, or character. In pursuing these speculations to this point, we do not so far meet any obvious dilemma or paradox – at most, there is a sense of strain, an increasing attenuation of content. A dilemma or real philosophical obstacle occurs, however, when one adds to these speculations another consideration: that it must also be true that I might not have existed. This we certainly want to agree to – few will be persuaded that their own existence is a necessary feature of the universe. Now it is clear that, if we admit the previous speculations, the 'I' of 'I might not have existed' must be the same attenuated 'I' that seemed to emerge from those speculations. For suppose we took 'I might not have existed' to mean (as it might naturally be taken to mean) that there might not have been someone who had such and such a history, such and such an appearance, etc., filling this out with a list of one's actual empirical properties. If the previous speculations in fact made sense, then this filling-out cannot be an adequate account of what it means to say 'I might not have existed'. For if, on the line of the previous speculations, I had been someone else, lived at a different time, and so forth, then it might well be true that there would not have existed someone with just the properties I actually have, and yet not be true that I did not exist – I would exist, but not with those properties. The same point can be approached from the opposite end: it looks as though we might admit that someone could exist with just those empirical properties of history, appearance, etc., that I as a matter of fact have, and yet that person not be me. So, by these arguments, 'I might not have existed' cannot mean 'there might not have existed a person with just this specification', where the specification is that of the properties I actually have. Nor will any other specification of properties do better. So it looks as though the 'I' of this statement must again be the attenuated 'I', the Cartesian centre of consciousness. But if this is so, what can 'I might not have existed' possibly mean? For it now looks as though there is absolutely nothing left to distinguish any Cartesian 'I' from any other, and it is impossible to see any more what would be subtracted from the universe by the removal of *me*.

Once the difficulty has presented itself in this form, it works back to the original set of speculations. For suppose I conceive it possible that I might have been Napoleon – and mean by this that there might have been a world which contained a Napoleon exactly the same as the Napoleon that our world contained, except that he would have been me. What could be the difference between the actual Napoleon and the imagined one? All I have to take to him in the imagined world is a Cartesian centre of consciousness; and that, the real Napoleon had already. Leibniz, perhaps, made something like this point when he said to one who expressed the wish that he were King of China, that all he wanted was that he should cease to exist and there should be a King in China.

Thus we seem to reach an impasse: on the one hand, we have a type of speculation which can, perhaps rather compulsively, seem to make sense; on the other hand, considerations which show that the speculations must fail. The way out of this impasse lies, I think, in diagnosing an illusion that lies in the speculations. This illusion has something to do with the nature of the imagination.

If the activity of imagining being Napoleon involves in any important way imagery, it is bound, I think, to involve participation imagery. Images of myself being Napoleon can scarcely merely be images of the physical figure of Napoleon, for they will not in themselves have enough of me in them – an external view would lose the essence of what makes such imaginings so much more compelling about myself than they are about another. They will rather be images of, for instance, the desolation at Austerlitz as viewed by me vaguely aware of my short stature and my cockaded hat, my hand in my tunic.

Consider now the *narration*, to revert to the model we used earlier, appropriate to this sort of imagination. It is going to be of the general form: 'I have conquered; the ideals of the Revolution in my hands are sweeping away the old world. Poor Maria Walewska, I wonder where she is now' and so on and so on, according to whatever knowledge or illusions I possess about Napoleon. Now suppose that we actually heard someone saying things like this. In general, when we hear utterances in the first person, there is only one question to be asked relative to the identity of the 'I' involved: 'Who is the speaker?' But in the case of utterances as unlikely as this, there are two questions: 'Who is the speaker?' and 'Who is it that he either believes that he is, or is pretending to be?' In the present case, the latter alternative is in question: a man engaged in an imaginative narration like this would be a man pretending to be, or playing the rôle of, Napoleon. The 'I' of his discourse is to be taken as an 'I' uttered by Napoleon; who it stands for, if it stands for anybody, is Napoleon. But, of course, this being the playing of a rôle, the actual utterer is someone else, who in the next moment may use 'I' in its ordinary way with respect to his ordinary self.

Now this narration does not, of course, have to be actually produced. I am using it, as I was using it before, as a model to display what the man is imagining; some of his imaginative activity may actually take the form of saying some of these things to himself, but much of it may take such forms as imagery of his doing and seeing things, of which this narrative merely represents the ideally best verbal expression. But what is true, as we have seen, for the public verbal performance is true also for the private fantasy; what I am doing, in fantasy, is something like playing the rôle of Napoleon. In this respect, if not more generally, I agree with Professor Ryle's association, in *The Concept of Mind*, of the imagination with pretending. In the description of this activity, only two people need figure: the real me and Napoleon. There is no place for a third item, the Cartesian 'I', regarding which I imagine that *it* might have belonged to Napoleon. To suppose that such an entity is involved seems, in some part at least, to follow from a confusion of two modes of the imagination: that of imagining with regard to a certain thing, distinct from myself, that it is such and such; and that of imagining being such and such.

I have used several times the formula 'imagining myself doing, being, etc., such and such'. Where this 'myself' is, roughly, my ordinary self, as in the case of the racing driver fantasy I discussed before, there is no great harm in this formula. But where the question is of imagining being, for instance, Napoleon, the formula 'imagining *myself* being Napoleon' is possibly misleading. It draws us near to a formula that may also be used, and which may be even more misleading – though misleading, of course, only when I start reflecting on it: the formula 'imagining that I am (or was) Napoleon'. For with regard to this formula, we may feel bound to ask what this 'I' is that turns up inside the expression of what I imagine. If it is the ordinary empirical one, as I am, what I imagine seems to be straightforwardly self-contradictory, which stops me in my tracks; and this will not do, for I know that, in imagining being Napoleon, I am not stopped in my tracks. Impressed by the fact that I am not stopped in my tracks, I may come to embrace the only apparent alternative: that this 'I' is a Cartesian one. The same sort of alternatives may seem to present themselves with the formula 'imagining myself being Napoleon', when we ask about the identity of the *myself*.

The mode of imagining appropriate to these fantasies, when they are not stopped in their tracks, is least misleadingly expressed as 'imagining being Napoleon': what this represents, the fantasy enactment of the rôle of Napoleon, is the only mode that has the power to sustain the speculations we have been discussing at all. And this mode, properly understood, does not introduce a further 'me' to generate these difficulties: there are only two persons involved in this, as I said, the real me and Napoleon. It is as unproblematic that I can imagine being Napoleon as that Charles Boyer could act the rôle of Napoleon.

It is perhaps in some such way, then, that we can explain why it is that although I can certainly imagine being Napoleon – or if I cannot, this is a limitation of mine – I still do not understand, and could not possibly understand, what it would be for me to have been Napoleon. For the fact that I can, in the only way that arouses my interest, imagine being Napoleon has no tendency at all to show that I can conceive, as a logical possibility, that I might have been Napoleon; any more than the fact that Charles Boyer can be Napoleon on the screen enables us to understand (in any serious sense) what it would be for Charles Boyer to have been Napoleon. Here we meet yet once more something that, in different ways, we have met twice before, once with Berkeley and once with Schlick; that at least with regard to the self, the imagination is too tricky a thing to provide a reliable road to the comprehension of what is logically possible.

4
The self and the future

Suppose that there were some process to which two persons, A and B, could be subjected as a result of which they might be said – question-beggingly – to have *exchanged bodies*. That is to say – less question-beggingly – there is a certain human body which is such that when previously we were confronted with it, we were confronted with person A, certain utterances coming from it were expressive of memories of the past experiences of A, certain movements of it partly constituted the actions of A and were taken as expressive of the character of A, and so forth; but now, after the process is completed, utterances coming from this body are expressive of what seem to be just those memories which previously we identified as memories of the past experiences of B, its movements partly constitute actions expressive of the character of B, and so forth; and conversely with the other body.

There are certain important philosophical limitations on how such imaginary cases are to be constructed, and how they are to be taken when constructed in various ways. I shall mention two principal limitations, not in order to pursue them further here, but precisely in order to get them out of the way.

There are certain limitations, particularly with regard to character and mannerisms, to our ability to imagine such cases even in the most restricted sense of our being disposed to take the later performances of that body which was previously A's as expressive of B's character; if the previous A and B were extremely unlike one another both physically and psychologically, and if, say, in addition, they were of different sex, there might be grave difficulties in reading B's dispositions in any possible performances of A's body. Let us forget this, and for the present purpose just take A and B as being sufficiently alike (however alike that has to be) for the difficulty not to arise; after the experiment, persons familiar with A and B are just *overwhelmingly struck* by the B-ish character of the doings associated with what was previously A's body, and conversely. Thus the feat of imagining an exchange of bodies is supposed possible in the most restricted sense. But now there is a further limitation which has to be overcome if the feat is to be not merely possible in the most restricted sense but also is to have an outcome which, on serious reflection, we are prepared to describe as *A* and *B* having changed bodies – that is, an outcome where, confronted with what was previously *A*'s body, we are prepared seriously to say that we are now confronted with *B*.

It would seem a necessary condition of so doing that the utterances coming from that body be taken as genuinely expressive of memories of *B*'s past. But memory is a causal notion; and as we actually use it, it seems a necessary condition of *x*'s present knowledge of *x*'s earlier experiences constituting memory of those experiences that the causal chain linking the experiences and the knowledge should not run outside *x*'s body. Hence if utterances coming from a given body are to be taken as expressive of memories of the experiences of *B*, there should be some suitable causal link between the appropriate state of that body and the original happening of those experiences to *B*. One radical way of securing that condition in the imagined exchange case is to suppose, with Shoemaker,[1] that the brains of A and of *B* are transposed. We may not need so radical a condition. Thus suppose it were possible to extract information from a man's brain and store it in a device while his brain was repaired, or even renewed, the information then being replaced: it would seem exaggerated to insist that the resultant man could not possibly have the memories he had before the operation. With regard to our knowledge of our own past, we draw distinctions between merely recalling, being reminded, and learning again, and those distinctions correspond (roughly) to distinctions between no new input, partial new input, and total new input with regard to the information in question; and it seems clear that the information-parking case just imagined would not count as new input in the sense necessary and sufficient for 'learning again'. Hence we can imagine the case we are concerned with in terms of information extracted into such devices from *A*'s and *B*'s brains and replaced in the other brain; this is the sort of model which, I think not unfairly for the present argument, I shall have in mind.

We imagine the following. The process considered above exists; two persons can enter some machine, let us say, and emerge changed in the appropriate ways. If A and *B* are the persons who enter, let us call the persons who emerge the *A-body-person* and the *B-body-person:* the A-body-person is that person (whoever it is) with whom I am confronted when, after the experiment, I am confronted with that body which previously was *A*'s body – that is

[1] *Self-Knowledge and Self-Identity* (Ithaca, N.Y., 1963), pp. 23 seq.

to say, that person who would naturally be taken for A by someone who just saw this person, was familiar with A's appearance before the experiment, and did not know about the happening of the experiment. A non-question-begging description of the experiment will leave it open which (if either) of the persons A and B the A-body-person is; the description of the experiment as 'persons changing bodies' of course implies that the A-body-person is actually B.

We take two persons A and B who are going to have the process carried out on them. (We can suppose, rather hazily, that they are willing for this to happen; to investigate at all closely at this stage why they might be willing or unwilling, what they would fear, and so forth, would anticipate some later issues.) We further announce that one of the two resultant persons, the A-body-person and the B-body-person, is going after the experiment to be given $100,000, while the other is going to be tortured. We then ask each of A and B to choose which treatment should be dealt out to which of the persons who will emerge from the experiment, the choice to be made (if it can be) on selfish grounds.

Suppose that A chooses that the B-body-person should get the pleasant treatment and the A-body-person the unpleasant treatment; and B chooses conversely (this might indicate that they thought that 'changing bodies' was indeed a good description of the outcome). The experimenter cannot act in accordance with both these sets of preferences, those expressed by A and those expressed by B. Hence there is one clear sense in which A and B cannot both get what they want: namely, that if the experimenter, before the experiment, announces to A and B that he intends to carry out the alternative (for example), of treating the B-body-person unpleasantly and the A-body-person pleasantly – then A can say rightly, 'That's not the outcome I chose to happen', and B can say rightly, 'That's just the outcome I chose to happen'. So, evidently, A and B before the experiment can each come to know either that the outcome he chose will be that which will happen, or that the one he chose will not happen, and in that sense they can get or fail to get what they wanted. But is it also true that when the experimenter proceeds after the experiment to act in accordance with one of the preferences and not the other, *then* one of A and B will have got what he wanted, and the other not?

There seems very good ground for saying so. For suppose the experimenter, having elicited A's and B's preference, says nothing to A and B about what he will do; conducts the experiment; and then, for example, gives the unpleasant treatment to the *B*-body-person and the pleasant treatment to the A-body-person. Then the *B*-body-person will not only complain of the unpleasant treatment as such, but will complain (since he has A's memories) that that was not the outcome he chose, since he chose that the *B*-body-person should be well treated; and since A made his choice in selfish spirit, he may add that he precisely chose in that way because he did not want the unpleasant things to happen to *him*. The A-body-person meanwhile will express satisfaction both at the receipt of the $100,000, and also at the fact that the experimenter has chosen to act in the way that he, *B*, so wisely chose. These facts make a strong case for saying that the experimenter has brought it about that *B* did in the outcome get what he wanted and A did not. It is therefore a strong case for saying that the *B*-body-person really is A, and the A-body-person really is *B*; and therefore for saying that the process of the experiment really is that of changing bodies. For the same reasons it would seem that A and *B* in our example really did choose wisely, and that it was A's bad luck that the choice he correctly made was not carried out, *B*'s good luck that the choice he correctly made was carried out. This seems to show that to care about what happens to me in the future is not necessarily to care about what happens to *this* body (the one I now have); and this in turn might be taken to show that in some sense of Descartes's obscure phrase, I and my body are 'really distinct' (though, of course, nothing in these considerations could support the idea that I could exist without a body at all).

These suggestions seem to be reinforced if we consider the cases where A and *B* make other choices with regard to the experiment. Suppose that A chooses that the A-body-person should get the money, and the *B*-body-person get the pain, and *B* chooses conversely. Here again there can be no outcome which matches the expressed preferences of both of them: they cannot both get what they want. The experimenter announces, before the experiment, that the A-body-person will in fact get the money, and the *B*-body-person will get the pain. So A at this stage gets what he wants (the announced outcome matches his expressed preference). After the experiment, the distribution is carried out as announced. Both the A-body-person and the *B*-body-person will have to agree that what is happening is in accordance with the preference that A originally expressed. The *B*-body-person will naturally express this acknowledgement (since he has A's memories) by saying that this is the distribution he chose; he will recall, among other things, the experimenter announcing this outcome, his approving it as what he chose, and so forth. However, he (the *B*-body-person) certainly does not like what is now happening to him, and would much prefer to be receiving what the *A*-body-person is receiving – namely, $100,000. The *A*-body-person will on the other hand recall choosing an outcome other than this one, but will reckon it good luck that the experimenter did not do what he recalls choosing. It looks, then, as though the *A*-body-person has got what he wanted, but not what he chose, while the *B*-body-person has got what he chose, but not what he wanted. So once more it looks as though they are, respectively, *B* and *A*; and that in this case the original choices of both *A* and *B* were unwise.

Suppose, lastly, that in the original choice *A* takes the line of the first case and *B* of the second: that is, *A* chooses that the *B*-body-person should get the money and the *A*-body-person the pain, and *B* chooses exactly the same thing. In this case, the experimenter would seem to be in the happy situation of giving both persons what they want – or at least, like God, what they have chosen. In this case, the *B*-body-person likes what he is receiving, recalls choosing it, and congratulates himself on the wisdom of (as he puts it) his choice; while the *A*-body-person does not like what he is receiving, recalls choosing it, and is forced to acknowledge that (as he puts it) his choice was unwise. So once more we seem to get results to support the suggestions drawn from the first case.

Let us now consider the question, not of *A* and *B* choosing certain outcomes to take place after the experiment, but of their willingness to engage in the experiment at all. If they were initially inclined to accept the description of the experiment as 'changing bodies' then one thing that would interest them would be the character of the other person's body. In this respect also what would happen after the experiment would seem to suggest that 'changing bodies' was a good description of the experiment. If *A* and *B* agreed to the experiment, being each not displeased with the appearance, physique, and so forth of the other person's body; after the experiment the *B*-body-person might well be found saying such things as: 'When I agreed to this experiment, I thought that *B*'s face was quite attractive, but now I look at it in the mirror, I am not so sure'; or the *A*-body-person might say 'When I agreed to this experiment I did not know that *A* had a wooden leg; but now, after it is over, I find that I have this wooden leg, and I want the experiment reversed.' It is possible that he might say further that he finds the leg very uncomfortable, and that the *B*-body-person should say, for instance, that he recalls that he found it very uncomfortable at first, but one gets used to it: but perhaps one would need to know more than at least I do about the physiology of habituation to artificial limbs to know whether the *A*-body-person would find the leg uncomfortable: that body, after all, has had the leg on it for some time. But apart from this sort of detail, the general line of the outcome regarded from this point of view seems to confirm our previous conclusions about the experiment.

Now let us suppose that when the experiment is proposed (in non-question-begging terms) *A* and *B* think rather of their psychological advantages and disadvantages. *A*'s thoughts turn primarily to certain sorts of anxiety to which he is very prone, while *B* is concerned with the frightful memories he has of past experiences which still distress him. They each hope that the experiment will in some way result in their being able to get away from these things. They may even have been impressed by philosophical arguments to the effect that bodily continuity is at least a necessary condition of personal identity: *A*, for example, reasons that, granted the experiment comes off, then the person who is bodily continuous with him will not have this anxiety, and while the other person will no doubt have some anxiety – perhaps in some sense his anxiety – at least that person will not be he. The experiment is performed and the experimenter (to whom *A* and *B* previously revealed privately their several difficulties and hopes) asks the *A*-body-person whether he has got rid of his anxiety. This person presumably replies that he does not know what the man is talking about; he never had such anxiety, but he did have some very disagreeable memories, and recalls engaging in the experiment to get rid of them, and is disappointed to discover that he still has them. The *B*-body-person will react in a similar way to questions about his painful memories, pointing out that he still has his anxiety. These results seem to confirm still further the description of the experiment as 'changing bodies'. And all the results suggest that the only rational thing to do, confronted with such an experiment, would be to identify oneself with one's memories, and so forth, and not with one's body. The philosophical arguments designed to show that bodily continuity was at least a necessary condition of personal identity would seem to be just mistaken.

Let us now consider something apparently different. Someone

in whose power I am tells me that I am going to be tortured tomorrow. I am frightened, and look forward to tomorrow in great apprehension. He adds that when the time comes, I shall not remember being told that this was going to happen to me, since shortly before the torture something else will be done to me which will make me forget the announcement. This certainly will not cheer me up, since I know perfectly well that I can forget things, and that there is such a thing as indeed being tortured unexpectedly because I had forgotten or been made to forget a prediction of the torture: that will still be a torture which, so long as I do know about the prediction, I look forward to in fear. He then adds that my forgetting the announcement will be only part of a larger process: when the moment of torture comes, I shall not remember any of the things I am now in a position to remember. This does not cheer me up, either, since I can readily conceive of being involved in an accident, for instance, as a result of which I wake up in a completely amnesiac state and also in great pain; that could certainly happen to me, I should not like it to happen to me, nor to know that it was going to happen to me. He now further adds that at the moment of torture I shall not only not remember the things I am now in a position to remember, but will have a different set of impressions of my past, quite different from the memories I now have. I do not think that this would cheer me up, either. For I can at least conceive the possibility, if not the concrete reality, of going completely mad, and thinking perhaps that I am George IV or somebody; and being told that something like that was going to happen to me would have no tendency to reduce the terror of being told authoritatively that I was going to be tortured, but would merely compound the horror. Nor do I see why I should be put into any better frame of mind by the person in charge adding lastly that the impressions of my past with which I shall be equipped on the eve of torture will exactly fit the past of another person now living, and that indeed I shall acquire these impressions by (for instance) information now in his brain being copied into mine. Fear, surely, would still be the proper reaction: and not because one did not know what was going to happen, but because in one vital respect at least one did know what was going to happen – torture, which one can indeed expect to happen to oneself, and to be preceded by certain mental derangements as well.

If this is right, the whole question seems now to be totally mysterious. For what we have just been through is of course merely one side, differently represented, of the transaction which we considered before; and it represents it as a perfectly hateful prospect, while the previous considerations represented it as something one should rationally, perhaps even cheerfully, choose out of the options there presented. It is differently presented, of course, and in two notable respects; but when we look at these two differences of presentation, can we really convince ourselves that the second presentation is wrong or misleading, thus leaving the road open to the first version which at the time seemed so convincing? Surely not.

The first difference is that in the second version the torture is throughout represented as going to happen to *me*: 'you', the man in charge persistently says. Thus he is not very neutral. But should he have been neutral? Or, to put it another way, does his use of the second person have a merely emotional and rhetorical effect on me, making me afraid when further reflection would have shown that I had no reason to be? It is certainly not obviously so. The problem just is that through every step of his predictions I seem to be able to follow him successfully. And if I reflect on whether what he has said gives me grounds for fearing that I shall be tortured, I could consider that behind my fears lies some principle such as this: that my undergoing physical pain in the future is not excluded by any psychological state I may be in at the time, with the platitudinous exception of those psychological states which in themselves exclude experiencing pain, notably (if it is a psychological state) unconsciousness. In particular, what impressions I have about the past will not have any effect on whether I undergo the pain or not. This principle seems sound enough.

It is an important fact that not everything I would, as things are, regard as an evil would be something that I should rationally fear as an evil if it were predicted that it would happen to me in the future and also predicted that I should undergo significant psychological changes in the meantime. For the fact that I regard that happening, things being as they are, as an evil can be dependent on factors of belief or character which might themselves be modified by the psychological changes in question. Thus if I am appallingly subject to acrophobia, and am told that I shall find myself on top of a steep mountain in the near future, I shall to that extent be afraid; but if I am told that I shall be psychologically changed in the meantime in such a way as to rid me of my acrophobia (and as with the other prediction, I believe it), then I have no reason to be afraid of the predicted happening, or at least not the same reason. Again, I might look forward to meeting a certain person again with either alarm or excitement because of my memories of our past relations. In some part, these memories operate in connexion with my emotion, not only on the present time, but projectively forward: for it is to a meeting itself affected by the presence of those memories that I look forward. If I am convinced that when the time comes I shall not have those memories, then I shall not have just the same reasons as before for looking forward to that meeting with the one emotion or the other. (Spiritualism, incidentally, appears to involve the belief that I have just the same reasons for a given attitude toward encountering people again after I am dead, as I did before: with the one modification that I can be sure it will all be very nice.)

Physical pain, however, the example which for simplicity (and not for any obsessional reason) I have taken, is absolutely minimally dependent on character or belief. No amount of change in my character or my beliefs would seem to affect substantially the nastiness of tortures applied to me; correspondingly, no degree of predicted change in my character and beliefs can unseat the fear of torture which, together with those changes, is predicted for me.

I am not at all suggesting that the *only* basis, or indeed the only rational basis, for fear in the face of these various predictions is how things will be relative to my psychological state in the eventual outcome. I am merely pointing out that this is one component; it is not the only one. For certainly one will fear and otherwise reject the changes themselves, or in very many cases one would. Thus one of the old paradoxes of hedonistic utilitarianism; if one had assurances that undergoing certain operations and being attached to a machine would provide one for the rest of one's existence with an unending sequence of delicious and varied experiences, one might very well reject the option, and react with fear if someone proposed to apply it compulsorily; and that fear and horror would seem appropriate reactions in the second case may help to discredit the interpretation (if anyone has the nerve to propose it) that one's reason for rejecting the option voluntarily would be a consciousness of duties to others which one in one's hedonic state would leave undone. The prospect of contented madness or vegetableness is found by many (not perhaps by all) appalling in ways which are obviously not a function of how things would then be for them, for things would then be for them not appalling. In the case we are at present discussing, these sorts of considerations seem merely to make it clearer that the predictions of the man in charge provide a double ground of horror: at the prospect of torture, and at the prospect of the change in character and in impressions of the past that will precede it. And certainly, to repeat what has already been said, the prospect of the second certainly seems to provide no ground for rejecting or not fearing the prospect of the first.

I said that there were two notable differences between the second presentation of our situation and the first. The first difference, which we have just said something about, was that the man predicted the torture for *me*, a psychologically very changed 'me'. We have yet to find a reason for saying that he should not have done this, or that I really should be unable to follow him if he does; I seem to be able to follow him only too well. The second difference is that in this presentation he does not mention the other man, except in the somewhat incidental rôle of being the provenance of the impressions of the past I end up with. He does not mention him at all as someone who will end up with impressions of the past derived from me (and, incidentally, with $100,000 as well – a consideration which, in the frame of mind appropriate to this version, will merely make me jealous).

But why *should* he mention this man and what is going to happen to him? My selfish concern is to be told what is going to happen to me, and now I know: torture, preceded by changes of character, brain operations, changes in impressions of the past. The knowledge that one other person, or none, or many will be similarly mistreated may affect me in other ways, of sympathy, greater horror at the power of this tyrant, and so forth; but surely it cannot affect my expectations of torture? But – someone will say – this is to leave out exactly the feature which, as the first presentation of the case showed, makes all the difference: for it is to leave out the person who, as the first presentation showed, will be you. It is to leave out not merely a feature which should fundamentally affect your fears, it is to leave out the very person for whom you are fearful. So of course, the objector will say, this makes all the difference.

But can it? Consider the following series of cases. In each case we are to suppose that after what is described, A is, as before, to be tortured; we are also to suppose the person A is informed beforehand that just these things followed by the torture will happen to him:

(i) A is subjected to an operation which produces total amnesia;
(ii) amnesia is produced in A, and other interference leads to certain changes in his character;

(iii) changes in his character are produced, and at the same time certain illusory 'memory' beliefs are induced in him: these are of a quite fictitious kind and do not fit the life of any actual person;

(iv) the same as (iii), except that both the character traits and the 'memory' impressions are designed to be appropriate to another actual person, *B*;

(v) the same as (iv), except that the result is produced by putting the information into A from the brain of *B*, by a method which leaves *B* the same as he was before;

(vi) the same happens to A as in (v), but *B* is not left the same, since a similar operation is conducted in the reverse direction.

I take it that no-one is going to dispute that A has reasons, and fairly straightforward reasons, for fear of pain when the prospect is that of situation (i); there seems no conceivable reason why this should not extend to situation (ii), and the situation (iii) can surely introduce no difference of principle – it just seems a situation which for more than one reason we should have grounds for fearing, as suggested above. Situation (iv) at least introduces the person *B*, who was the focus of the objection we are now discussing. But it does not seem to introduce him in any way which makes a material difference; if I can expect pain through a transformation which involves new 'memory'-impressions, it would seem a purely external fact, relative to that, that the 'memory'-impressions had a model. Nor, in (iv), do we satisfy a causal condition which I mentioned at the beginning for the 'memories' actually being memories; though notice that if the job were done thoroughly, I might well be able to elicit from the A-body-person the kinds of remarks about his previous expectations of the experiment – remarks appropriate to the original *B* – which so impressed us in the first version of the story. I shall have a similar assurance of this being so in situation (v), where, moreover, a plausible application of the causal condition is available.

But two things are to be noticed about this situation. First, if we concentrate on A and the A-body-person, we do not seem to have added anything which from the point of view of his fears makes any material difference; just as, in the move from (iii) to (iv), it made no relevant difference that the new 'memory'-impressions which precede the pain had, as it happened, a model, so in the move from (iv) to (v) all we have added is that they have a model which is also their cause: and it is still difficult to see why that, to him looking forward, could possibly make the difference between expecting pain and not expecting pain. To illustrate that point from the case of character: if A is capable of expecting pain, he is capable of expecting pain preceded by a change in his dispositions – and to that expectation it can make no difference, whether that change in his dispositions is modelled on, or indeed indirectly caused by, the dispositions of some other person. If his fears can, as it were, reach through the change, it seems a mere trimming how the change is in fact induced. The second point about situation (v) is that if the crucial question for A's fears with regard to what befalls the A-body-person is whether the A-body-person is or is not the person *B*,[2] then that condition has not yet been satisfied in situation (v): for there we have an undisputed *B* in addition to the A-body-person, and certainly those two are not the same person.

But in situation (vi), we seemed to think, that is finally what he is. But if A's original fears could reach through the expected changes in (v), as they did in (iv) and (iii), then certainly they can reach through in (vi). Indeed, from the point of view of A's expectations and fears, there is less difference between (vi) and (v) than there is between (v) and (iv) or between (iv) and (iii). In those transitions, there were at least differences – though we could not see that they were really relevant differences – in the content or cause of what happened to him; in the present case there is absolutely no difference at all in what happens to him, the only difference being in what happens to someone else. If he can fear pain when (v) is predicted, why should he cease to when (vi) is?

I can see only one way of relevantly laying great weight on the transition from (v) to (vi); and this involves a considerable difficulty. This is to deny that, as I put it, the transition from (v) to (vi) involves merely the addition of something happening to *somebody else;* what rather it does, it will be said, is to involve the reintroduction of A himself, as the *B*-body-person; since he has reappeared in this form, it is for this person, and not for the unfortunate A-body-person, that A will have his expectations. This is to reassert, in effect, the viewpoint emphasised in our first presentation of the experiment. But this surely has the consequence that A should not have fears for the A-body-person who appeared in situation (v). For by the present argument, the A-body-person in (vi) is not A; the *B*-body-person is. But the A-body-person in (v) is, in character, history, everything, exactly the same as the A-body-person in (vi); so if the latter is not A, then neither is the former.

2 This of course does not have to be the crucial question, but it seems one fair way of taking up the present objection.

(It is this point, no doubt, that encourages one to speak of the difference that goes with (vi) as being, on the present view, the *reintroduction* of A.) But no-one else in (v) has any better claim to be A. So in (v), it seems, A just does not exist. This would certainly explain why A should have no fears for the state of things in (v) – though he might well have fears for the path to it. But it rather looked earlier as though he could well have fears for the state of things in (v). Let us grant, however, that that was an illusion, and that A really does not exist in (v); then does he exist in (iv), (iii), (ii), or (i)? It seems very difficult to deny it for (i) and (ii); are we perhaps to draw the line between (iii) and (iv)?

Here someone will say: you must not insist on drawing a line – borderline cases are borderline cases, and you must not push our concepts beyond their limits. But this well-known piece of advice, sensible as it is in many cases, seems in the present case to involve an extraordinary difficulty. It may intellectually comfort observers of A's situation; but what is A supposed to make of it? To be told that a future situation is a borderline one for its being myself that is hurt, that it is conceptually undecidable whether it will be me or not, is something which, it seems, I can do nothing with; because, in particular, it seems to have no comprehensible representation in my expectations and the emotions that go with them.

If I expect that a certain situation, S, will come about in the future, there is of course a wide range of emotions and concerns, directed on S, which I may experience now in relation to my expectation. Unless I am exceptionally egoistic, it is not a condition on my being concerned in relation to this expectation, that I myself will be involved in S – where my being 'involved' in S means that I figure in S as someone doing something at that time or having something done to me, or, again, that S will have consequences affecting me at that or some subsequent time. There are some emotions, however, which I will feel only if I will be involved in S, and fear is an obvious example.

Now the description of S under which it figures in my expectations will necessarily be, in various ways, indeterminate; and one way in which it may be indeterminate is that it leaves open whether I shall be involved in S or not. Thus I may have good reason to expect that one of us five is going to get hurt, but no reason to expect it to be me rather than one of the others. My present emotions will be correspondingly affected by this indeterminacy. Thus, sticking to the egoistic concern involved in fear, I shall presumably be somewhat more cheerful than if I knew it was going to be me, somewhat less cheerful than if I had been left out altogether. Fear will be mixed with, and qualified by, apprehension; and so forth. These emotions revolve around the thought of the eventual determination of the indeterminacy; moments of straight fear focus on its really turning out to be me, of hope on its turning out not to be me. All the emotions are related to the coming about of what I expect: and what I expect in such a case just cannot come about save by coming about in one of the ways or another.

There are other ways in which indeterminate expectations can be related to fear. Thus I may expect (perhaps neurotically) that something nasty is going to happen to me, indeed expect that when it happens it will take some determinate form, but have no range, or no closed range, of candidates for the determinate form to rehearse in my present thought. Different from this would be the fear of something radically indeterminate – the fear (one might say) of a nameless horror. If somebody had such a fear, one could even say that he had, in a sense, a perfectly determinate expectation: if what he expects indeed comes about, there will be nothing more determinate to be said about it after the event than was said in the expectation. Both these cases of course are cases of *fear* because one thing that is fixed amid the indeterminacy is the belief that it is me to whom the things will happen.

Central to the expectation of S is the thought of what it will be like when it happens – thought which may be indeterminate, range over alternatives, and so forth. When S involves me, there can be the possibility of a special form of such thought: the thought of how it will be for me, the imaginative projection of myself as participant in S.[3] I do not have to think about S in this way, when it involves me; but I may be able to. (It might be suggested that this possibility was even mirrored in the language, in the distinction between 'expecting to be hurt' and 'expecting that I shall be hurt'; but I am very doubtful about this point, which is in any case of no importance.)

Suppose now that there is an S with regard to which it is for conceptual reasons undecidable whether it involves me or not, as is proposed for the experimental situation by the line we are discussing. It is important that the expectation of S is not *indeterminate* in any of the ways we have just been considering. It is not like the nameless horror, since the fixed point of that case was that

[3] For a more detailed treatment of issues related to this, see 'Imagination and the Self', pp. 38 *seq.*

it was going to happen to the subject, and that made his state unequivocally fear. Nor is it like the expectation of the man who expects one of the five to be hurt; his fear was indeed equivocal, but its focus, and that of the expectation, was that when S came about, it would certainly come about in one way or the other. In the present case, fear (of the torture, that is to say, not of the initial experiment) seems neither appropriate, nor inappropriate, nor appropriately equivocal. Relatedly, the subject has an incurable difficulty about how he may think about S. If he engages in projective imaginative thinking (about how it will be for him), he implicitly answers the necessarily unanswerable question; if he thinks that he cannot engage in such thinking, it looks very much as if he also answers it, though in the opposite direction. Perhaps he must just refrain from such thinking; but is he just refraining from it, if it is incurably undecidable whether he can or cannot engage in it?

It may be said that all that these considerations can show is that fear, at any rate, does not get its proper footing in this case; but that there could be some other, more ambivalent, form of concern which would indeed be appropriate to this particular expectation, the expectation of the conceptually undecidable situation. There are, perhaps, analogous feelings that actually occur in actual situations. Thus material objects do occasionally undergo puzzling transformations which leave a conceptual shadow over their identity. Suppose I were sentimentally attached to an object to which this sort of thing then happened; it might be that I could neither feel about it quite as I did originally, nor be totally indifferent to it, but would have some other and rather ambivalent feeling towards it. Similarly, it may be said, toward the prospective sufferer of pain, my identity relations with whom are conceptually shadowed, I can feel neither as I would if he were certainly me, nor as I would if he were certainly not, but rather some such ambivalent concern.

But this analogy does little to remove the most baffling aspect of the present case – an aspect which has already turned up in what was said about the subject's difficulty in thinking either projectively or non-projectively about the situation. For to regard the prospective pain-sufferer *just* like the transmogrified object of sentiment, and to conceive of my ambivalent distress about his future pain as just like ambivalent distress about some future damage to such an object, is of course to leave him and me clearly distinct from one another, and thus to displace the conceptual shadow from its proper place. I have to get nearer to him than that. But is there any nearer that I can get to him without expecting his pain? If there is, the analogy has not shown us it. We can certainly not get nearer by expecting, as it were, *ambivalent* pain; there is no place at all for that. There seems to be an obstinate bafflement to mirroring in my expectations a situation in which it is conceptually undecidable whether I occur.

The bafflement seems, moreover, to turn to plain absurdity if we move from conceptual undecidability to its close friend and neighbour, conventionalist decision. This comes out if we consider another description, overtly conventionalist, of the series of cases which occasioned the present discussion. This description would reject a point I relied on in an earlier argument – namely, that if we deny that the A-body-person in (vi) is A (because the B-body-person is), then we must deny that the A-body-person in (v) is A, since they are exactly similar. 'No', it may be said, 'this is just to assume that we say the same in different sorts of situation. No doubt when we have the very good candidate for being A – namely, the B-body-person – we call him A; but this does not mean that we should not call the A-body-person A in that other situation when we have no better candidate around. Different situations call for different descriptions.' This line of talk is the sort of thing indeed appropriate to lawyers deciding the ownership of some property which has undergone some bewildering set of transformations; they just have to decide, and in each situation, let us suppose, it has got to go to somebody, on as reasonable grounds as the facts and the law admit. But as a line to deal with a person's fears or expectations about his own future, it seems to have no sense at all. If A's fears can extend to what will happen to the A-body-person in (v), I do not see how they can be rationally diverted from the fate of the exactly similar person in (vi) by his being told that someone would have a reason in the latter situation which he would not have in the former for deciding to call another person A.

Thus, to sum up, it looks as though there are two presentations of the imagined experiment and the choice associated with it, each of which carries conviction, and which lead to contrary conclusions. The idea, moreover, that the situation after the experiment is conceptually undecidable in the relevant respect seems not to assist, but rather to increase, the puzzlement; while the idea (so often appealed to in these matters) that it is conventionally decidable is even worse. Following from all that, I am not in the least clear which option it would be wise to take if one were presented with them before the experiment. I find that rather disturbing.

Whatever the puzzlement, there is one feature of the arguments which have led to it which is worth picking out, since it runs counter to something which is, I think, often rather vaguely supposed. It is often recognised that there are 'first-personal' and 'third-personal' aspects of questions about persons, and that there are difficulties about the relations between them. It is also recognised that 'mentalistic' considerations (as we may vaguely call them) and considerations of bodily continuity are involved in questions of personal identity (which is not to say that there are mentalistic and bodily criteria of personal identity). It is tempting to think that the two distinctions run in parallel: roughly, that a first-person approach concentrates attention on mentalistic considerations, while a third-personal approach emphasises considerations of bodily continuity. The present discussion is an illustration of exactly the opposite. The first argument, which led to the 'mentalistic' conclusion that *A* and *B* would change bodies and that each person should identify himself with the destination of his memories and character, was an an argument entirely conducted in third-personal terms. The second argument, which suggested the bodily continuity identification, concerned itself with the first-personal issue of what *A* could expect. That this is so seems to me (though I will not discuss it further here) of some significance.

I will end by suggesting one rather shaky way in which one might approach a resolution of the problem, using only the limited materials already available.

The apparently decisive arguments of the first presentation, which suggested that *A* should identify himself with the *B*-body-person, turned on the extreme neatness of the situation in satisfying, if any could, the description of 'changing bodies'. But this neatness is basically artificial; it is the product of the will of the experimenter to produce a situation which would naturally elicit, with minimum hesitation, that description. By the sorts of methods he employed, he could easily have left off earlier or gone on further. He could have stopped at situation (v), leaving *B* as he was; or he could have gone on and produced two persons each with A-like character and memories, as well as one or two with *B*-like characteristics. If he had done either of those, we should have been in yet greater difficulty about what to say; he just chose to make it as easy as possible for us to find something to say.

Now if we had some model of ghostly persons in bodies, which were in some sense actually moved around by certain procedures, we could regard the neat experiment just as the *effective* experiment: the one method that really did result in the ghostly persons' changing places without being destroyed, dispersed, or whatever. But we cannot seriously use such a model. The experimenter has not in the sense of that model *induced* a change of bodies; he has rather produced the one situation out of a range of equally possible situations which we should be most disposed to call a change of bodies. As against this, the principle that one's fears can extend to future pain whatever psychological changes precede it seems positively straightforward. Perhaps, indeed, it is not; but we need to be shown what is wrong with it. Until we are shown what is wrong with it, we should perhaps decide that if we were the person A then, if we were to decide selfishly, we should pass the pain to the B-body-person. It would be risky: that there is room for the notion of a *risk* here is itself a major feature of the problem.

5

Are persons bodies?

Problems of mind and body arise at two levels. On the one hand, there are general issues concerning the relations between a subject's mental states and his possession of a body, including in particular their relations to his observable behaviour. On the other hand, there are questions concerning the relations between a subject's mental states and certain internal states of his organism (in particular, states of the central nervous system) which might in a developed psycho-physical science be correlated with the mental states – the term 'correlated' here being not intended to beg any questions.

This second range of problems, which we might call problems at the micro-level, particularly concern how such a correlation may most illuminatingly and economically be characterised; and the most notable recent contribution to this area has been the group of views often called the 'identity theory' or 'central state materialism'. It is not, however, with this range of problems that I shall for the most part be concerned in this paper, but rather with the first range of problems, problems at the macro-level. But it is worth noticing in passing one very important area of overlap between the two ranges: if the occurrence of a mental state (e.g., a sensation) is cited as the *explanation* of a piece of observable behaviour, the question arises of how such an explanation is related to an explanation in terms of physical mechanisms, and this, at the inner end, constitutes a problem at the micro-level.

Among problems at the macro-level, some of the most general may conveniently be labelled 'metaphysical'. They include such questions as: What sorts of things do there have to be in the world for there to be mental states? Do there have to be physical bodies (e.g., organisms)? If so, is this because the sort of thing that 'has' mental states must itself be a physical thing? It is with this sort of question that the present paper will be concerned.

I start with some remarks on Mr Strawson's well-known treatment of the subject.[1] It will be recalled that Strawson distinguishes among predicates ascribed to persons, two classes, of M-predicates and P-predicates. These are introduced, under those labels, by his saying: 'The first kind of predicate consists of those which are also properly

[1] *Individuals* (London: Methuen, 1959), Ch. 3.

applied to material bodies to which we would not dream of applying predicates ascribing states of consciousness[2]. . . The second kind consists of all the other predicates we apply to persons.'[3] This distinction I am deliberately going to treat in a simplified form, by regarding *P*-predicates as those 'we would not dream' of applying to material bodies, and *M*-predicates as those we can apply to material bodies. This is a simplification, since Strawson himself recognises that not all *P*-predicates ascribe 'states of consciousness';[4] but this is a point which he himself is disposed to take pretty lightly, on the grounds that all *P*-predicates imply the possession of consciousness on the part of that to which they are ascribed. I do not think that anything in my remarks will turn essentially on the adoption of the simplification. In terms of this distinction among predicates we ascribe to ourselves, I take it to be Strawson's view that the concept of a person is the (primitive) concept of a subject to which both these sorts of predicates can be applied.

I shall sustain the fiction for the purposes of discussion that we can roughly individuate predicates in the relevant ways – though this is in fact a fiction which conceals some major difficulties. 'Running down hill' presumably does not express the same predicate when used in connexion with a river and with a man; but perhaps it does when used in connexion with a man and with a dog. Does 'digging a hole' express the same predicate when used in connexion with a man, a dog, and a mechanical excavator? Does 'adding up the accounts' when used in connexion with a bank clerk and a computer? Presumably if we could answer these questions, we would be well on the way with many of our problems; but, for the present discussion, I shall not go on about it.

If it is Strawson's view that the concept of a person is that of a subject to which both *M*- and *P*-predicates can be ascribed, the first difficulty is whether this means that a person is the sort of thing

[2] This sentence is grammatically ambiguous. I have taken the expression 'material bodies to which we would not dream of applying predicates ascribing states of consciousness' as meaning 'material bodies, namely those things to which we would not dream of applying etc.'; and taking it in this way is indeed central to my argument. It could, however, mean 'those among material bodies to which we would not dream of applying etc.'; that is to say, as implying that persons were themselves included among material bodies. This latter interpretation seems scarcely consistent with other features, and the general emphasis, of Strawson's theory; it would make it, in fact, little different from the view I advance. But if this is what he actually meant, then my criticisms should be read as attaching not to Strawson but to a prevalent interpretation of Strawson.

[3] *Individuals*, p. 105.

[4] *Ibid.* p. 105.

to which any *P*-predicate can be ascribed, or the sort of thing to which some *P*-predicate can be ascribed. If the latter, then the concept is not that of a person, but of (something like) an animal. If the former, then it may perhaps be the concept of a person; but even this is not clear, because of the unclarity attached to such expressions as 'can be ascribed', 'ascribable', etc. We might have some creatures to which the whole range of *P*-predicates was *ascribable* – in whatever sense it is in which Strawson thinks that to material bodies they are not ascribable – but of which they were not all true; and those that were not true were those that imparted precisely the characteristic of *being a person*.

But suppose that we say that persons are just picked out as those to which (as well as M-predicates) *any* P-predicate is ascribable. Then material bodies will be those things to which no *P*-predicate is ascribable. And we shall have to admit a further class of things to which both M-predicates and some *P*-predicates are ascribable, namely other animals. And this point seems to me to show a difficulty in Strawson's approach which is not merely minor. Strawson's view was, it seems, that the concept of a person was unique in admitting the joint ascription to things that fall under it of the two sorts of predicate, and this seems important to his thesis in terms of the explications he gives of the possibility of such joint ascription, which connect that possibility intimately with the possibility of self-ascription. There must, it now seems, be something wrong with this; and if the concept of a person is, with regard to the ascription of the two sorts of predicates, primitive, then it looks as though there will have to be other such primitive concepts, or at least one such.

I suspect that this difficulty is one aspect of a general and odd feature of Strawson's account, namely the noticeably Cartesian materials out of which it is constructed.[5] Neither Strawson nor Descartes shows much disposition to relate *persons* to any classification of living things; but it can scarcely be an insignificant fact that our paradigm (to put it mildly) of a person is a human being, and human beings form a sub-class of living things. The neglect of the continuity of our ascriptions of predicates to human beings and to other animals is bound to produce an artificial (and highly Cartesian) dichotomy between persons and everything else.

I pass to a second difficulty which, if it is real, is more fundamental than this. It turns on what is meant by saying that (in the

[5] There is some more on this point, and on the individuation of P-predicates, in 'Strawson on individuals', pp. 120–6.

simplified version of the thesis) *P*-predicates are predicates which 'we would not dream of applying to material bodies'. I shall take this, in the first instance, to mean something which could also be expressed by saying that it would *make no sense* to apply such predicates to material bodies: that something on these lines is what Strawson actually means seems to me to receive some support from a passage in which he speaks of '. . . an enormous class of predicates (sc. *P*-predicates) such that the applicability of those predicates or their negations defines a major logical type or category of individuals':[6] but I shall not pursue the exegetical issue.

There is certainly an unclarity in saying that it does not make sense to ascribe a certain predicate to a certain type of thing. Category doctrines, notoriously, are often expressed in such terms: thus it may be said that it does not make sense to assert or deny greenness of a prime number. But there is something unsatisfactory about such formulations: they express a doctrine which should surely be about sense, in terms of reference. 'That is green' does not itself become a senseless form of words if someone tries to refer to a prime number in uttering the sentence; nor does 'the thing he's talking about is green' if it turns out that the thing he is talking about is a prime number. What surely are categorially senseless, if anything is categorially senseless, are sentences such as 'the prime number 7 is green'. The point is emphasised by the fact that category-senselessness can equally be diagnosed, if at all, in non-referential statements, e.g., 'Any number which is prime is green.' If these considerations are right, then it seems that what are categorially senseless (if anything) are conjunctions of predicates; and what we should more accurately say is not that 'green' cannot sensibly be ascribed to a prime number, but that 'green and a prime number' cannot be ascribed to anything, because it does not make sense.

The thesis which, on the present interpretation, Strawson holds is that *P*-predicates cannot be sensibly ascribed to material bodies. If what I just said is right, then this must admit of a more accurate paraphrase to the effect that there is some class of predicates – material body predicates – such that the conjunction of them and any *P*-predicate does not make sense and cannot be ascribed to anything. But at least among such predicates must be the *M*-predicates; and indeed this class might be thought to be coextensive with the class of *M*-predicates, for while we have supposedly been told something about predicates which can be sensibly ascribed to persons but not to material bodies, we have been told nothing about any predicates

[6] *Individuals*, p. 99 note.

which can be sensibly ascribed to material bodies and not to persons – perhaps any predicate ascribable to a material body can be sensibly, if patently falsely, ascribed to a person. But on this second showing, and perhaps even on the first, it begins to look as though P-predicates and M-predicates cannot be sensibly conjoined, and hence cannot be jointly ascribed to anything. So if persons are precisely things which admit of such joint ascription, there cannot be any persons.

To jump to that conclusion from these premises would of course be unjustified. What the premises entail is that there are various predicates or conjunctive sets of predicates, instantiation of which by a thing constitutes that thing a material body; and that the conjunction of any such set with a P-predicate is senseless. The premises do not entail, what the direct inference of the unpalatable conclusion requires, that the conjunction of a P-predicate with any member, or any proper subset, of such sets would be senseless.

Though we do not get to the unpalatable conclusion so directly, we shall see in a minute that we do get to it eventually. First, however, we must notice that there is a total obscurity about how these conjunctive sets of material-body predicates are in general to be characterised. We can in fact produce a dummy to stand in place of each such set: the predicate 'being a material body'. But if we try to get the hang of them by taking this seriously, we get nowhere. For what is, in the required sense, a material body? It certainly cannot be merely anything to which M-predicates are ascribable: for then the unpalatable conclusion does follow, instantly. It will have, rather, to be a *merely* material body; and that is, it would seem, just something to which M-predicates are ascribable and P-predicates are not, which gets us nowhere at all. So there seems to be no short way (or at least very short way) of characterising what it is, the conjunctive ascription of which with P-predicates is senseless.

But, it may be said, why look for such a general characterisation? We can provide examples enough of the sorts of predicates and conjunctions of predicates which fall into the 'material body' list, such as 'being a rock', perhaps, or 'being a table', or 'being made entirely of sodium', or 'being many light-years across and at a surface temperature of 6,000°K'. But now we have to recall that the requirements of the thesis with the present interpretation are that the conjunctions of these various items and P-predicates are supposed to be *senseless*. It is not the claim of the thesis that these predicates *empirically* exclude P-predicates – obviously enough. Nor is it the claim that they form logically inconsistent, contradictory conjunctions when conjoined with P-predicates: that would be an interesting line to take, but it is different from, and indeed incompatible with, the 'category-senselessness' approach: in order to form a *contradictory* conjunction, predicates must surely belong to the same category (cf. the difference between 'all prime numbers are green' and 'all prime numbers are divisable without remainder by two'). But we are surely going to be hard put to it to find a doctrine of sense by which, of the following pairs of predicates, for example, the first in each case will make a senseless conjunction with P-predicates, while the second makes a sensible conjunction: being made of the same stuff as the Apollo Belvedere, having the same weight as the Apollo Belvedere; being made entirely of sodium, being made of carbon, oxygen, etc.; frequently to be found in slate, frequently to be found in slate quarries; being a waxwork, looking like a waxwork; being a sponge, being a primate. Perhaps the first members of these pairs are not to be allocated to the (merely) material body list; if not, it is unclear why, or what is.

Apart from these considerations, a more particular argument can be advanced which really does seem to lead back to the original unpalatable conclusion. Let there be an object which has just the properties of a human body; which is, if you like, a human body, save that it is not the body of a person. No P-predicates go with it. The possibility of this, it seems to me, cannot be excluded on the thesis under discussion; for it would be excluded, surely, only if the instantiation of all these properties together entailed the instantiation of P-predicates, and this (on the thesis) seems to be excluded. Now this object is surely a material body. But P-predicates cannot be sensibly ascribed to any material body. This means that P-predicates cannot be sensibly conjoined with any set of predicates which sufficiently specify a thing which is a material body. But since the body just mentioned is a material body, the predicates which specify it must be such a set. Hence they cannot be sensibly conjoined with P-predicates. Hence no human being, at least, is a person, since this conjunction is exactly what would be true of him if he were. The argument, moreover, could be repeated with regard to any other body which was supposedly the body of a person. Hence indeed there are no persons.

These difficulties seem to me to make hopeless the version of Strawson's position which represents it as a thesis about sense. Perhaps, however, the phrase 'which we would not dream of applying to material bodies' does not mean 'which it would make no sense to apply to material bodies'. Perhaps it just means that there are certain predicates which we ascribe to ourselves which we would never for a moment think could be truly ascribed to material bodies: such ascriptions would just, as we all know, be false. If this is what is meant, no category style of difference would have been suggested, and the previous objections would not apply. There is, however, a different objection which will apply. For if it is just false of certain material bodies that psychological predicates apply to them, what obstacle can there be to saying that it is just true of others (e.g., ourselves) that such predicates do apply to them? If we do say this, the concept of a person will be in no way primitive. For now we can say, quite simply, that while many material bodies do not, and no doubt cannot, think (etc.), others (very complex ones) can, and a person is such a body. We shall then have reached the third corner of a triangle with Descartes and with Strawson: saying neither that a person is a mind who has a body, nor yet that he is an unanalysable subject of mind-predicates and body-predicates; but that he is a material body which thinks (etc.).

Why should we not say that persons form a class of material bodies? Certainly not merely on the ground that they have psychological attributes, as we have seen: that seems to rest either on the view that no material bodies have psychological attributes, which at best begs the question, or on the view that merely material bodies do not have psychological attributes, which is vacuously true.

For the rest of this paper, I shall consider four leading objections to the view that persons are material bodies, and say something against them; what I say will not in every case be very full, but will, I hope, be discouraging, if no more, to the objections – though in the case of the last objection, a certain qualification to the view may be required.

Objection 1: We can conceive of disembodied persons. I shall not here attempt to refute this position, and shall not even consider it in full generality with respect to *non*-bodied persons, but consider only a more restricted idea, of strictly *dis*embodied persons, i.e., of persons formerly embodied who have become disembodied. Even this I shall not argue against categorically, but will confine myself to trying to show merely this, that if we admit the possibility of persons previously embodied becoming disembodied, then we are committed to giving a Cartesian or dualistic account of those persons in their embodied state. Anyone who thinks the Cartesian account mistaken will, if I am right, have reason to give up an idea of a transition to a disembodied state; and since anyone who believes in a permanently non-bodied person is presumably something like a Cartesian anyway, only Cartesians or near-Cartesians will be left.

Let us consider, if we can, the state of a person previously embodied but now disembodied. Somebody raises such questions as 'what weight has he?' 'what height has he?'; having regard to his disembodied state, it seems that there are two rather different things that might be said about such questions, (*a*) that they have no answer, (*b*) that they have an answer, and the answers are zero lb, zero in., etc. I shall take up these two lines in turn.

(*a*) The force of this seems to be that a person is a thing which, though it can, does not have to, exemplify determinates under physical determinables. But this has many difficulties. For surely the understanding of what a given sort of thing is closely involves an understanding of under what determinables a thing of that sort exemplifies determinates. Connected with this, we can recall an important remark of Leibniz: that the real is the fully determinate. If we are given a specification of a thing of a certain sort, and are told that it exemplifies no determinates under determinables associated with things of that sort, we can standardly conclude that it is not the specification of any real thing of that sort, but, e.g., of a fictional thing: part of what it is for Lady Macbeth to be a fictional woman is that there are many questions to which with regard to any real woman, there must be answers (though we may not know what they are), but which have no answers in the case of Lady Macbeth.

Considerations on these admittedly sketchy lines may well give us reason to say that it is impossible for one and the same thing to have a given collection of determinables apply to it at one time and not at another. If so, we shall say that the possibility of disembodiment would show, not just that a person was a sort of thing that *did not necessarily* exemplify physical determinables, but that it was a sort of thing that *necessarily did not* exemplify such determinables. Then even embodied persons would not have physical attributes, but would be nonphysical things associated with a body, i.e., a Cartesian account would apply.

This is only the sketch of an answer to (*a*), but I think that very serious difficulties will be found for (*a*) on these lines. Admittedly, there are some determinables which a given sort of thing can, as it were, lose: thus a material body might become totally colourless (at the extreme, by becoming invisible). This possibility may be taken to show that *having a colour* is not essential to being a physical body. The case of a person's losing all his physical attributes would seem in any case graver than that, and more significant for one's understanding of what sort of thing a person was; but in any case, it would certainly show that having physical attributes was not essential to being a person. Now this would not lead directly, of course, to what I have called the Cartesian conclusion; for the fact that persons did not essentially have physical attributes would not (contrary to an inference possibly conducted by Locke with regard to primary and secondary qualities) show in itself that they never had them at all. But this is not all that we have to work from: for it seems true that all the current arguments against the Cartesian position (e.g., Strawson's) do involve saying that it is essential that persons have, at least some of the time, physical attributes. I am not sure that any coherent account can be given of a sort of thing to which it is essential that it display at some time determinates under a wide range of determinables, but not essential that it do this at all times; yet this is required by line (*a*).

(*b*) cuts cleanly through that sort of difficulty, at least; but it succumbs to a more clearly definable difficulty. Here we must remember the disembodied person's *body*, which evidently may still exist (embalmed, buried, or whatever). This will display physical attributes like any other material body; let us take the particular case of its weight and suppose its weight $= k$ (which of course $\neq$ 0. Now at some earlier time t before disembodiment, something which for the moment we might call this body displayed weight; let us suppose that weight $= m$ ($m \neq 0$, and, we may plausibly suppose, $\neq k$). So we have at t something which weighs m; while at t' (after disembodiment) we have a person who weighs 0 and a body which weighs k. Now something has, between t and t' changed from weighing m to weighing k; and that thing would seem to be the body.

But it looks also as though there were something that had changed between t and t' from weighing m to weighing 0; suppose that there is such a thing. If there is, it cannot be the same thing as the thing we considered last, i.e., the body: for the two predicates '. . . changes just between t and t' from weighing m to weighing 0' and 'changes just between t and t' from weighing m to weighing k ($k \neq 0$)' are incompatible with one another. So this thing, if it exists, must be a different thing: it would seem to be, in fact, the person (it is, after all, the person who ends up at t' weighing 0). So now we have two things, one of which in the given time has changed from weighing m to weighing k, the other from weighing m to weighing 0.

This entails that there are two different things, each of which at t weighed m. So what are we to say about the weight at t of something which consists just of those two things? It might seem that such a thing would have to weigh $2m$: in which case, a person together with his body must weigh twice as much as his body weighs, which is absurd. Perhaps there is another possibility. Consider, for instance, a car and the materials of which it is made. These are not identical things since the materials, independently identified, can have a different history from that of the car. The concept of weight can be applied to each; yet the car and the total of materials of which it consists at a given time do not of course weigh more than the car weighs. So the weight-doubling paradox can be avoided by saying that a person consists of, is made of, his body. But one who believes in disembodiment surely cannot say *that*; for how can a thing which consists at a given time of certain materials come to consist of nothing at all, save by ceasing to exist? If there are any merits to the quasi-Aristotelian model of *consisting of* for the relations of persons and bodies (and I am doubtful of them), it certainly cannot be consistently combined with the possibility of disembodiment.

The assumption that there were two things which had undergone different changes of weight led to two possible conclusions about the embodied person and his weight, neither of them acceptable. So the only thing left is to deny that the two different changes have occurred. But certainly the body has undergone the change specified (from weighing m to weighing k). Hence the only way out is to say that the person, who afterwards weighs 0, always did weigh 0: i.e., that it has always been a weightless (and by variants of the same argument, extensionless etc.) item associated with a body. That is to say, the Cartesian account of embodied persons follows, on line (b), from the possibility of disembodiment.

Objection 2: 'Jones' (taken as referring to a person) and 'Jones's body' are not interchangeable SALVA VERITATE. Thus, it might be speciously argued, 'Jones feels cold' and 'Jones's body feels cold' do not have the same truth-conditions. But this is because 'feels cold' has two different senses, one of which is naturally suggested by the choice of the one referential expression, the other by the other; if we take the same sense (imagining, for instance, the doctor laying his hand on Jones's body and saying 'Jones feels cold') they do have the same truth-conditions. There are of course many and strong conventions which govern the selection of the expressions 'Jones' and 'Jones's body'; but what has to be demonstrated is that the grotesqueness of many sentences which result from breaching these conventions suffices to show that Jones and Jones's body are not the same thing; and I doubt whether this can be demonstrated. A rather simple argument to the conclusion that they are not the same thing rests on the point that at least 'Jones's body' cannot be substituted for 'Jones' *in the context 'Jones's body'*. But this by itself is obviously a facile objection: an exactly parallel argument could be used to show that 'Marks and Spencer's' does not refer to the same thing as 'the firm of Marks and Spencer's' or 'Marks and Spencer's shop'.

Again, Aristotelian enthusiasts will point out that, leaving aside immortality, when Jones (or his body) dies, Jones ceases to exist ('he is no more'), while his body does not. There may be something here: but it surely cannot be pressed too hard. For, taken strictly, it should lead to the conclusion that 'living person' is pleonasm and 'dead person' a contradiction; nor should it be possible to see a person dead, since when I see what is usually called that, I see something that exists. And if it is said that when I see a dead person I see the dead but existent body which was the body of a sometime person, this rewriting seems merely designed to preserve the thesis from the simpler alternative that in seeing a dead body I see a dead person because that is what it is.

Behind the conventions I have already referred to, there are deep and important concerns reflected in the ways we talk about persons and their bodies. To take one of thousands, it is certainly not exactly the same thing to love a person and to love his or her body. But this does not show that the many and various things which that distinction says may not be said in ways which make it plainer that it does not entail that persons and bodies are two different things. The thesis is, after all, that bodies are the subjects of psychological attributes; particularly in ascribing such attributes, or in connexions which involve them, we do not, and no doubt never will, use the expression 'X's body'. But a demonstration is lacking that that comprehensible fact shows the thesis to be false.

Objection 3: If persons are material bodies, then all properties of persons are material properties; but this is false. This attacks head-on the issue of bodies having psychological attributes; but it attacks it so head-on as to be suspect of begging the question. We can ask, what are 'material properties'? If they are just whatever properties material bodies have, then it painlessly follows from the thesis that psychological properties are included among material ones. If it is just defined to exclude psychological predicates, it patently begs the question. What the objection needs is a plausible independent characterisation of material properties which excludes peculiar, e.g., psychological, properties of persons. But what is this going to be? Descartes had a clear answer to this question: a material property will be a mode or determination of the attributes fundamental to physical theory (in his view, extension). But this condition, while clear, is absurdly too strong if we are also to say that quite ordinary material bodies have only material properties; it excludes, for instance, 'observed by physicists' as a property of material bodies (a point I owe to Sidney Morgenbesser).

There are much deeper issues in this area which involve the relations between psychological states and the physical states which we must suppose to underlie them – the problems at the micro-level which I mentioned at the beginning. I cannot discuss these here; but there is just one point that I should like very briefly to raise, since it has a close relation to the thesis of this paper. Some psychological concepts are clearly causal concepts, in the sense that to apply such a concept to a person implies a claim about the causation of some mental state or disposition of his, whether this be by features of his environment or by others of his mental states, dispositions, or experiences. Perception is one such concept; memory is another; and I think it is plausible to suppose that the same is true of knowledge in general. Let us take memory, a case which can scarcely be disputed. If it is agreed that it is a necessary condition on *A*'s remembering an event *E* that he should have present knowledge of *E* which is caused by earlier experience of *E*, the question arises of how we can conceive of such causation's acting.

Armstrong[7] has rightly said that it is a philosophical proposition that memory and other psychological functions involve such causal relations; but has said further that it will be a contingent fact (one of several contingencies which must obtain if Central State Materialism is actually to be true, and not merely a conceptual possibility) that these causal relations obtain at a physical level, and not in an immaterial substance. This seems to me a rather odd position to take. It is certainly a philosophical question whether there could be an immaterial substance, and another, whether, if there could, we can form any coherent idea of causal relations obtaining in it. If the answers to both these questions were positive, then what Armstrong regards as a contingency would be a contingency. But it seems to me very far from clear that the answers to these questions could be positive; and, in particular, far from clear that the idea of causal

[7] David M. Armstrong, A *Materialist Theory of the Mind* (London: Routledge & Kegan Paul, 1968).

relations obtaining in an immaterial substance could be anything but utterly mysterious. If this idea were incurably confused, then it would at least not be a contingency that the causal relations involved in memory were not realised in an immaterial substance; and it might well be wondered whether there were any coherent alternative in fact to the relations' being realised in states of the person's body. If there were not, then of course there would be no contingency left at this point of the materialist programme.

If we did think that there was no alternative to the causal relations running through the body, then there would be a further argument for the view that persons are bodies. It does not immediately follow: it might be said that the most that could follow was that persons had to have bodies. But support would surely be lent to the stronger view by the consideration that the very application of central psychological concepts involves something which, when properly understood, is seen to make an indeterminate reference to internal states of the body.

There may be an objection, of a familiar kind, to the idea that an everyday concept such as memory could possibly involve, even indirectly, such a reference to internal physical states. For, it may be said, people have used a concept of memory for centuries, and people use it now, with no conception of internal physical causation in this regard; and often, indeed, in conjunction with views which are inconsistent with such a requirement. This is not an impressive argument. People successfully use, and there is much point in their using, a concept which implies causal relations between a person's states at different times: the manifest signs of such causation guide their use of the concept, and form the basis of such useful distinctions as those between recalling, being reminded, and learning again. But their successful use of such notions does not mean they need have reflected, or reflected effectively, on how the causation might be conceived as acting; and they can have beliefs (and obviously do have beliefs) which depend on their not having reflected effectively on this point. Thus the argument seems to me a poor one; but it may be considerations on the lines of the argument which have led some materialists to overestimate, at this point at least, the amount of contingency in materialism.

Objection 4: The identity of persons is not the same as the identity of bodies. This is the last objection I shall consider, and also, I think, the most forceful one. If persons are a class of bodies, then 'same person' must imply 'same body', just as, whales being a species of mammal, 'same whale' implies 'same mammal', and soldiers being a class of men, 'same soldier' implies 'same man'. But to this requirement that bodily identity be a necessary condition of personal identity, there seems to be at least one persuasive counter-example, namely Shoemaker's example of two men whose brains are taken out and replaced in one another's bodies, with (it is supposed) consequent transfer of character- and memory-traits. If judgements of personal identity in such a case went the way of the character- and memory-traits, as it seems they reasonably might, we would have here a divergence from bodily identity; since clearly it would be absurd to suggest that what governs the identity of the *body* is the identity of the brain, i.e., that the body which now contains the brain of Smith must be the same body as the body which earlier contained the brain of Smith – it quite evidently is not.

I am not happy about Shoemaker's case as a clear case of 'changing bodies'; for one thing, I remain unclear about the relation between giving that description of the case, and what is to be said about the expectations of the original persons with regard to their own futures. I discuss that problem elsewhere.[8] What can be said for Shoemaker's case over many putative counter-examples against the necessity of bodily identity, is that it avoids the *reduplication problem:* that is to say, the principle of personal identity which can be elicited from it is not such as to allow of two contemporaneous persons, not identical with each other, each of which precisely satisfies the principle. For it cannot be the case that there be two bodies, each of which contains at the same time precisely Smith's brain. Of course, as Wiggins has discussed in his book,[9] Smith's brain might be split, and it is imaginable that exactly the same character- and memory-traits should go with the implanting of each half, as go with the implanting of the whole. This is fundamentally no different from the possibility attached to a criterion based on the identity of the whole body, that the whole body should, amoeba-like, split: this is a logical possibility to which all material bodies are heir. This possibility does not show, however, that criteria based on the continuity of material things (whether whole bodies or whole brains) are in absolutely no different case with regard to the reduplication problem than are other criteria not so based. For the reduplication problem arises if a supposed criterion of identity allows

[8] 'The Self and the Future', pp. 46–63. The discussion there actually uses the information-transfer model introduced below (p. 79), and not the model of physical brain-transfer.

[9] David Wiggins, *Identity and Spatio-Temporal Continuity* (Oxford: Blackwell, 1967), pp. 52 *seq.*

there to be two distinct items, B and C, each of which satisfies the criterion in just the way that it would if the other did not exist. But this is not so with bodily continuity; what is true of B when it is in the ordinary way continuous with A is just not the same as what is true of it when, together with C, it has been produced from A by fission.

Someone may suggest that we can reproduce this feature with purely 'mental' criteria as well. For let R be the relation of 'having memory- and character-resemblance to' (suitably strongly interpreted). 'Bearing R to A' cannot by itself provide the criterion of identity with A, since it is liable to the reduplication problem. But 'uniquely bearing R to A' can; since if B uniquely bears R to A, then something is true of it which is just not true of it if C bears R to A as well. But this dodge, while it establishes a surface similarity between the two cases, does not eliminate a deeper difference. For there is a fairly clear sense in which what is true of B when it uniquely bears R to A is just the same as what is true of it when it non-uniquely bears R to A; the 'uniquely', representing as it does merely the conjunction of a negative existential statement to the original statement about B, makes in this sense no real difference to B. Whereas the difference between being straightforwardly continuous with A, and being a fission-product of A, is a genuine difference in the history of B. Being so, it is also an unalterable feature of B, that B came about in the one way or the other. Whereas, if 'uniquely bearing R to A' were a criterion of identity, it looks as though one could *bring it about* that B, not previously identical with A, became identical with A – just by suppressing the rival candidate C: and this seems to show clearly the inadequacy of such a criterion.[10]

The avoidance of the reduplication problem is, then, one feature of the Shoemaker case as it stands. If we accept that case, then the principle of identity underlying it should be represented in such a way as to embody the feature that avoids the reduplication problem: very roughly put, it will come out as something like 'A and B are the same person if and only if B displays the same memory- and character-traits as A, and does so because the body of B contains the same brain as the body of A.'[11] On this principle, persons will not be bodies, since the identity of persons will diverge from the identity of bodies.

[10] At least this will be so on a tensed interpretation of the negative existential statement implied by 'uniquely'. It would not be so on an untensed (or omnitemporal) interpretation; but I think that further difficulties would be found with such an interpretation.

[11] A sophisticated version of such a criterion is suggested by Wiggins, *Identity and Spatio-Temporal Continuity*, p. 55.

Correspondingly, the ascription of properties to persons will not be the ascription of properties to bodies: not even the *bodily* properties which are ascribed to persons will be ascribed to bodies. For if the Shoemaker case is possible, it will be possible truly to say of a certain person that he used to have red hair and weigh 200 lb, but that he now has black hair and weighs 150 lb; and it is not true of any body that it used to have the one set of properties and now has the other. Accepting the Shoemaker case will at any rate leave us with a job still to do, namely to make clear how the ascription of bodily properties to persons is not the ascription of anything to bodies, a problem which, in criticising the (admittedly very strong) version of such a divergence advanced by Strawson, we found to have its difficulties.

I shall not pursue that further here; but will turn lastly to a class of cases which constitute a very natural extension of the Shoemaker case, but, unlike that case, do admit the reduplication problem. These will arise if we consider, not the physical transfer of brains, but the transfer of information between brains. Thus we can imagine the removal of the information from a brain into some storage device (the device, that is, is put into a state information-theoretically equivalent to the total state of the brain), and is then put back into the same or another brain. (Such a process may, perhaps, be forever impossible, but it does not seem to present any purely logical or conceptual difficulty.) One thing at least seems clear about the consequences of this; we shall get this out of the way first. If this were done to one man, information being removed from his brain (for purposes of brain-repair, for instance) and then put back – then, supposing that he recovered all the dispositions, with regard to memory, that he had had before, we should not dream of saying that he did not, at the later stage, really remember. The passage of the information *via* the device would not be counted as the kind of causal route to his later knowledge which is incompatible with that knowledge's being memory. As things are, the sorts of causal route that go outside the body do not count for memory: if a man learns anew of his past experiences by reading what he earlier wrote about them in his diary, then precisely he does not remember his earlier experiences (there is of course the intermediate case of *being reminded*). But the imagined passage of the information *via* the device is obviously not a case which would fall under this ban: the replacement of the information is not, as such, 'learning again'. So at least we can be clear that passage of information *via* the device is not in itself incompatible with later knowledge's being memory.

It seems also pretty clear that under these circumstances a person could be counted the same if this were done to him, and in the process he were given a new brain (the repairs, let us say, actually required a new part). This shows that the crude principle of identity extracted from the Shoemaker case must indeed be too crude; here we have personal identity without the same brain, though of course we have identity of the rest of the body to hold onto. But now it looks as though the information could be put back, not merely into a new brain, but into a new brain in a new body – 'new', that is to say, relative to the body the person originally had, whether it was or was not newly manufactured. And here we have a process which is open to the reduplication problem: for we could of course print off more than one person in accordance with these conditions.

Now I think we *can* give a sense to the statement that all the resultant persons are the same person as the original prototype and indeed – consonant with the transitivity of identity – the same person as each other. This will be in a *type* sense of 'same person'. If the prototype person was Smith, all the resultants will be, significantly, *Smiths*; and 'person', like other type-token words, will have a plural differently applicable under two different principles of counting – a room containing two Smiths and three Robinsons will contain, in the one sense, five, in the other, two, persons.

Under these arrangements, would persons be bodies? A type-person would be something (very roughly) like a class of bodies; and to be confronted with the same type-person would be to be confronted with either the same body of the same type or with different bodies of the same type. However, we have to notice that the question of what set of bodies a type-person would be equivalent to, is one that might have to be made relative to time; both because fresh token-persons might be later printed off, and because (presumably) a given particular body might be changed from exemplifying one type to exemplifying another. However – though I think this needs further investigation – I do not think that this would force on us the conclusion that *token*-persons were not bodies, since remarks about personal identity which were not equivalent to remarks about bodily identity could be adequately represented in terms of bodies belonging to the same or different person-types.

There are many intriguing consequences of this situation. One very important feature of the situation is this. Since we are not supposing that the token-persons, once printed off from the same prototype, have intercommunicating experiences (and it might be very far from clear what it would be to suppose this), they will be divergently affected by different experiences, and will tend to get increasingly dissimilar. Looked at as copies of the prototype, they will become copies which are increasingly blurred or written-over; looked at in their own right, they will become increasingly individual personalities. This might be welcomed. For someone who loved one of these token-persons might well love her not because she was a Mary Smith, but despite the fact that she was a Mary Smith (a weak version of which arises even now with regard to members of families who share very pronounced characteristics). The more they diverged, the more secure hold the lover might feel he had on what particularly he loved.

If someone loved a token-person *just* as a Mary Smith, then it might well be unclear that the token-person was really what he loved. What he loves is *Mary Smith*, and that is to love the type-person. We can see dimly what this would be like. It would be like loving a work of art in some reproducible medium. One might start comparing, as it were, performances of the type; and wanting to be near the person one loved would be like wanting very much to hear some performance, even an indifferent one, of *Figaro* – just as one will go to the scratch provincial performance of *Figaro* rather than hear no *Figaro* at all, so one would see the very run-down Mary Smith who was in the locality, rather than see no Mary Smith at all.

Much of what we call loving a person would begin to crack under this, and reflection on it may encourage us not to undervalue the deeply body-based situation we actually have. While in the present situation of things to love a person is not exactly the same as to love a body, perhaps to say that they are basically the same is more grotesquely misleading than it is a deep metaphysical error; and if it does not sound very high-minded, the alternatives that so briskly grow out of suspending the present situation do not sound too spiritual, either.

6

The Makropulos case: reflections on the tedium of immortality

This essay started life as a lecture in a series 'on the immortality of the soul or kindred spiritual subject'.[1] My kindred spiritual subject is, one might say, the mortality of the soul. Those among previous lecturers who were philosophers tended, I think, to discuss the question whether we are immortal; that is not my subject, but rather what a good thing it is that we are not. Immortality, or a state without death, would be meaningless, I shall suggest; so, in a sense, death gives the meaning to life. That does not mean that we should not fear death (whatever force that injunction might be taken to have, anyway). Indeed, there are several very different ways in which it could be true at once that death gave the meaning to life and that death was, other things being equal, something to be feared. Some existentialists, for instance, seem to have said that death was what gave meaning to life, if anything did, just because it was the fear of death that gave meaning to life; I shall not follow them. I shall rather pursue the idea that from facts about human desire and happiness and what a human life is, it follows both that immortality would be, where conceivable at all, intolerable, and that (other things being equal) death is reasonably regarded as an evil. Considering whether death can reasonably be regarded as an evil is in fact as near as I shall get to considering whether it should be feared: they are not quite the same question.

My title is that, as it is usually translated into English, of a play by Karel Čapek which was made into an opera by Janaček and which tells of a woman called Elina Makropulos, *alias* Emilia Marty, *alias* Ellian Macgregor, alias a number of other things with the initials 'EM', on whom her father, the Court physician to a sixteenth-century Emperor, tried out an elixir of life. At the time of the action she is aged 342. Her unending life has come to a state of boredom, indifference and coldness. Everything is joyless: 'in the end it is the same', she says, 'singing and silence'. She refuses to take the elixir again; she dies; and the formula is deliberately destroyed by a young woman among the protests of some older men.

[1] At the University of California, Berkeley, under a benefaction in the names of Agnes and Constantine Foerster. I am grateful to the Committee for inviting me to give the 1972 lecture in this series.

EM's state suggests at least this, that death is not necessarily an evil, and not just in the sense in which almost everybody would agree to that, where death provides an end to great suffering, but in the more intimate sense that it can be a good thing not to live too long. It suggests more than that, for it suggests that it was not a peculiarity of EM's that an endless life was meaningless. That is something I shall follow out later. First, though, we should put together the suggestion of EM's case, that death is not necessarily an evil, with the claim of some philosophies and religions that death is necessarily not an evil. Notoriously, there have been found two contrary bases on which that claim can be mounted: death is said by some not to be an evil because it is not the end, and by others, because it is. There is perhaps some profound temperamental difference between those who find consolation for the fact of death in the hope that it is only the start of another life, and those who equally find comfort in the conviction that it is the end of the only life there is. That both such temperaments exist means that those who find a diagnosis of the belief in immortality, and indeed a reproach to it, in the idea that it constitutes a consolation, have at best only a statistical fact to support them. While that may be just about enough for the diagnosis, it is not enough for the reproach.

Most famous, perhaps, among those who have found comfort in the second option, the prospect of annihilation, was Lucretius, who, in the steps of Epicurus, and probably from a personal fear of death which in some of his pages seems almost tangible, addresses himself to proving that death is never an evil. Lucretius has two basic arguments for this conclusion, and it is an important feature of them both that the conclusion they offer has the very strong consequence – and seems clearly intended to have the consequence – that, for oneself at least, it is all the same whenever one dies, that a long life is no better than a short one. That is to say, death is never an evil in the sense not merely that there is no-one for whom dying is an evil, but that there is no time at which dying is an evil – sooner or later, it is all the same.

The first argument[2] seeks to interpret the fear of death as a confusion, based on the idea that we shall be there after death to repine our loss of the *praemia vitae*, the rewards and delights of life, and to be upset at the spectacle of our bodies burned, and so forth. The fear of death, it is suggested, must necessarily be the fear of some experiences had when one is dead. But if death is annihilation, then there are no such experiences: in the Epicurean phrase,

[2] *de Rerum Natura* III, 870 *seq*, 898 *seq*.

when death is there, we are not, and when we are there, death is not. So, death being annihilation, there is nothing to fear. The second argument[3] addresses itself directly to the question of whether one dies earlier or later, and says that one will be the same time dead however early or late one dies, and therefore one might as well die earlier as later. And from both arguments we can conclude *nil igitur mors est ad nos, neque pertinet hilum* – death is nothing to us, and does not matter at all.[4]

The second of these arguments seems even on the face of things to contradict the first. For it must imply that if there *were* a finite period of death, such that if you died later you would be dead for less time, then there *would* be some point in wanting to die later rather than earlier. But that implication makes sense, surely, only on the supposition that what is wrong with dying consists in something undesirable about the condition of being dead. And that is what is denied by the first argument.

More important than this, the oddness of the second argument can help to focus a difficulty already implicit in the first. The first argument, in locating the objection to dying in a confused objection to being dead, and exposing that in terms of a confusion with being alive, takes it as genuinely true of life that the satisfaction of desire, and possession of the *praemia vitae,* are good things. It is not irrational to be upset by the loss of home, children, possessions – what is irrational is to think of death as, in the relevant sense, *losing* anything. But now if we consider two lives, one very short and cut off before the *praemia* have been acquired, the other fully provided with the *praemia* and containing their enjoyment to a ripe age, it is very difficult to see why the second life, by these standards alone, is not to be thought better than the first. But if it is, then there must be something wrong with the argument which tries to show that there is nothing worse about a short life than a long one. The argument locates the mistake about dying in a mistake about consciousness, it being assumed that what commonsense thinks about the worth of the *praemia vitae* and the sadness of their (conscious) loss is sound enough. But if the *praemia vitae* are valuable; even if we include as necessary to that value consciousness that one possesses them; then surely getting to the point of possessing them is better than not getting to that point, longer enjoyment of them is better than shorter, and more of them, other things being equal, is better than less of them. But if so, then it just will not be true that to die earlier is all the same as to die later, nor that death is never an evil –

[3] *Ibid,* 1091. [4] *Ibid,* 830.

and the thought that to die later is better than to die earlier will not be dependent on some muddle about thinking that the dead person will be alive to lament his loss. It will depend only on the idea, apparently sound, that if the *praemia vitae* and consciousness of them are good things, then longer consciousness of more *praemia* is better than shorter consciousness of fewer *praemia*.

Is the idea sound? A decent argument, surely, can be marshalled to support it. If I desire something, then, other things being equal, I prefer a state of affairs in which I get it from one in which I do not get it, and (again, other things being equal) plan for a future in which I get it rather than not. But one future, for sure, in which I would not get it would be one in which I was dead. To want something, we may also say, is to that extent to have reason for resisting what excludes having that thing: and death certainly does that, for a very large range of things that one wants.[5] If that is right, then for any of those things, wanting something itself gives one a reason for avoiding death. Even though if I do not succeed, I will not know that, nor what I am missing, from the perspective of the wanting agent it is rational to aim for states of affairs in which his want is satisfied, and hence to regard death as something to be avoided; that is, to regard it as an evil.

It is admittedly true that many of the things I want, I want only on the assumption that I am going to be alive; and some people, for instance some of the old, desperately want certain things when nevertheless they would much rather that they and their wants were dead. It might be suggested that not just these special cases, but really all wants, were conditional on being alive; a situation in which one has ceased to exist is not to be compared with others with respect to desire-satisfaction – rather, if one dies, all bets are off. But surely the claim that all desires are in this sense conditional must be wrong. For consider the idea of a rational forward-looking calculation of suicide: there can be such a thing, even if many suicides are not rational, and even though with some that are, it may be unclear to what extent they are forward-looking (the obscurity of this with regard to suicides of honour is an obscurity in the notion of shame). In such a calculation, a man might consider what lay

[5] Obviously the principle is not exceptionless. For one thing, one can want to be dead: the content of that desire may be obscure, but whatever it is, a man presumably cannot be *prevented* from getting it by dying. More generally, the principle does not apply to what I elsewhere call *non-I desire*: for an account of these, see 'Egoism and Altuism', pp. 260 *seq.* They do not affect the present discussion, which is within the limits of egoistic rationality.

before him, and decide whether he did or did not want to undergo it. If he does decide to undergo it, then some desire propels him on into the future, and *that* desire at least is not one that operates conditionally on his being alive, since it itself resolves the question of whether he is going to be alive. He has an unconditional, or (as I shall say) a *categorical* desire.

The man who seriously calculates about suicide and rejects it, only just has such a desire, perhaps. But if one is in a state in which the question of suicide does not occur, or occurs only as total fantasy – if, to take just one example, one is happy – one has many such desires, which do not hang from the assumption of one's existence. If they did hang from that assumption, then they would be quite powerless to rule out that assumption's being questioned, or to answer the question if it is raised; but clearly they are not powerless in those directions – on the contrary they are some of the few things, perhaps the only things, that have power in that direction. Some ascetics have supposed that happiness required reducing one's desires to those necessary for one's existence, that is, to those that one has to have granted that one exists at all; rather, it requires that some of one's desires should be fully categorical, and one's existence itself wanted as something necessary to them.

To suppose that one can in this way categorically want things implies a number of things about the nature of desire. It implies, for one thing, that the reason I have for bringing it about that I get what I want is not merely that of avoiding the unpleasantness of not getting what I want. But that must in any case be right – otherwise we should have to represent every desire as the desire to avoid its own frustration, which is absurd.

About what those categorical desires must be, there is not much of great generality to be said, if one is looking at the happy state of things: except, once more against the ascetic, that there should be not just enough, but more than enough. But the question might be raised, at the impoverished end of things, as to what the minimum categorical desire might be. Could it be *just* the desire to remain alive? The answer is perhaps 'no'. In saying that, I do not want to deny the existence, the value, or the basic necessity of a sheer reactive drive to self-preservation: humanity would certainly wither if the drive to keep alive were not stronger than any perceived reasons for keeping alive. But if the question is asked, and it is going to be answered calculatively, then the bare categorical desire to stay alive will not sustain the calculation – that desire itself, when things have got that far, has to be sustained or filled out by some desire for something else, even if it is only, at the margin, the desire that future desires of mine will be born and satisfied. But the best insight into the effect of categorical desire is not gained at the impoverished end of things, and hence in situations where the question has actually come up. The question of life being desirable is certainly transcendental in the most modest sense, in that it gets by far its best answer in never being asked at all.

None of this – including the thoughts of the calculative suicide – requires my reflection on a world in which I never occur at all. In the terms of 'possible worlds' (which can admittedly be misleading), a man could, on the present account, have a reason from his own point of view to prefer a possible world in which he went on longer to one in which he went on for less long, or – like the suicide – the opposite; but he would have no reason of this kind to prefer a world in which he did not occur at all. Thoughts about his total absence from the world would have to be of a different kind, impersonal reflections on the value *for the world* of his presence or absence: of the same kind, essentially, as he could conduct (or, more probably, not manage to conduct) with regard to anyone else. While he can think egoistically of what it would be for him to live longer or less long, he cannot think egoistically of what it would be for him never to have existed at all. Hence the sombre words of Sophocles[6] 'Never to have been born counts highest of all . . .' are well met by the old Jewish reply – 'how many are so lucky? Not one in ten thousand'.

Lucretius' first argument has been interestingly criticised by Thomas Nagel,[7] on lines different from those that I have been following. Nagel claims that what is wrong with Lucretius' argument is that it rests on the assumption that nothing can be a misfortune for a man unless he knows about it, and that misfortunes must consist in something nasty *for* him. Against this assumption, Nagel cites a number of plausible counter-instances, of circumstances which would normally be thought to constitute a misfortune, though those to whom they happen are and remain ignorant of them (as, for instance, certain situations of betrayal). The difference between Nagel's approach and mine does not, of course, lie in the mere point of whether one admits misfortunes which do not consist of or involve nasty experiences: anyone who rejects Lucretius' argument must admit them. The difference is that the reasons which a man would have for avoiding death are, on the present account, grounded in desires – categorical desires – which he has; he, on the basis of

[6] *Oedipus at Colonus* 1224 *seq.*

[7] 'Death', *Nous* IV.1 (1970), pp. 73 *seq.* Reprinted with some alterations in Rachels ed., *Moral Problems.*

these, has reason to regard possible death as a misfortune to be avoided, and we, looking at things from his point of view, would have reason to regard his actual death as his misfortune. Nagel, however, if I understand him, does not see the misfortune that befalls a man who dies as necessarily grounded in the issue of what desires or sorts of desires he had; just as in the betrayal case, it could be a misfortune for a man to be betrayed, even though he did not have any desire not to be betrayed. If this is a correct account, Nagel's reasoning is one step further away from Utilitarianism on this matter than mine,[8] and rests on an independent kind of value which a sufficiently Utilitarian person might just reject; while my argument cannot merely be rejected by a Utilitarian person, it seems to me, since he must if he is to be consistent, and other things being equal, attach disutility to any situation which he has good reason to prevent, and he certainly has good reason to prevent a situation which involves the non-satisfaction of his desires. Thus, granted categorical desires, death has a disutility for an agent, although that disutility does not, of course, consist in unsatisfactory experiences involved in its occurrence.

The question would remain, of course, with regard to any given agent, whether he had categorical desires. For the present argument, it will do to leave it as a contingent fact that most people do: for they will have a reason, and a perfectly coherent reason, to regard death as a misfortune, while it was Lucretius' claim that no-one could have a coherent reason for so regarding it. There may well be other reasons as well; thus Nagel's reasoning, though different from the more Utilitarian type of reason I have used against Lucretius, seems compatible with it and there are strong reasons to adopt his kind of consideration as well. In fact, further and deeper thought about this question seems likely to fill up the apparent gap between the two sorts of argument; it is hard to believe, for one thing, that the supposed contingent fact that people have categorical desires can really be as contingent as all that. One last point about the two arguments is that they coincide in not offering – as I mentioned earlier – any considerations about worlds in which one does not occur at all; but there is perhaps an additional reason why this should be so in the Utilitarian-type argument, over and above the one it shares with Nagel's. The reason it shares with Nagel's is that the type of misfortune we are concerned with in thinking about X's death is X's misfortune (as opposed to the misfortunes of the state

8 Though my argument does not in any sense imply Utilitarianism; for some further considerations on this, see the final paragraphs of this paper.

or whatever); and whatever sort of misfortune it may be in a given possible world that X does not occur in it, it is not X's misfortune. They share the feature, then, that for anything to be X's misfortune in a given world, then X must occur in that world. But the Utilitarian-type argument further grounds the misfortune, if there is one, in certain features of X, namely his desires; and if there is no X in a given world, then *a fortiori* there are no such grounds.

But now – if death, other things being equal, is a misfortune; and a longer life is better than a shorter life; and we reject the Lucretian argument that it does not matter when one dies; then it looks as though – other things always being equal – death is at any time an evil, and it is always better to live than die. Nagel indeed, from his point of view, does seem to permit that conclusion, even though he admits some remarks about the natural term of life and the greater misfortune of dying in one's prime. But wider consequences follow. For if all that is true, then it looks as though it would be not only always better to live, but better to live always, that is, never to die. If Lucretius is wrong, we seem committed to wanting to be immortal.

That would be, as has been repeatedly said, with other things equal. No-one need deny that since, for instance, we grow old and our powers decline, much may happen to increase the reasons for thinking death a good thing. But these are contingencies. We might not age; perhaps, one day, it will be possible for some of us not to age. If that were so, would it not follow then that, more life being *per se* better than less life, we should have reason so far as that went (but not necessarily in terms of other inhabitants) to live for ever? EM indeed bears strong, if fictional, witness against the desirability of that; but perhaps she still laboured under some contingent limitations, social or psychological, which might once more be eliminated to bring it about that really other things were equal. Against this, I am going to suggest that the supposed contingencies are not really contingencies; that an endless life would be a meaningless one; and that we could have no reason for living eternally a human life. There is no desirable or significant property which life would have more of, or have more unqualifiedly, if we lasted for ever. In some part, we can apply to life Aristotle's marvellous remark about Plato's Form of the Good:[9] 'nor will it be any the more good for being eternal: that which lasts long is no whiter than that which perishes in a day'. But only in part; for, rejecting Lucretius, we have already admitted that more days may give us more than one day can.

[9] *Ethica Nicomachea* 1096^b 4.

If one pictures living for ever as living as an embodied person in the world rather as it is, it will be a question, and not so trivial as may seem, of what age one eternally is. EM was 342; because for 300 years she had been 42. This choice (if it was a choice) I am personally, and at present, well disposed to salute – if one had to spend eternity at any age, that seems an admirable age to spend it at. Nor would it necessarily be a less good age for a woman: that at least was not EM's problem, that she was too old at the age she continued to be at. Her problem lay in having been at it for too long. Her trouble was it seems, boredom: a boredom connected with the fact that everything that could happen and make sense to one particular human being of 42 had already happened to her. Or, rather, all the sorts of things that could make sense to one woman of a certain character; for EM has a certain character, and indeed, except for her accumulating memories of earlier times, and no doubt some changes of style to suit the passing centuries, seems always to have been much the same sort of person.

There are difficult questions, if one presses the issue, about this constancy of character. How is this accumulation of memories related to this character which she eternally has, and to the character of her existence? Are they much the same kind of events repeated? Then it is itself strange that she allows them to be repeated, accepting the same repetitions, the same limitations – indeed, *accepting* is what it later becomes, when earlier it would not, or even could not, have been that. The repeated patterns of personal relations, for instance, must take on a character of being inescapable. Or is the pattern of her experiences not repetitious in this way, but varied? Then the problem shifts, to the relation between these varied experiences, and the fixed character: how can it remain fixed, through an endless series of very various experiences? The experiences must surely happen to her without really affecting her; she must be, as EM is, detached and withdrawn.

EM, of course, is in a world of people who do not share her condition, and that determines certain features of the life she has to lead, as that any personal relationship requires peculiar kinds of concealment. That, at least, is a form of isolation which would disappear if her condition were generalised. But to suppose more generally that boredom and inner death would be eliminated if everyone were similarly becalmed, is an empty hope: it would be a world of Bourbons, learning nothing and forgetting nothing, and it is unclear how much could even happen.

The more one reflects to any realistic degree on the conditions of

EM's unending life, the less it seems a mere contingency that it froze up as it did. That it is not a contingency, is suggested also by the fact that the reflections can sustain themselves independently of any question of the particular character that EM had; it is enough, almost, that she has a human character at all. Perhaps not quite. One sort of character for which the difficulties of unending life would have less significance than they proved to have for EM might be one who at the beginning was more like what she is at the end: cold, withdrawn, already frozen. For him, the prospect of unending cold is presumably less bleak in that he is used to it. But with him, the question can shift to a different place, as to why he wants the unending life at all; for, the more he is at the beginning like EM is at the end, the less place there is for categorical desire to keep him going, and to resist the desire for death. In EM's case, her boredom and distance from life both kill desire and consist in the death of it; one who is already enough like that to sustain life in those conditions may well be one who had nothing to make him want to do so. But even if he has, and we conceive of a person who is stonily resolved to sustain for ever an already stony existence, his possibility will be of no comfort to those, one hopes a larger party, who want to live longer because they want to live more.

To meet the basic anti-Lucretian hope for continuing life which is grounded in categorical desire, EM's unending life in this world is inadequate, and necessarily so relative to just those desires and conceptions of character which go into the hope. That is very important, since it is the most direct response, that which should have been adequate if the hope is both coherent and what it initially seemed to be. It also satisfied one of two important conditions which must be satisfied by anything which is to be adequate as a fulfilment of my anti-Lucretian hope, namely that it should clearly be *me* who lives for ever. The second important condition is that the state in which I survive should be one which, to me looking forward, will be adequately related, in the life it presents, to those aims which I now have in wanting to survive at all. That is a vague formula, and necessarily so, for what exactly that relation will be must depend to some extent on what kind of aims and (as one might say) prospects for myself I now have. What we can say is that since I am propelled forward into longer life by categorical desires, what is promised must hold out some hopes for those desires. The limiting case of this might be that the promised life held out some hope just to that desire mentioned before, that future desires of mine will be born and satisfied; but if that were the only categorical desire that carried me forward into it, at least this seems demanded, that any image I have of those future desires should make it comprehensible to me how in terms of my character they could be my desires.

This second condition, the EM kind of survival failed, on reflection, to satisfy; but at least it is clear why, before reflection, it looked as though it might satisfy the condition – it consists, after all, in just going on in ways in which we are quite used to going on. If we turn away now from EM to more remote kinds of survival, the problems of those two conditions press more heavily right from the beginning. Since the major problems of the EM situation lay in the indefinite extension of one life, a tempting alternative is survival by means of an indefinite series of lives. Most, perhaps all, versions of this belief which have actually existed have immediately failed the first condition: they get nowhere near providing any consideration to mark the difference between rebirth and new birth. But let us suppose the problem, in some way or another, removed; some conditions of bodily continuity, minimally sufficient for personal identity, may be supposed satisfied. (Anyone who thinks that no such conditions could be sufficient, and requires, for instance, conditions of memory, may well find it correspondingly difficult to find an alternative for survival in this direction which both satisfies the first requirement, of identity, and also adequately avoids the difficulties of the EM alternative.) The problem remains of whether this series of psychologically disjoint lives could be an object of hope to one who did not want to die. That is, in my view, a different question from the question of whether it will be him – which is why I distinguished originally two different requirements to be satisfied. But it is a question; and even if the first requirement be supposed satisfied, it is exceedingly unclear that the second can be. This will be so, even if one were to accept the idea, itself problematical, that one could have reason to fear the future pain of someone who was merely bodily continuous with one as one now is.[10]

There are in the first place certain difficulties about how much a man could consistently be allowed to know about the series of his lives, if we are to preserve the psychological disjointness which is the feature of this model. It might be that each would in fact have to seem to him as though it were his only life, and that he could not have grounds for being sure what, or even that, later lives were to come. If so, then no comfort or hope will be forthcoming in this

[10] One possible conclusion from the dilemma discussed in 'The Self and the Future'. For the point, mentioned below, of the independence of physical pain from psychological change, see p. 54.

model to those who want to go on living. More interesting questions, however, concern the man's relation to a future life of which he did get some advance idea. If we could allow the idea that he could fear pain which was going to occur in that life, then we have at least provided him with one kind of reason which might move him to opt out of that life, and destroy himself (being recurrent, under conditions of bodily continuity, would not make one indestructible). But physical pain and its nastiness are to the maximum degree independent of what one's desires and character are, and the degree of identification needed with the later life to reject that aspect of it is absolutely minimal. Beyond that point, however, it is unclear how he is to bring this later character and its desires into a relation to his present ones, so as to be satisfied or the reverse with this marginal promise of continued existence. If he can regard this future life as an object of hope, then equally it must be possible for him to regard it with alarm, or depression, and – as in the simple pain case – opt out of it. If we cannot make sense of his entertaining that choice, then we have not made sense of this future life being adequately related to his present life, so that it could, alternatively, be something he might want in wanting not to die. But can we clearly make sense of that choice? For if we – or he – merely wipe out his present character and desires, there is nothing left by which he can judge it at all, at least as something *for him*; while if we leave them in, we – and he – apply something irrelevant to that future life, since (to adapt the Epicurean phrase), when they are there, it is not, and when it is there, they are not. We might imagine him considering the future prospects, and agreeing to go on if he found them congenial. But that is a muddled picture. For whether they are congenial to him as he is now must be beside the point, and the idea that it is not beside the point depends on carrying over into the case features that do not belong to it, as (perhaps) that he will remember later what he wanted in the earlier life. And when we admit that it is beside the point whether the prospects are congenial, then the force of the idea that the future life could be something that he *now* wanted to go on to, fades.

There are important and still obscure issues here,[11] but perhaps enough has been said to cast doubt on this option as coherently satisfying the desire to stay alive. While few will be disposed to think that much can be made of it, I must confess that out of the

11 For a detailed discussion of closely related questions, though in a different framework, see Derek Parfitt, 'Personal Identity', *Philosophical Review*, LXXX (1971), pp. 3–27.

alternatives it is the only one that for me would, if it made sense, have any attraction – no doubt because it is the only one which has the feature that what one is living at any given point is actually *a life*. It is singular that those systems of belief that get closest to actually accepting recurrence of this sort seem, almost without exception, to look forward to the point when one will be released from it. Such systems seem less interested in continuing one's life than in earning one the right to a superior sort of death.

The serial and disjoint lives are at least more attractive than the attempt which some have made, to combine the best of continuous and of serial existence in a fantasy of very varied lives which are nevertheless cumulatively effective in memory. This might be called the *Teiresias* model. As that case singularly demonstrates, it has the quality of a fantasy, of emotional pressure trying to combine the uncombinable. One thing that the fantasy has to ignore is the connexion, both as cause and as consequence, between having one range of experiences rather than another, wishing to engage in one sort of thing rather than another, and having a character. Teiresias cannot have a character, either continuously through these proceedings, or cumulatively at the end (if there were to be an end) of them: he is not, eventually, a person but a phenomenon.

In discussing the last models, we have moved a little away from the very direct response which EM's case seemed to provide to the hope that one would never die. But perhaps we have moved not nearly far enough. Nothing of this, and nothing much like this, was in the minds of many who have hoped for immortality; for it was not in this world that they hoped to live for ever. As one might say, their hope was not so much that they would never die as that they would live after their death, and while that in its turn can be represented as the hope that one would not really die, or, again, that it was not really oneself that would die, the change of formulation could point to an after-life sufficiently unlike this life, perhaps, to earth the current of doubt that flows from EM's frozen boredom.

But in fact this hope has been and could only be modelled on some image of a more familiar untiring or unresting or unflagging activity or satisfaction; and what is essentially EM's problem, one way or another, remains. In general we can ask, what it is about the imaged activities of an eternal life which would stave off the principle hazard to which EM succumbed, boredom. The Don Juan in Hell joke, that heaven's prospects are tedious and the devil has the best tunes, though a tired fancy in itself, at least serves to show up a real and (I suspect) a profound difficulty, of providing any model of an unending, supposedly satisfying, state or activity which would not rightly prove boring to anyone who remained conscious of himself and who had acquired a character, interests, tastes and impatiences in the course of living, already, a finite life. The point is not that for such a man boredom would be a tiresome consequence of the supposed states or activities, and that they would be objectionable just on the utilitarian or hedonistic ground that they had this disagreeable feature. If that were all there was to it, we could imagine the feature away, along no doubt with other disagreeable features of human life in its present imperfection. The point is rather that boredom, as sometimes in more ordinary circumstances, would be not just a tiresome effect, but a reaction almost perceptual in character to the poverty of one's relation to the environment. Nothing less will do for eternity than something that makes boredom *unthinkable*. What could that be? Something that could be guaranteed to be at every moment utterly absorbing? But if a man has and retains a character, there is no reason to suppose that there is anything that could be that. If, lacking a conception of the guaranteedly absorbing activity, one tries merely to think away the reaction of boredom, one is no longer supposing an improvement in the circumstances, but merely an impoverishment in his consciousness of them. Just as being bored can be a sign of not noticing, understanding or appreciating enough, so equally not being bored can be a sign of not noticing, or not reflecting, enough. One might make the immortal man content at every moment, by just stripping off from him consciousness which would have brought discontent by reminding him of other times, other interests, other possibilities. Perhaps, indeed, that is what we have already done, in a more tempting way, by picturing him just now as at every moment totally absorbed – but that is something we shall come back to.

Of course there is in actual life such a thing as justified but necessary boredom. Thus – to take a not entirely typical example – someone who was, or who thought himself, devoted to the radical cause might eventually admit to himself that he found a lot of its rhetoric excruciatingly boring. He might think that he ought not to feel that, that the reaction was wrong, and merely represented an unworthiness of his, an unregenerate remnant of intellectual superiority. However, he might rather feel that it would not necessarily be a better world in which no-one was bored by such rhetoric and that boredom was, indeed, a perfectly worthy reaction to this rhetoric after all this time; but for all that, the rhetoric might be necessary. A man at arms can get cramp from standing too long at his post, but sentry-duty can after all be necessary. But the threat of monotony in eternal activities could not be dealt with in that way, by regarding immortal boredom as an unavoidable ache derived from standing ceaselessly at one's post. (This is one reason why I said that boredom in eternity would have to be *unthinkable.*) For the question would be unavoidable, in what campaign one was supposed to be serving, what one's ceaseless sentry-watch was for.

Some philosophers have pictured an eternal existence as occupied in something like intense intellectual enquiry. Why that might seem to solve the problem, at least for them, is obvious. The activity is engrossing, self-justifying, affords, as it may appear, endless new perspectives, and by being engrossing enables one to lose oneself. It is that last feature that supposedly makes boredom unthinkable, by providing something that is, in that earlier phrase, at every moment totally absorbing. But if one is totally and perpetually absorbed in such an activity, and loses oneself in it, then as those words suggest, we come back to the problem of satisfying the conditions that it should be me who lives for ever, and that the eternal life should be in prospect of some interest. Let us leave aside the question of people whose characteristic and most personal interests are remote from such pursuits, and for whom, correspondingly, an immortality promised in terms of intellectual activity is going to make heavy demands on some theory of a 'real self' which will have to emerge at death. More interesting is the content and value of the promise for a person who *is*, in this life, disposed to those activities. For looking at such a person as he now is, it seems quite unreasonable to suppose that those activities would have the fulfilling or liberating character that they do have for him, if they were in fact all he could do or conceive of doing. If they are genuinely fulfilling, and do not operate (as they can) merely as a compulsive diversion, then the ground and shape of the satisfactions that the intellectual enquiry offers him, will relate to *him*, and not just to the enquiry. The *Platonic introjection*, seeing the satisfactions of studying what is timeless and impersonal as being themselves timeless and impersonal, may be a deep illusion, but it is certainly an illusion.

We can see better into that illusion by considering Spinoza's thought, that intellectual activity was the most active and free state that a man could be in, and that a man who had risen to such activity was in some sense most fully individual, most fully himself. This conclusion has been sympathetically expounded by Stuart Hampshire, who finds on this point a similar doctrine in Spinoza and in Freud:[12] in particular, he writes '[one's] only means of achieving this distinctness as an individual, this freedom in relation to the common order of nature, is the power of the mind freely to follow in its thought an intellectual order'. The contrast to this free intellectual activity is 'the common condition of men that their conduct and their judgements of value, their desires and aversions, are in each individual determined by unconscious memories' – a process which the same writer has elsewhere associated with our having any character at all as individuals.[13]

Hampshire claims that in pure intellectual activity the mind is most free because it is then least determined by causes outside its immediate states. I take him to mean that rational activity is that in which the occurrence of an earlier thought maximally explains the occurrence of a later thought, because it is the rational relation between their contents which, granted the occurrence of the first, explains the occurrence of the second. But even the maximal explanatory power, in these terms, of the earlier thought does not extend to total explanation: for it will still require explanation why this thinker on this occasion continued on this rational path of thought at all. Thus I am not sure that the Spinozist consideration which Hampshire advances even gives a very satisfactory sense to the *activity* of the mind. It leaves out, as the last point shows, the driving power which is needed to sustain one even in the most narrowly rational thought. It is still further remote from any notion of creativity, since that, even within a theoretical context, and certainly in an artistic one, precisely implies the origination of ideas which are not fully predictable in terms of the content of existing ideas. But even if it could yield one sense for 'activity', it would still offer very little, despite Spinoza's heroic defence of the notion, for *freedom*. Or – to put it another way – even if it offered something for freedom of the intellect, it offers nothing for freedom of the individual. For when freedom is initially understood as the absence of 'outside' determination, and in particular understood in those terms as an unquestionable *value*, my freedom is reasonably not taken to include freedom from my past, my character and my desires. To suppose that those are, in the relevant sense, 'outside' determinations, is merely to beg the vital question about the boundaries of the self, and not to prove from premisses acceptable to any clear-headed man

[12] *Spinoza and the Idea of Freedom*, reprinted in *Freedom of Mind* (Oxford: Clarendon Press, 1972), pp. 183 *seq*; the two quotations are from pp. 206–7.

[13] *Disposition and Memory*, *Freedom of Mind*, pp. 160 *seq*; see especially pp. 176–7.

who desires freedom that the boundaries of the self should be drawn round the intellect. On the contrary, the desire for freedom can, and should, be seen as the desire to be free in the exercise and development of character, not as the desire to be free of it. And if Hampshire and others are right in claiming that an individual character springs from and gets its energies from unconscious memories and unclear desires, then the individual must see them too as within the boundaries of the self, and themselves involved in the drive to persist in life and activity.

With this loss, under the Spinozist conception, of the individual's character, there is, contrary to Hampshire's claim, a loss of individuality itself, and certainly of anything that could make an eternity of intellectual activity, so construed, a reasonable object of interest to one concerned with individual immortality. As those who totally wish to lose themselves in the movement can consistently only hope that the movement will go on, so the consistent Spinozist – at least on this account of Spinozism – can only hope that the intellectual activity goes on, something which could be as well realised in the existence of Aristotle's prime mover, perhaps, as in anything to do with Spinoza or any other particular man.

Stepping back now from the extremes of Spinozist abstraction, I shall end by returning to a point from which we set out, the sheer desire to go on living, and shall mention a writer on this subject, Unamuno, whose work *The Tragic Sense of Life*[14] gives perhaps more extreme expression than anyone else has done to that most basic form of the desire to be immortal, the desire not to die.

> I do not want to die – no, I neither want to die nor do I want to want to die; I want to live for ever and ever and ever. I want this 'I' to live – this poor 'I' that I am and that I feel myself to be here and now, and therefore the problem of the duration of my soul, of my own soul, tortures me.'[15]

Although Unamuno frequently refers to Spinoza, the spirit of this is certainly far removed from that of the 'sorrowful Jew of Amsterdam'. Furthermore, in his clear insistence that what he desperately wants is this life, the life of this self, not to end, Unamuno reveals himself at equal removes from Manicheanism and from Utilitarianism; and that is correct, for the one is only the one-legged descendant of the other. That tradition – Manichean, Orphic, Platonic,

[14] *Del sentimiento trágico de la vida*, translated by J. E. Crawford Flitch (London: 1921). Page references are to the Fontana Library edition, 1962.
[15] *Ibid.*, p. 60.

Augustinian – which contrasts the spirit and the body in such a sense that the spiritual aims at eternity, truth and salvation, while the body is adjusted to pleasure, the temporary, and eventual dissolution, is still represented, as to fifty per cent, by secular Utilitarianism: it is just one of the original pair of boots left by itself and better regarded now that the other has fallen into disrepair. Bodies are all that we have or are: hence for Utilitarianism it *follows* that the only focus of our arrangements can be the efficient organisation of happiness. Immortality, certainly, is out, and so life here should last as long as we determine – or eventually, one may suspect, others will determine – that it is pleasant for us to be around.

Unamuno's outlook is at the opposite pole to this and whatever else may be wrong with it, it salutes the true idea that the meaning of life does not consist either in the management of satisfactions in a body or in an abstract immortality without one. On the one hand he had no time for Manicheanism, and admired the rather brutal Catholic faith which could express its hopes for a future life in the words which he knew on a tombstone in Bilbao:[16]

> Aunque estamos in polvo convertidos
> en Ti, Señor, nuestra esperanza fía,
> que tornaremos a vivir vestidos
> con la carne y la piel que nos cubria.

At the same time, his desire to remain alive extends an almost incomprehensible distance beyond any desire to continue agreeable experiences:

> For myself I can say that as a youth and even as a child I remained unmoved when shown the most moving pictures of hell, for even then nothing appeared quite so horrible to me as nothingness itself.[17]

The most that I have claimed earlier against Lucretius is not enough to make that preference intelligible to me. The fear of sheer nothingness is certainly part of what Lucretius rightly, if too lightly, hoped to exorcise; and the *mere* desire to stay alive, which is here stretched to its limit, is not enough (I suggested before) to answer the question, once the question has come up and requires an answer in rational terms. Yet Unamuno's affirmation of existence even through limitless suffering[18] brings out something which is implicit in the claim

[16] *Ibid.*, p. 79. [17] *Ibid.*, p. 28.

[18] An affirmation which takes on a special dignity retrospectively in the light of his own death shortly after his courageous speech against Millán Astray and the obscene slogan '!Viva la Muerte!' See Hugh Thomas, *The Spanish Civil War* (Harmondsworth: Pelican, 1961), pp. 442–4.

against Lucretius. It is not necessarily the prospect of pleasant times that create the motive against dying, but the existence of categorical desire, and categorical desire can drive through both the existence and the prospect of unpleasant times.

Suppose, then, that categorical desire does sustain the desire to live. So long as it remains so, I shall want not to die. Yet I also know, if what has gone before is right, that an eternal life would be unliveable. In part, as EM's case originally suggested, that is because categorical desire will go away from it: in those versions, such as hers, in which I am recognisably myself, I would eventually have had altogether too much of myself. There are good reasons, surely, for dying before that happens. But equally, at times earlier than that moment, there is reason for not dying. Necessarily, it tends to be either too early or too late. EM reminds us that it can be too late, and many, as against Lucretius, need no reminding that it can be too early. If that is any sort of dilemma, it can, as things still are and if one is exceptionally lucky, be resolved, not by doing anything, but just by dying shortly before the horrors of not doing so become evident. Technical progress may, in more than one direction, make that piece of luck rarer. But as things are, it is possible to be, in contrast to EM, *felix opportunitate mortis* – as it can be appropriately mistranslated, lucky in having the chance to die.

7
Strawson on individuals

P. F. Strawson's book *Individuals*[1] is subtitled *An Essay in Descriptive Metaphysics*. 'Descriptive metaphysics', he writes (p. 9), 'is content to describe the actual structure of our thought about the world', whereas 'revisonary metaphysics is concerned to produce a better structure'; it is distinguished from logical or conceptual analysis in scope and generality, rather than in fundamental intention. The book is divided into two parts; in Strawson's words (pp. 11–12), 'the first part aims at establishing the central position which material bodies and persons occupy among particulars in general. . . In the second part of the book the aim is to establish and explain the connexion between the idea of a particular in general and that of an object of reference or logical subject.'

In the first part, Strawson introduces the notion of identification, and gives an account of the identification of particulars and the rôle played in this, in our actual thought, by material bodies (Ch. 1). He then considers the possibilities of identification in a hypothetical world containing no material bodies, but only sounds (Ch. 2). In the third chapter, he discusses persons, and in the fourth offers some engaging and largely self-contained Leibnizian reflections ('Monads'). The second part starts with a long discussion of subject and predicate, in which various criteria for the distinction are considered. This is followed by a consideration of 'language without particulars', and the book ends with a chapter called 'Logical Subjects and Existence', in which existence itself, objects of reference which are not particulars, and some questions of reductionism are discussed.

These comments fall into four sections. In the first I discuss Strawson's account of particular-identification, and in the second certain problems in his treatment of space and time. These sections are almost entirely concerned with the first chapter of the book, and, in both, questions are raised about the notion of reference. In the third section I consider Strawson's concept of a *basic particular*, and go on to discuss the relation of this to his treatment of individuals as a whole, and to some theses of the second part of the book. The fourth section offers, fairly independently of the rest, some criticisms of

[1] London: Methuen, 1959.

Strawson's chapter on persons. I do not consider at all the chapter on sounds, nor that on monads, nor much of the logical matter in the second part.

There is one general question raised by *Individuals*, which is of great importance, but which I touch on only obliquely. This concerns the nature and limits of what Strawson calls 'descriptive metaphysics'; it may be felt that there is too little determinacy in the idea of 'our actual conceptual system', and in the canons of argument that seek to establish, as Strawson does, the primacy of certain things in this system over others, for the aims of descriptive metaphysics to be entirely clear. These seem to me to be genuine questions; but as Strawson has written a book that admirably seeks not to describe descriptive metaphysics, but to produce some, I have correspondingly tried in this notice to consider the results rather than the nature of the activity. The third section, however, on basic particulars, does raise issues that concern the ultimate purpose of Strawson's type of enquiry.

1 *Identification*. Strawson introduces the concept of the identification of particulars in the context of a speaker–hearer situation, and first in connexion with the hearer: a hearer can *identify* a particular mentioned by a speaker if he knows what particular the speaker is talking about. A speaker is said to *make an identifying reference* to a particular, if he uses an expression to refer to a particular, a standard function of which expression is to enable the hearer to identify the particular referred to; and the speaker himself *identifies* a particular if he makes an identifying reference to it, and enables his hearer to identify it. These accounts are, and are no doubt meant to be, fairly rough. In particular, they presuppose the notion of *referring*, which is not itself examined; though a little is said about it in the second part of the book (pp. 181 *seq.*, 190).

It may be that the hearer can identify a mentioned particular, but identify it only relative to a range of particulars itself only identified as the range being talked about by the speaker; thus if the speaker is telling an anecdote about three men, the hearer may know which of the three men is at a particular point being referred to, but not know who any of the three men are. This Strawson calls *story-relative identification*. It is clear that such identification could not suffice for the purpose of discourse: we need also *non-relative identification*. A sufficient condition of this is the ability to pick out sensibly the mentioned particular, knowing it to be that particular; this is called *direct location* or *demonstrative identification*. However, we can, and must be able to, identify non-relatively particulars that are not immediately given to perception; hence there must also be *non-demonstrative identification.*

Non-demonstrative identification raises a familiar problem. If the mentioned particular cannot be directly located, then it must be located via a verbal specification, and this verbal specification must rely on descriptions or names or both, and names in their turn must be backed by descriptions: hence we are forced back on to descriptions. But descriptions seem to be essentially general, so that any description may be multiply satisfied; and if this is so, it is a puzzle how we can non-demonstratively *identify*, as opposed to offering sets of descriptions which may, with luck, be uniquely satisfied, but can never be known to be uniquely satisfied. To this familiar problem Strawson offers two answers. The first, which he calls the 'practical' answer, is that the hearer may just know what range of particulars the speaker means, so that the question whether there may be other particulars which satisfy the descriptions need not bother him. The second, or 'theoretical', answer is that the descriptions given need not be in the objectionable sense general, since they may serve to relate uniquely the particular which is to be indirectly located to some other particular which is directly located. Strawson passes some strictures on the first of these two answers, as (roughly) not going far enough. He does not, however, pass on it what seems to be the most obvious stricture, that it is not an answer at all. If we ask *how* the hearer might know what range of particulars the speaker means, we shall surely be forced to say that the hearer must ultimately be able to relate, in a way to which the speaker would agree, the range of particulars being mentioned to a directly located particular; i.e. we shall straightaway be forced into the second, or 'theoretical', answer.

Strawson does not here say, and perhaps never directly says, that it is *essential* to non-demonstrative identification that the mentioned particular be locatable in unique relation to some demonstratively identified particular, although the tenor of his argument in general strongly suggests that he believes this to be so. He does in the end state a general condition of hearer-identification in the non-demonstrative case, which seems to embody this belief. He says that the condition will be fulfilled if the hearer knows that the particular being referred to was identical with some particular about which he knew some *individuating fact* or facts (other than the fact that it was the particular being referred to), where to know an individuating fact about a particular is to know that such-and-such a thing is true of that particular and of no other particular whatsoever; and he mentions no conditions under which a hearer could know something of this form, except that the particular in question should be uniquely related in some way to a directly located particular. Strawson adds that it is not a requirement of this condition's being satisfied that the hearer should be able to make his knowledge fully articulate.

The condition is qualified to exclude purely story-relative identification (p. 23). This qualification need not detain us, except to remark that it excludes – perhaps designedly, but not explicitly – more than story-relative identification relative to a range of particulars mentioned by *the speaker*. The qualification rules out as cases of non-relative identification, any identification which is relative to the discourse of anybody, and so has the result that we cannot identify in the strongest sense, e.g. the characters of fiction.

One further concept of this group that must be mentioned is that of *re-identification*. To re-identify a particular is to identify 'a particular encountered on one occasion, or described in respect of one occasion, as *the same individual* [Strawson's emphasis] as a particular encountered on another occasion, or described in respect of another occasion' (p. 31). Strawson says that it is not surprising that it should be natural to use the same word for this activity, and for the activity, previously called (hearer-)identification, of recognising what particular a speaker is referring to: 'in both kinds of case, identifying involves thinking that something is *the same* [Strawson's emphasis]: that the particular copy I see in the speaker's hand is the same particular as that to which he is referring; that the copy in his hand is the same particular as the copy I bought yesterday' (*ibid.*).

There is something very odd about this argument. For, if it is correct, it follows that 'the x he is referring to is the x which is . . .' (where follows some individuating description) expresses a genuine identity judgement, as does 'the x he is holding is the x I bought yesterday'. Now the latter judgement has existential presuppositions: in order for it to be true (at least) there must be an x which he is holding, and an x which I bought. These presuppositions Strawson himself has elsewhere expressed by saying that the two individuating expressions 'must have a reference'. How do these considerations apply to the former judgement just quoted, and in particular to the first individuating expression that occurs in it, 'the x he is referring to'? If this expression has no existential presupposition of any sort, then the two judgements are evidently not analogous, and the argument collapses. If it does have an existential presupposition, there is more than one possibility for what this presupposition may be, and whichever possibility is chosen, Strawson is in difficulties.

First, it might be suggested that it was a sufficient condition of there being an *x* which A referred to that A did seriously, non-quotingly, etc., use, in an appropriate syntactic context, some individuating expression which purported to mention an *x*. This would, of course, be an extremely weak interpretation of the existential presupposition – so weak, in fact, that it is doubtful whether it could be called an *existential* presupposition at all. In this form, it could scarcely serve Strawson's purposes. For one thing, it would divorce the truth conditions of 'there was an *x* which A was referring to when he used the expression "*E*"' from those of 'the expression "*E*", as used by A, had a reference', since there would be many occasions on which the first would be true and the latter false.

Another, and stronger, interpretation of the existential presupposition would be this: that if A seriously, etc., used the individuating expression '*E*' which purported to mention an *x*, we are to say that there is an *x* which A referred to, if and only if there is an *x* which answers to the description contained in '*E*'. This interpretation of course brings together again the truth conditions of 'there was an *x* which A referred to by "*E*"' and '"*E*", as used by A, had a reference', and this is a result which, it would seem from his other writings on this subject, Strawson would want to secure. Under this interpretation, there always corresponds to the identification statement attributed to the hearer – 'the *x* he is referring to is the *x* which is . . .' – another statement, of the form 'the *x* which answers to the description contained in "E" is the *x* which . . .', where 'E' is the expression referringly used by the speaker. Thus, in order to identify what the speaker has referred to, the hearer must always have *another* description in hand which applies to the thing that the speaker's original description applied to. But this has difficulties for the notion of speaker-identification; for the speaker is said to have identified what he was talking about if he made an identifying reference to it which enabled the hearer to identify it, and it follows from the present account that he could never, by what he said, enable the hearer to identify the thing in question, unless the hearer already had a description which applied to it. This seems drastically to limit the notion of identification. Moreover, it limits it in a manner which Strawson cannot want to accept. In the second chapter of the book, Strawson extends the notion of identification of particulars in thought (pp. 60 *seq.*), i.e. to situations in which a thinker picks out or identifies a particular for himself, as it were. It cannot be a condition of performing this feat that, for every description by means of which the thinker tries to identify a particular, he must already have another description which applies to the same thing: if it were so, the thinker could never get started.

A further difficulty here is that there are many referring expressions that a speaker may use, for which it is extremely unclear what sense can be attached to the formula 'the x which answers to the description contained in "*E*"'. This will be the case with direct demonstrative reference, which is central to Strawson's account. Suppose a speaker says something that starts 'that matchstick . . .', and the hearer has to identify which he means. The hearer cannot be pictured as making some judgement of the form 'the matchstick which is that matchstick . . .' or 'the matchstick which answers to "that matchstick" . . .', since these make no sense. His judgement must rather be of the form 'the matchstick which he meant when he said "that matchstick" . . .', which once more imports the speaker's reference essentially into the hearer's identification. In his later account (p. 182), Strawson agrees that a description like 'the one he has in mind' may enter into the hearer's characterisation of the speaker's reference, but argues, correctly, that such a description cannot serve for the speaker himself to pick out what he has in mind. 'So', he continues, 'there must be some description he could give, though it need not be the description he does give, which applies uniquely to the thing he has in mind and does not include the phrase "the one I have in mind".' This does not follow. The argument assumes that nothing can be picked out except by *some* uniquely instantiated description. This assumption cannot be correct; for if descriptions are ultimately rooted in demonstratives, as Strawson himself seems elsewhere to suggest, it cannot be the case that demonstratives are themselves rooted in descriptions.

These difficulties cast doubt on Strawson's procedure of starting with hearer-identification, moving back to speaker-identification, and then on to identification in thought. Hearer-identification is essentially the act of catching on to a reference, and is expressible in the form 'the thing he is referring to is the thing which . . .' This, on Strawson's account, reduces essentially to 'the thing that falls under the description which he used is the thing which . . .' If speaker-identification is defined by reference to hearer-identification, it will be a necessary condition of speaker-identification that the hearer has an independent description in hand; and this notion cannot be generalised to cover speaker-identification without benefit of hearer, as identification in thought. So what are these latter notions? Some of what Strawson says suggests that they effectively reduce to *referring* itself. But if so, first it would seem that this sense of 'identification' should be primary even in the speaker–hearer situation; second, the notion has not been made clear, since the only notion of 'referring' that has been introduced seems to be that of using, in certain sets of context, a description under which something falls, and this must be an inadequate notion of referring.

2 *Space and Time.* Among the ways in which particulars that are not directly located can be related in identification to others that are, or more generally to others already identified, there is one set of relations of outstanding importance and generality, at least for our conceptual system as it actually is: the set of spatial and temporal relations. Strawson identifies the space-time structure as the framework of our actual thought about particulars, and makes important claims for it in its rôle as this framework, and draws from these claims consequences important for his thesis in the first part of the book.

Strawson's claims for the spatio-temporal system in our actual thought about particulars are basically threefold. First, the system is *unique* and *unified*. There are (in the Kantian phrase) only one space and one time, and every element in space and time can be related to every other both spatially and temporally: 'of things of which it makes sense to inquire about the spatial position, we think it always significant not only to ask how any two such things are spatially related at any one time, the same for each, but also to enquire about the spatial relations of any one thing at any moment of its history to any other thing at any moment of its history, when the moments may be different' (p. 31). Second, it is not a contingent matter, relatively to our actual conceptual system, that empirical reality forms such a structure; rather, it is a condition of the *reality* of any supposed empirical thing or event that it can be located in the structure (p. 29). Third, the structure is of use to us in the identification of particulars, because it enables us to relate all particulars which belong to it to ourselves; for we ourselves not only have a place in this scheme, but know this place (p. 30).

The special importance of these claims for Strawson's thesis is that he argues from them to the conclusion that material bodies are in a certain sense basic to our identification of particulars. A class of *basic particulars*, in Strawson's terminology, is a class of particulars such that 'as things are, it would not be possible to make all the identifying references which we do make to particulars of other classes, unless we made identifying references to particulars of that class, whereas it would be possible to make all the identifying references we do make to particulars of that class without making identifying reference to particulars of other classes' (pp. 38–9). Strawson emphasises that the basicness of basic particulars concerns only their basicness in identification – he does not wish to say that non-basic particulars are in any sense less real than basic ones; nevertheless, he tells us that it seems to him 'unobjectionable' to say that basic particulars are 'ontologically prior' to others (p. 59).

I shall postpone until the next section some more general questions about Strawson's notion of a basic particular, confining myself here to the connexions he makes between the basicness of material bodies, and the nature of the spatio-temporal system. The thesis that material bodies are in the defined sense basic follows, in Strawson's view, from the claims made for the spatio-temporal system, in conjunction with the thesis that the spatio-temporal system does not exist independently of the things that occupy it, but is defined only by the relations of those things. Thus, if we ask what constitutes the framework, we must look to the objects that occupy it; and we shall find that only some among them have the properties that could constitute a framework of the required kind: 'three-dimensional objects with some endurance in time' (p. 39; for the whole argument, see pp. 38 *seq.*). The category of material bodies 'is the only one competent to constitute' the framework actually used in particular-identification, viz. the structure of one temporal and three spatial dimensions (p. 56).

This is, in bare outline, the way in which Strawson connects his thesis about the basicness of material bodies with his claims for the spatio-temporal system. Two difficulties in particular seem to me to arise at this stage: first, about the sense of the claim that we know our own place in the system; and second, about the argument to the basicness of material bodies among spatio-temporal particulars. In addition, I think that doubts could be raised about Strawson's Kantian confidence in the unique system of one temporal and three spatial dimensions as the framework of all empirical reality; it is perhaps unduly simple to deal with all that natural science might want to say about either sub-atomic or astronomical events. Strawson presumably cannot want to say that such things are not encompassed by 'our conceptual system'; he himself makes a passing reference to 'theoretical entities' of natural science (p. 44), and if 'our conceptual system' were to be so restricted, his conclusions would be trivialised. But this type of difficulty I shall not attempt to pursue.

First, then, there is a problem about what Strawson means when he says that 'we know our own place' in the spatio-temporal system: an assertion essential to his argument since it is supposed to explain how our own various identifications, and the world at large, are linked together. If we did not know our place in the system, it seems no set of descriptions relating various particulars one to another in the spatio-temporal system would ultimately be of identificatory use to us. An argument for this conclusion might be given as follows: either such a set of descriptions would relate these particulars to ourselves, or it would not. If it did, but we did not know our own place in the spatio-temporal system at large, the particulars would not have been related to that system at large, and hence would not have been ultimately pinned down in the world of reality. But if the set of descriptions did not relate the particulars to ourselves, we should be just as far off from ultimate identification of them: any identification of them in terms of each other could at most be 'story-relative'.

Strawson does not give such an argument, but it looks as though some such considerations underlie his emphasis on our 'knowing our place in the system'. In any case, it certainly seems that he attaches some special importance to our knowledge of our place in the system. The problem is that, in terms of Strawson's theory, it is hard in fact to give this supposed knowledge the importance that it requires, because it is hard to see how the supposed knowledge can both be genuine knowledge, and be in any special position as compared with our knowledge of any other particulars. It is clearly not enough, in order that I should know my place in the system, that I should merely know that I am *here now*; such *cogito*-like knowledge clearly does not relate me to anything. (A similar point seems to be made by Strawson himself when, in a different connexion, he remarks that 'it cannot be maintained that "now" or "here" independently identifies a time or place' (p. 216; cf. p. 221).) What I need to know is that *here* is such-and-such a place, and that *now* is such-and-such a time, where the identification of the place and time serve to relate them to some general geographical and chronological scheme. But this relating will rely on reference to some other particulars, such as the Greenwich meridian or the birth of Christ. Thus it seems that if I have any real knowledge of my place in the scheme, I have it in virtue of reliance on the identification of some other particulars. Thus it is hard to see that my knowledge of my place in the scheme plays any special rôle in my system of identifications at all; for if my identification of *here* (in the only sense in which it is going to be any use to me) depends on my identification of, say, the Greenwich meridian, why should I not be able to get on just as well by merely identifying the Greenwich meridian?

Yet Strawson does need to say that I could not get on as well, at least from the theoretical point of view, by starting with the identification of the Greenwich meridian, since that itself will not be satisfactorily identified save by relation to what is sensibly located, i.e. what is located in terms of the here and now. The odd thing is that he gives no account of our knowledge of the here and now which serves to explain why or how sensible location and our knowledge of our own place in the system play the rôles they are supposed to play.

Indeed, he says one thing about sensible location and immediate reference which seems to make the problem yet more difficult. He says at one point that 'we may admit, if we like, that an implicit reference to speaker and hearer is involved in any demonstrative reference made in the presence of the object referred to' (pp. 42–3); but he regards such implicit reference, because it is 'absolutely general in such situations', as being 'discountable' (p. 43; cf. p. 46). He regards it as so discountable, in fact, that he is prepared to say that directly located objects can 'be identified without a mediating reference to any other particular at all' (p. 45). When he says that this implicit reference to speaker and hearer is absolutely general, he has in mind the two connected points, first, that it is present in any demonstrative reference whatsoever, and not merely in such reference to some special class of particulars, and, second, that it is an implicit reference to persons merely in their capacity as speaker or hearer of the utterances that bear the reference, and not in any more substantial sense. When he says that these implicit references are discountable, he no doubt has primarily in mind something that indeed follows immediately from their absolute generality, namely that they would not have to be mentioned in characterising demonstrative reference to one class of particulars as against another. But it does not follow from this that they are discountable in the different sense that they would not have to be mentioned in giving a general account of what sort of identification presupposed what: for it might well be – if the 'implicit reference' account is correct – that *any* identification of a particular which had been demonstratively indicated presupposed identification of the speaker.

If it were the case that the understanding of any demonstrative reference presupposed the identification of the speaker, Strawson's theory would be in difficulties on more than one count. The appeal to direct location as the foundation stone of our system of identifications would be unsatisfactory, since direct location itself would be a complex notion presupposing identification of speakers; and the procedure of starting with hearer-identification would, once more, turn out to conceal difficulties, since any hearer's identification of something mentioned by a speaker would presuppose an identification carried out by the hearer without (in the same sense) benefit of speaker, since it would presuppose the hearer's identification of something not mentioned by the speaker, namely the speaker himself.

These difficulties, again, are primarily connected with Strawson's taking for granted the notion of reference. The account of identifying reference stated or implicit in the book is, very roughly speaking, a close relative of Russell's, with genuine context-dependent token-reflexives in place of Russell's logically proper names. As part of studying genuine token-reflexives instead of logically proper names, Strawson rightly emphasises the rôle of actual speaker–hearer confrontations, instead of looking at propositions all by themselves *in vacuo*. So far, so good; but Strawson does not seem to have pressed sufficiently firmly into the consequences of accepting this kind of theory of reference, with the result that the token-reflexives are left doing very much the same job as the logically proper names were supposed to do, unambiguously hooking onto the world. Onto these hooks, Strawson hangs the weight of our system of identifications in apparent confidence. But from his account of reference, it should follow that the confidence is premature; one must further ask how the use and understanding of token-reflexives is related to the speaker–hearer situation, and this Strawson does not seem to have done, or at least not sufficiently to dispel doubts about the anchorage of identifications to the here and now.

The doubts that I have discussed so far in connexion with space and time have largely been concerned with the completeness of Strawson's account, and with certain ambiguities that seem to surround its foundations. There is, however, another sort of doubt that the theory invites – a doubt of circularity. Strawson says that in our conceptual system as it is, the identification of material particulars, at least, involves relating them to the one unique spatio-temporal structure. Space and time, however, are held to be relational, and the argument to the basicness of material bodies indeed relies precisely on this: 'it is a conceptual truth . . . that places are defined by the relations of material bodies' (p. 58). Hence it seems that places and times are identified in terms of material bodies, and material bodies in terms of places and times.

Strawson acknowledges this circularity himself, in one connexion: as concerns the reidentificaton of material bodies (p. 36). This is an extremely important connexion, since the possibility of such reidentification is explicitly argued to be essential, 'if we are to operate the scheme of a single unified spatio-temporal system or framework of particulars' (p. 31). So Strawson is committed to this: that we must be able to identify times and places if we are to re-identify material bodies, and we must be able to reidentify material bodies if we are, at least, to operate a thorough-going system of spatial and temporal location. This is not yet a complete circle, since there is, if only formally, a gap between being able to identify such times and places as are necessarily identified in reidentifying some material bodies, and operating the thorough-going spatio-temporal system. But this gap is not a real one; from Strawson's other arguments, to the effect that location in the unified spatio-temporal system is a condition of the reality of an empirical particular, it follows that the reidentification of any material particular presupposes its location in the unified system. Hence the circle is in fact complete.

Strawson is undisturbed by this circularity. 'There is no mystery about this mutual dependence. To exhibit its detail is simply to describe the criteria by which we criticise, amend and extend our ascription of identity to things and places' (p. 37). He disclaims any attempt to 'exhibit its detail in full', and confines himself to some remarks to the effect that a decision whether a thing is or is not in the same place as before depends on one's choice of co-ordinates or reference points.

Yet surely Strawson should be more disturbed than he is by this circularity. It cannot be enough to say that 'to exhibit its detail is simply to describe the criteria' by which we identify things and places, for the problem is why, when we set about describing these criteria, we should find ourselves describing things that are joined by a presuppositional circle; and this must be a problem for Strawson, since an important part of his aim is precisely to show what parts of our identificatory conceptual system depend on or presuppose what.

3 *Basic Particulars*. Strawson's notion of a *basic particular* has already been mentioned, at the beginning of the last section; it will be recalled that the basicness in question is one of identification, but that Strawson finds it 'unobjectionable' to say that basic particulars are 'ontologically prior' (p. 59). However, it is not clear how

much this permissive gesture in fact permits, since it is not clear to what senses of 'ontologically prior' it extends. There is indeed one possible sense (or, perhaps, class of senses) of the term in which it would appear that we were not merely permitted by Strawson's system, but required by it, to say that if x's are basic particulars with respect to y's, then x's are ontologically prior to y's. This is the sense, or senses, in which 'x is ontologically prior to y' means 'if y is included in our ontology, then x must be, but not conversely'. For Strawson claims that the possibility of identifying particulars of a certain type is a necessary condition of 'the inclusion of that type in our ontology' (p. 16). Now if x's are (identificationally) basic with respect to y's, and it is a necessary condition of including either x's or y's in our ontology that we can identify them, it follows that it is a necessary condition of including y's in our ontology that we can identify x's. But it seems very difficult to avoid, as a consequence of this, the conclusion that it is a necessary condition of including y's in our ontology that we include x's in it. For the only condition under which it would seem plausible to say that we could identify x's without including them in our ontology would be the situation in which x's, though identifiable, were thought to be insufficiently basic. But this is not so in the case under discussion, where *ex hypothesi* the x's are more basic than the y's already included in our ontology. Hence it is hard to avoid the conclusion that if 'ontologically prior' means 'having priority for inclusion in our ontology', then basic particulars must, in virtue of Strawson's earlier, unqualified, claim, necessarily be ontologically prior.

However, it is far from clear whether this is the sense of the phrase, or indeed what 'inclusion in our ontology' itself means. If it were merely a question of the application of these forms of words, it would not matter greatly, since these are not forms of words to which Strawson is greatly attached. Behind these forms of words, however, there lies a question which is central to the evaluation of Strawson's argument: the question of what importance or significance attaches to the fact that certain named classes of particulars are in his sense basic. That this fact is important is the presupposition of most of the book; their basicness is supposed to show why 'a central place' must be given to these among other particulars, and indeed (in virtue of certain arguments in the second half of the book which I shall consider in a moment) among individuals or logical subjects in general (cf. e.g. p. 246). It is very hard, taking the book as a whole, to resist the impression that this emphasis is in some way connected with questions of the reality or ontological status that is to be ascribed to various types of thing, despite the disclaimers that Strawson makes of such an interpretation. This impression seems to be confirmed in the closing sentences of the book when Strawson, perhaps less guardedly than earlier, says that he 'may even be said to have found some reason in the idea that persons and material bodies are what primarily exist' (p. 247).

Yet it is not easy to make entirely precise the connexions between Strawson's argument and questions of ontology. On the one hand, it is certain that he is not concerned with one sort of 'ontological priority' that philosophers have discussed, by which x is ontologically prior to y if x could exist without y, but not y without x. Thus Strawson holds that the identification of 'theoretical' particles in physics depends on the identification of macroscopic material bodies (p. 44), but he presumably does not think that there could not be any particles unless there were macroscopic material bodies. On the other hand, he is not merely concerned with structural priorities in language, for so far as these are concerned, conceptual dependence is as important as identification-dependence, and Strawson, in a passage which I do not find easy to follow, seems to find conceptual dependence less important or significant than identification-dependence (pp. 45, 50–2). It seems rather that what he is concerned with is structural dependences in language in so far as these are concerned with statements or presuppositions of existence, i.e. with what things we must take as existent if we are to take other things as existent. Yet this, as it stands, is rather too wide; for if 'take as existent' here meant merely 'think of as existent', it seems that we could, once more, think of physical particles as existent without thinking of macroscopic bodies as existent, since we could imagine the universe as containing e.g. only a highly rarefied gas. Hence 'take as existent' would have to be understood more narrowly than this, as meaning perhaps 'speaking of, or being able to speak of, as individually existent'. This indeed yields a correct account of Strawson's concerns; the trouble is that it does little to explain them, as opposed to merely restating them.

However, the 'ontological connexions' of Strawson's enquiry can perhaps be put like this: that it is a necessary condition of our ascribing reality to a thing that we can identify it, and hence that the establishment of priorities of identification does in a weak sense go to show why we should think of one sort of thing as 'more real' than another. It is only in a weak sense that it goes to show this, since it might well be that even within the context of 'our ordinary conceptual system', there were criteria of 'reality' or 'primacy' other than basicness in identification; and Strawson never really produces an argument to show that basicness in identification is the only, or the chief, such criterion. Yet he needs such an argument, if the statement that basic particulars are primary is to be more than the simplest tautology, and he clearly does not intend it to be that. This seems to be an incompleteness *within* the range of 'descriptive metaphysics'. There are, of course, or might be, further criteria of reality or primacy, the consideration of which would go *beyond* descriptive metaphysics – criteria in terms of which it might be asked whether our ordinary implicit criteria of reality or primacy (whatever these turned out to be) were correct. Such questions are not the concern of Strawson as descriptive metaphysician, and this is perhaps what he has in mind when he makes his disclaimers about the connexions of basicness and reality. The trouble is that he needs to establish some such connexions even within the limits he has set himself, if the characteristic of basicness is to have the philosophical significance he clearly does attribute to it.

Whatever account is to be assumed of the importance of basic particulars among particulars, it is important to see that in Strawson's theory a decision of what particulars are basic particulars does not, by itself, provide any answer to the question of why basic particulars should be thought of as primary among things in general. Basic particulars are basic only among particulars; the determination of their position among things in general requires, further, a determination of the position of particulars among things in general, and it is with that problem that he is, in part, concerned in the second part of the book.

For Strawson, particulars seem to be things in space or time. This, if it is so, is so by definition, though he does not explicitly state the definition as such; indeed he (unlike the publisher's blurb) does not unequivocally state that they are all in space or time. At the beginning of the first chapter he writes that in his use of the word 'particular', 'as in most familiar philosophical uses, historical occurrences, material objects, people and their shadows are all particulars; whereas qualities and properties, numbers and species are not' (p. 15). Later he says: 'perhaps not all particulars are in both time *and* space [Strawson's emphasis]. But it is at least plausible to assume that every particular which is not, is uniquely related in some other way to one which is' (pp. 22–3). These somewhat ambiguous statements are meant to admit the possibility, I think, only of particulars that are in one of the pair time and space (presumably time) without being in the other, and not the possibility of particulars that are not in either. The same goes, presumably, for another passage in which Strawson says: 'every particular either has its place in this [sc. spatio-temporal] system, or is of a kind the members of which cannot in general be identified except by reference to particulars of other kinds which have their place in it' (p. 25). For while this latter passage, and another in much the same terms (p. 233), could very easily be taken to suggest that there were particulars which were *completely* outside the spatio-temporal system (though related to others within it), Strawson never seems to mention any such particular, and another passage (p. 119), though not itself free from ambiguity on this point, seems to support the interpretation that puts every particular into at least one of time and space; especially in approving a view ascribed to Kant, that 'space and time are our only forms of intuition' (which should presumably read 'are the forms of our only form of intuition'). If Strawson has any reservations on this point, they are presumably in favour of some sorts of psychological occurrence.

In any case, all particulars for Strawson are certainly empirical particulars. In this sense of 'particular', it is clearly not merely the correlative term of 'universal', since many things fall under universals that are not empirical particulars, as the number five falls under the universal 'prime number'. Such things can be referred to, and the universals ascribed to them; the reference can be understood, and thus the things, in Strawson's terminology, can be identified. The class of things in general that can be identifyingly referred to Strawson calls the class of *individuals*; only some individuals are particulars. It will presumably be a condition of reality of individuals in general that they can be identified. Now, as has already been remarked, no considerations about the identification-dependence of particulars between themselves can by itself tell us anything about the ontological status of individuals which are not particulars, either with respect to each other, or with respect to particulars; here we need some account of the relation of particulars to individuals in general.

Such an account does emerge from the second part of the book. There, Strawson primarily tackles the problem of giving an explanation and justification of the distinction of subject and predicate; and, after a complex and interesting discussion which I shall not attempt to summarise, finds such an explanation in the idea that the introduction of the subject term into a proposition is based on and presupposes a statement of empirical fact, whereas the introduction of the predicate or universal term does not. Thus, to take the simplest case, the statement 'the man over there is smoking' introduces as its subject term *the man over there*, and this introduction is based on and presupposes the empirical fact *that there is a man over there*; whereas the introduction of the predicate term *smoking*, which is joined to the subject term by what Strawson calls 'a non-relational tie' (a genus of which he distinguishes various species), does not presuppose any such empirical fact. This explanation, which I have stated in its roughest form, undergoes various refinements to deal with different sorts of both subject and predicate terms; but this is its essence. In it, Strawson finds an explanation of why we feel that there is a genuine distinction between subject and predicate terms, and, in particular, of why we feel that the subject term is complete in itself in some way in which the predicate term is not.

It will be at once apparent that this explanation is not an account of the distinction between subject and predicate in general; it applies only to those propositions in which the subject term is a particular, for it is only particulars whose introduction is based on an empirical fact. Having established this explanation in the case of particulars, however, Strawson proceeds to examine predications about other sorts of individual as being in some sense analogical extensions of the basic or central case of predication about a particular. In so far as we are prepared to make assertions about other sorts of things, making identifying references to them, so far do we tend to ascribe reality to them, as genuine individuals. Strawson's approach is well illustrated by the question he puts in his chapter on 'Logical Subjects and Existence': 'why are some non-particulars better entrenched than others as individuals?' (p. 232). To this question he does not think that there is any one general answer; though his discrimination of non-particular individuals into the better and the worse entrenched (on the whole, in favour of sentence-types, numbers, works of art, and against qualities, states, processes and even species: see e.g. p. 231) is guided by the possibilities of reduction. He does not at any point press the question very hard, and it is clear that he has no great brief for the possibility or interest of reductionism in any formalist sense. On the whole the considerations he employs concern the possibility of producing in our actual language a natural paraphrase which eliminates the supposed reference to an individual (cf. p. 231); and where no thorough-going reduction is possible, he will be satisfied if talk about one sort of entity can be shown to be based on talk about another (cf. p. 201). Even for supposed individuals which are not well entrenched, it seems that he has no tendency to say that they do not really exist; he shows approval of the proposal that 'exist' be used in a formal way, to apply correctly to things of any category (pp. 239 *seq.*).

How far, then, does this theory give any grounds for saying that basic particulars have a primary position among individuals as a whole? The only grounds are contained in the thesis that predication about particulars is the primary form of predication, to which other applications of the subject-predicate structure can be seen as analogically related. But is this enough? For, first of all, we meet again the question that arose when basic particulars were considered merely with respect to other particulars, of the *sense* of 'primary'. Here this question is yet more pressing: for one may well wonder what implicit criteria of primacy, or centrality, or reality are concealed in Strawson's very informal notion of better and worse 'entrenchment'. Why should the possibilities of ordinary language paraphrase, and the other considerations that Strawson raises in connexion with reduction, be in any way connected with the centrality or, in any sense, ontological importance of the individuals in question? In formalistic reductionist programmes one finds an attempt at a theoretical justification of such a connexion, in terms of the necessities of quantification. Strawson rejects, perhaps rightly, the presuppositions of such a procedure, but produces nothing in justification of his own. Here one suspects that descriptive metaphysics is leading a rather parasitic existence, by relying on a weaker and less precise form of considerations proper to a certain sort of revisionary, or at least legislative, metaphysics, without showing the appropriateness of such criteria to its own way of life.

But leaving that aside, there is another doubt about the sufficiency of Strawson's argument. For what grounds are there for saying that predication about particulars *is* primary, save that particulars are already regarded as primary? To this, I think Strawson would answer that it is by concentrating on predications about particulars in the first place that one can see the rationale of the subject-predicate distinction. So that the argument would now run: the reality of the subject-predicate distinction can be understood and justified if one sees predication about particulars as primary; if one does so, one sees reference to and identification of particulars as primary, with respect to other individuals; hence one sees particulars, and *a fortiori* basic particulars, as primary among individuals.

But now what about the first premiss of this argument? This raises the further question: how much significance is to be attached to the fact, if it is a fact, that concentration on predication about particulars peculiarly helps to understand and justify the subject-predicate distinction? For perhaps this distinction is of no ultimate importance. Now this is not a question that Strawson ignores or dismisses; he in fact introduces his discussion by mentioning Ramsey's doubts about the subject-predicate distinction, and claims that he can answer them. His answer, however, consists in producing a rationale of the subject-predicate distinction, which rationale rests on taking predication about particulars as primary. Thus we have come round in a circle.

Does this circle matter? It might be said that it does not: that if a coherent account of the connexion of a set of notions between themselves can be given, this is the most that can be wanted; at any rate, the most that can be wanted from descriptive metaphysics. However, I think that the existence of this circle matters rather more to Strawson's arguments than this reply allows. For it is at least very easy to see Strawson as setting about attempting *two* tasks, within the context of descriptive metaphysics: that of explaining a natural tendency to think of basic particulars as primary among individuals, and that of explaining why we think of subject and predicate as importantly different. If his argument is connected as I have suggested, he cannot be said in the end to have carried out either of these tasks. If there are these two tasks, it must be that we do not understand the basis of either of the two beliefs in question; hence explanations of each which rely on the other cannot be ultimate explanations.

The point can perhaps be put in another way, to fit an account that Strawson explicitly gives of what he is trying to do. He mentions a 'traditional view', according to which there is an asymmetry between particulars and universals in respect of their relations to the subject–predicate distinction' and which 'accords particulars a special place among logical subjects' (p. 138); and he says that he wants 'to discover the rationale of the traditional view, if it has one'. This formulation rolls the two tasks into one, that of finding a rationale for a 'traditional view' which has the form of a conjunctive proposition: that subjects and predicates are different, and that particulars are the primary subjects. Strawson does not seem in the end to have found a rationale for the proposition expressing the conjunction of these two theses, but at best for a different proposition, expressing their mutual implication.

I say 'at best', for all this is to assume that Strawson's account of the subject-predicate distinction and its primary connexion with predication about particulars is in fact correct. I think that this is doubtful, though I cannot pursue the question at any length here.

But on general grounds, one may wonder why our notions of the completeness, etc., of the subject term should be peculiarly connected with the empirical nature of the fact on which its introduction is based. The notions of completeness, 'saturation', etc., of the subject seem to apply as directly to 'the sum of seven and four is odd' as to 'the man over there is smoking', without benefit of the alleged analogy from empirical cases; and there seems to be as big a difference between the facts on which the introduction of the two terms is based – to use Strawson's terminology – in this case as in the other, although in this case the difference is not that between an empirical and a non-empirical fact. Strawson's argument here clearly needs close investigation, to which mathematical cases (to which he pays surprisingly little attention) will be specially relevant.

4 *Persons.* Strawson bases his discussion of persons, which occupies the third chapter of the book, on a distinction between two kinds of predicates that we can ascribe to ourselves, which he calls *M*-predicates and *P*-predicates. *M*-predicates are those that could ascribe also to material objects; *P*-predicates are those that could not possibly be ascribed to material objects, and include such things as actions and intentions, thoughts and feelings, perceptions, memories and sensations (pp. 89, 104). Of the *P*-predicates, there is, apparently, a sub-class the ascription of any of which to a person constitutes the ascription to him of a 'state of consciousness'.[2] Strawson's first questions are: 'why are they ascribed to the same thing as certain corporeal characteristics, a certain physical situation, etc.?' – i.e. as certain *M*-predicates (p. 90).

Strawson then considers two theories which deny, respectively, the presuppositions of these two questions. That which denies the presupposition of the first he calls 'the no-ownership view', a theory, indications of which are perhaps to be found in the writings of Schlick and others, to the effect that states of consciousness do not genuinely have any subject, all that is true being the contingent fact that different sets of experiences are causally dependent on the corporeal states of different bodies. The theory that denies the presupposition of the second question he calls 'the Cartesian view'; on this view, states of consciousness and corporeal predicates are not really ascribed to the same thing, but to two different subjects which happen in some way to be joined.

Strawson then attempts to show the incoherence of these two

[2] For further comment on the distinction, see 'Are Persons Bodies?', pp. 64–70; and in particular, for the interpretation of Strawson, p. 65 and note.

views. His fundamental argument against the no-ownership view is that it cannot be stated without presupposing that which it sets out to deny. For of *what* set of experiences or states of consciousness is it contingently true that they depend on the corporeal states of my body, where *my body* is identified in purely physical terms? The no-ownership theorist must answer this question; but he can answer it only by saying '*my* experiences', which reintroduces the type of ownership of experience which he was trying to do without (pp. 96 *seq.*).

Against the Cartesian view, Strawson argues as follows: 'One can ascribe states of consciousness to oneself only if one can ascribe them to others. One can ascribe them to others only if one can identify other subjects of experience. And one cannot identify others if one can identify them *only* [Strawson's emphasis] as subjects of experience, possessors of states of consciousness' (p. 100). But it is this last that the Cartesian theorist must suppose to be possible. The only alternative for him would be to identify other subjects of experience *via* their perceived bodies. This he would have to do by extrapolation from his own case; but this would presuppose that he already had the notion of *his* experiences (his Cartesian ego, as opposed to his body), and this notion, by the earlier argument, he is not yet in a position to have (pp. 100–1).

The incoherence of these theories should lead us, in Strawson's view, to recognise the *primitiveness* of the concept of 'a person', or an entity to which both sorts of predicates can be ascribed. He then explores some consequences of this conclusion. We must recognise, for instance, that there are certain among the P-predicates which we ascribe to ourselves on grounds different from those on which we ascribe them to others; nevertheless the grounds on which we ascribe them to others are logically adequate grounds. It is important that these predicates are 'self-ascribable and other-ascribable to the same individual' (p. 110); this is one basis of our learning these predicates as having these two sorts of grounds of ascription. The fact that we can learn such predicates – 'that P-predicates are possible' – can be more readily understood when we see certain of them, those concerned with certain sorts of overt bodily action, as central (pp. 111 *seq.*).

A vast range of questions is raised by Strawson's concentrated and ingenious assault on these problems; his criticisms of the 'Cartesian' and 'no-ownership' views, his notion of 'logically adequate grounds' in connexion with the self-ascription and other-ascription of P-predicates, his account of 'I' as a referring expression (p. 100, cf.

p. 103), and the sense of the term 'primitive', all invite discussion. I shall confine myself to just one question: the initial distinction between two sorts of predicates.

Strawson's principle for distinguishing between the two classes of predicates is, interestingly enough, to be found already in Descartes, though in a form that suggests their ascription to different subjects: 'Everything that we discover in ourselves, which we see could also be in completely inanimate bodies, should be attributed only to our body; on the other hand, everything that is in us, which we could not conceive of as possibly belonging to a (physical) body, should be attributed to our soul' (*Passions of the Soul*, Art. 3). This rule requiries, for Descartes' purposes, at least a good deal of interpretation. Its application yields as members of the second class, as Strawson remarks of his rule, a very heterogeneous collection of predicates, large numbers of which, such as 'is smiling', 'is going for a walk' – to take examples mentioned by Strawson (p. 104) – Descartes could not ascribe as they stand to the soul. Descartes perhaps thought that such predicates were really complex, and could be analysed into a mental part and a physical part. Strawson of course is not in just the same difficulties, but his use of this Cartesian rule seems to lead to some.

Taking the second class – *P*-predicates – as a whole, for large numbers of them there is no difficulty at all in seeing why they are ascribed to the same individuals as are corporeal predicates, since they involve or imply corporeal predicates. Strawson realises this, since he mentions the examples just quoted; and his realisation of it is signalled by the fact that when he comes to the heart of his discussion, he conducts it, not in terms of *P*-predicates in general, but in terms of 'states of consciousness'. This term is slipped in without introduction; it presumably stands for what are ascribed by some sub-class of *P*-predicates, but by what sub-class Strawson does not make clear. Thus for the main part of the discussion it is not clear what predicates are in fact being considered, and since the whole question is of how these predicates can be predicated, there is a corresponding unclarity about what the question is. Indeed, there is an unclarity about what a *person* is, since a person is said to be 'a type of entity such that *both* predicates ascribing states of consciousness *and* [Strawson's emphasis in both cases] predicates ascribing corporeal characteristics . . . are equally applicable to a single individual of that single type' (p. 102). This might suggest that 'states of consciousness' are ascribed by that sub-class of *P*-predicates that cannot be applied to animals. But this would yield a rather impoverished sub-class, and Strawson does not seem to recognise in what follows any such restriction; though perhaps he should, since it is the concept of 'a person', and not that of 'an animal', which is supposedly proved to be 'primitive'.

This unclarity extends in fact beyond the distinction between different sorts of *P*-predicates, to the distinction between *P*-predicates and *M*-predicates. For once we see that many *P*-predicates are highly corporeal, we may begin to wonder which corporeal predicates really are *M*-predicates. Strawson mentions, apparently among *M*-predicates, colouring and physical position, where the latter includes both location and attitude (p. 89). Yet it is extremely unclear that '. . . is sitting down' is a predicate that can be ascribed to a material object; not merely because the form of words would be unnatural, but because 'he is sitting down' in the standard case implies 'he sat down'. (Could it be said of a man whose legs were bent up in a fit, and who had been put in a chair, that he was sitting down?) Similar difficulties arise with colour; are we making the same predication when we say of a man's face, and of litmus paper, that it 'went red'? Similarly, again, with another example that Strawson gives: 'I am cold' (p. 93); for surely there is some logical connexion between 'I am cold' and 'I feel cold', and if so, this can scarcely be straightforwardly the same '. . . cold' as is ascribed to cups of tea.

Here it might be said that Strawson has confused two things: predicates that can be ascribed either to persons or to material objects, and predicates that can indeed be ascribed only to persons, but to persons merely as corporeal beings. But to make such a distinction would not help. For what does 'merely as corporeal beings' mean? Either it means 'as physical objects', in which case the test for distinguishing this type of predicate would turn out to be the same as the one for the type of predicate from which they were supposed to be distinguished, i.e. the test just found to be unsatisfactory; or else 'persons merely as corporeal beings' would have to be defined by contrast with 'persons as more than corporeal beings' or even 'as incorporeal beings', to which no sense has at this stage been given, or perhaps could be given.

This initial unclarity in the distinction between the two sorts of predicates is not a matter merely of roughness or vagueness. Strawson lacks any criterion for the notion of 'same predicate' in this connexion. He can scarcely hold that it is a sufficient condition of the same predicate's being applied to persons and to material objects that the same *words* are applied to both. If this were the condition, the distinction would fall in some odd places – thus 'walk' would seem to be a *P*-predicate, but 'run' would not. Moreover, the class of *P*-predicates would be unacceptably small. A vast range of words which to persons ascribe actions can without any hesitation be applied to machines, which Strawson would presumably count as material objects. With the development of computers, the range of words that can be so applied becomes notoriously more and more 'psychological'.

Here it may be replied that the words are not applied to persons and to machines in the same sense: that the two sorts of application are not applications of the same predicate. But now some criterion is needed for deciding when the same predicate is, and is not, being applied; and not only has Strawson failed to provide any such criterion, but it is evident, I think, that he could not provide it without presupposing some positions in the philosophy of mind. It is only if one *already* has some concept of the mental as opposed to the physical that one can claim that e.g. computers do not 'remember', or that cranes do not 'lift', in the same sense as that in which men do these things. The presupposition of Strawson's approach that a distinction between his two sorts of predicate is already given, seems to me fundamentally misguided.

Strawson's reliance on this distinction, and on the unanalysed notion of 'states of consciousness' that is used to help it out, leads to some curious consequences.

It encourages him to divorce 'states of consciousness' from bodily states in a way that invites the Cartesian spectre in at the back door while Strawson is wheedling it out of the front. He introduces, for instance, again without explanation, the notion of *perceptual experience*, and argues that it is a contingent fact that our perceptual experience is connected in the way it is with our bodies. In support of this, he suggests that it is logically possible that there should be a subject of perceptual experience, *S*, to which three different bodies were relevant, *A*, *B* and *C*. For *S* to see, *A*'s eyes must be open; those of *B* and *C* may be shut. However, for *S* to see things in place x, what matters is that C should be in place x; where A and *B* may be does not matter. But, lastly, the direction of the heads and eyeballs of A and C do not matter for *S*'s experience: the direction depends on *B* (pp. 90–1).

It seems to me an illusion to suppose that this fantasy is intelligible; for where, to put it crudely, is the *will* that governs these various movements? We move as a result of perceiving, and in order to perceive; and opening and closing of the eyes, the inclination of the head, and the movement of the limbs are of a piece in this. If, in Strawson's model, someone in the C place directs a blow at C's face, can C turn his head aside to avoid the blow and look for somewhere to move to? It seems that *S* – who after all saw the blow coming – must turn C's head aside to avoid the blow, but turn *B*'s head aside to look for escape; which will help little, since *B* is elsewhere. It is not a contingent fact that we perceive, move and act from the same place, for this is one foundation of the notion of genuine perception as opposed to illusion (cf. Hampshire, *Thought and Action*, Ch. 1, on this point). Strawson's 'subject of perceptual experience' seems to be an unregenerate Cartesian relic.

If Strawson is prepared to admit such a notion, it is not entirely clear what weight is to be attached to his conclusions in this chapter. For if it is a contingent fact that a subject of perceptual experience uses only one body, it may well be a contingent fact that he uses any body at all. Indeed, Strawson is prepared to admit this; at the end of the chapter he entertains the fancy that after death people might continue for a while in a disembodied state (pp. 115–16). He remarks of such a person that he would rapidly lose his sense of individuality, dependent as that would be only on his previous incarnation. But it is unclear that it follows from what Strawson has said that this would be so. For on Strawson's admissions, this disembodied person could perceive from a point of view, observe others, think about them, no doubt have sensations and emotions – at least nothing has been said to exclude these from 'states of consciousness' only contingently dependent on bodies. All that he would lack is bodily contact with others, and being identified by them. He might survive well on such a mental diet. Indeed, it is not certain that Strawson has proved, as he claims, that a person might not exist who had always been disembodied. For if, as Strawson supposes, it is possible to perceive disembodiedly from a point of view, why should a disembodied person not be able to identify others by their bodies, and himself by his point of view? He could not, on Strawson's argument, suppose the other, embodied, persons to be merely bodies plus something like himself; but perhaps he would not suppose this.

Thus Strawson's Cartesian conception of some *P*-predicates to a certain extent undermines the general tenor of his argument. Moreover, it makes his later account of the nature of *P*-predicates less persuasive than it need be. For, although he asserts that the public grounds of other-ascription and the grounds of self-ascription (which are presumably private – he apparently feels no Wittgensteinian doubts about talking of 'grounds' here) are linked in the same predicate, he says little on how or why this should be so; and on his approach, it seems bound to remain something of a mystery.

Those who sympathise with the spirit of Strawson's conclusions on this topic will tend to wish, I think, that he had carried it more radically into his arguments. As it is, he discusses it in terms, and on assumptions, excessively borrowed from those to whom he is opposed. His attempt to build up his conclusion from such materials is a remarkable *tour-de-force*, but they do not inspire confidence in its solidity.

8

Knowledge and meaning in the philosophy of mind

I shall consider some points which bear on certain general methods of argument that Shoemaker uses in his book, *Self-Knowledge and Self-Identity*.[1] They are methods of argument that enjoy considerable currency, and Shoemaker's very effective use of them invites one to consider their validity.

The first sentence of Shoemaker's book is: 'What we mean when we assert something to be the case cannot be different from what we know when we know that thing to be the case' (p. 1). This is incontestable, if it is taken to claim merely that no equivocation on '*P*' is involved in 'X asserts that *P*' and 'X knows that *P*'. In this form, while the principle is incontestable, it is also not of much philosophical use; in particular, not of much use for combating scepticism. Scepticism is compatible with it, and indeed can be partly based upon it; as when the sceptic claims that what we mean in making assertions about, say, other minds, refers to something sufficiently inaccessible for us not to be able to know anything about other minds.

The principle gets into a philosophical stride when assisted by certain other considerations. Thus there may be two classes of propositions A and B such that (*a*) B is the class of what would normally be called reports of tests, experiments, or observations relevant to the truth of the members of A, but (*b*) there is no way of coming to know members of A more direct than through knowing members of B. In this case it is tempting to say that *what we know* if we know a member of A is some member or members of B; and hence (by the principle) that what we mean when we assert a member of A is such members of B. Taking the step – if it is a further step – that what we mean when we assert *P* is what *P* means, we arrive at a drastic form of verificationism; which, apart from no doubt more subtle disadvantages, might lead us to be puzzled about the meaning of propositions about, for instance, a state of the universe in which it contained sub-atomic particles but no cloud chambers or similar apparatus.

There is a more general way in which the principle can exert a verificationist (or even an idealist) influence; again, not in itself and taken strictly – for in itself and taken strictly it is incontestable – but,

[1] Ithaca: Cornell University Press, 1963.

rather, perhaps because it selects *knowledge* as the notion to associate with meaning, rather than saying (what would be equally incontestable) that what we mean when we assert that something is the case cannot be different from what we believe when we believe that it is the case, or from what we doubt when we doubt whether it is the case, or from what we want when we want it to be the case, and so forth. This selection suggests a particular connexion between knowledge that *P* and the meaning of '*P*': a connexion which, together with the selection of the phrase 'What *we* mean when . . .' might possibly encourage something like the following argument schema:

1 '*P*' has the meaning we give it.
2 We would not have succeeded in giving '*P*' a meaning unless we knew when it applies and when it does not.
3 A necessary condition of our knowing when '*P*' applies and when not is Q. Therefore
4 Q is a necessary condition of our having succeeded in giving '*P*' a meaning (by 2 and 3); and therefore
5 Q is a necessary condition of '*P*' having a meaning (by 1 and 4). Evidently
6 '*P*' having a meaning is a necessary condition of '*P*' being true; therefore
7 Q is a necessary condition of '*P*' being true (5, 6).

Few people, presumably, would accept this argument schema in its unrestricted form; for one thing, an interpretation of Q which makes (3) come out true for any *P* whatsoever is that we exist, use concepts, and so forth. (Some interpreters of Kant, who represent his transcendental arguments as being very roughly of this type, perhaps pay insufficient attention to Kant's insistence that his transcendental arguments gave knowledge of how things must be only because the things were not things in themselves. The idealism was what was supposed to make the whole enterprise possible.)

Obviously, various sorts of criticism could be made of the schema as it stands. The interesting question is what sorts of restrictions, if any, could serve to turn this uninviting sophism into a sound line of philosophical argument, while retaining something of its better inclinations (which are, after all, favourably construed, inclinations against rubbish). This question is raised implicitly by certain central points of Shoemaker's book; I shall consider it below. First, however, I shall consider his refutation of the sceptic about other people's pains, which also involves an important connexion between meaning and knowledge.

Shoemaker's argument against the sceptic is a version of the 'public language' considerations that have been extensively brought to bear on this question; it is a notably clear and succint version. The argument (pp. 168–9) can be fairly set out, I think, as follows:

1 Barring slips of the tongue, one who understands 'I am in pain' cannot utter these words with the intention of making a true assertion unless he is in pain. Therefore

2 If X understands 'I am in pain', then, if X says, 'I am in pain', intending to make a true assertion, X is in pain. Therefore

3 If it is possible to know that X understands 'I am in pain', it is possible to know that X is in pain. But

4 If 'I am in pain' has an established meaning, then it is possible for one language-user to know that another language-user understands it.

Let 'S' = 'It is impossible for one person to know of another that he is in pain.' Then

5 If S, then 'I am in pain' does not have an established meaning (3, 4). But

6 If 'pain' has an established meaning, 'I am in pain' has an established meaning; and only if 'pain' has an established meaning does 'S' have a meaning, since 'S' uses and does not just mention the expression 'pain'. So

7 If a true, and hence intelligible, assertion is made by the utterance of 'S', 'I am in pain' has an established meaning (6). Therefore

8 Not S (or rather 'there is a logical absurdity in uttering "S" intending to make a true statement') (5, 7).

This is an impressive argument; but if its intention is, as it seems to be, to knock the sceptic flat, I doubt whether it succeeds. His objection to it could best be focused on this point: whether the minimum sense of 'understand' necessary to make (4) true is sufficient to make (3) true. Shoemaker perhaps displays some uneasiness about (4) himself, in that what he says is necessary to 'pain' having an established meaning is that we can know of another that he 'uses it correctly' or 'has correctly learned its meaning'. The latter formulation adds nothing except a red herring: it cannot be a (logically) necessary condition of understanding a creature's discourse that I know he has learned it correctly, since it is not a logically necessary condition of a creature's understanding and using discourse that he has *learned* it at all – indeed, it is a conspicuous merit of Shoemaker's formulation of his argument that it is free of the irrelevant considerations about language-learning which bedevil these issues. So (4) turns on 'uses it correctly'; and the sceptic will no doubt reply that he agrees to (4) under this interpretation, but that the fact that he can tell in that sense that someone else understands 'pain' is compatible with his scepticism; it is a less ambitious sense of 'understand' than that involved in (3). He might indeed agree with (3), with the stronger sense of 'understand' that it involves, but deny that in order for 'pain' to have an established meaning each person must know that others understand, in that sense, the expression.

The difficulty can also be formulated in another way. What is the warrant for the crucial premiss (3)? Shoemaker would claim, if I understood him, that (3) follows from (2), and that (2) is a formulation of 'incorrigibility' with respect to first-person pain statements, which the sceptic would be neither entitled nor disposed to deny. Let us grant (2) for the moment; and let us further assume that the persons whose understanding of 'I am in pain' is in question do actually use this sentence to make assertions, and that this is known: this point might itself be a focus of the sceptic's attention, but let us ignore it. Does (3) follow from (2)? The inference appears to be of the form: 'If *P*, then Q; so if it is possible to know that *P*, it is possible to know that Q.' As a general pattern of argument, this is invalid. For suppose that there is just one man, Robinson, who is fiendish and clever enough to commit a certain type of crime. Then it will be true that if a crime of that type is committed, it is committed by Robinson; but it does not follow from that that if it is possible to know that such a crime has been committed, it is possible to know that it has been committed by Robinson (he may make it impossible). In order to get from 'If *P*, then Q' to 'If it is possible to know that *P*, it is possible to know that Q', one needs the further premiss that *it is possible to know that if P then* Q. Shoemaker presumably thinks that there is no difficulty with this extra premiss in the present case, since he represents (2) as being a necessary truth.

But the sceptic, merely reorganising his well-known materials, might surely express a doubt whether it was a necessary truth, and wonder whether he *knew* it to be true at all. The very force of the argument might show him that to claim to know this came excessively close to claiming to know the sort of thing which he is claiming not to know.

I do not think that this second formulation of the difficulty presents the sceptical position as having any more interest or plausibility than the first one; one may agree that they are fairly small anyway, and that Shoemaker's argument is, while falling short of a conclusive rebuttal, a good way of indicating some of the implausibility. But the second formulation has at least this much interest: it shows that in order to escape Shoemaker's argument, the sceptic does not in fact have to deny any of its premisses; he merely has to deny that he knows premiss (2) to be true. The effect of the denial is not merely that thereby he could claim not to know the conclusion to be true; it would be that, robbed of the concealed premiss that one *knows* (2) to be true, the argument ceases to be valid at all.

Apart from its success or failure as a rebuttal of scepticism, Shoemaker's argument here raises more interesting and fundamental questions about what sort of concept he regards 'pain' as being: these I go on to consider.

A point on which Shoemaker lays great emphasis is that, while there is a logical correspondence between first- and third-person statements, and 'A sees a tree' is true if and only if 'I see a tree', said by A, is true, nevertheless the grounds on which the two statements are made are different: the sorts of considerations used by others in establishing that A sees a tree are not characteristically used by A to establish that he sees a tree (pp. 170–1). A special case of this is the case of memory: while criteria of personal identity are involved in another's claiming that A remembers a certain event, no such criteria are involved in A's claiming that he remembers the event.

It follows that the applicability of the concepts of memory, perception, and so forth involves a non-contingent relationship between the sorts of grounds on which third-person claims are made and the sorts of psychological situations in which first-person claims are sincerely made. This conclusion, similar to Strawson's views in *Individuals* – to which here, as elsewhere, it is a little surprising to find no reference – constitutes one version of the *non-contingency thesis*: it is a necessary truth that there obtains *in general* a relation between psychological states and the sorts of bodily states observation of which figures in establishing third-person claims about such psychological states. It is agreed that such relationships need not be universal; that they might not in every respect be the correlations with which we are familiar (thus we might find application for 'He sees out of his back'); it is even allowed that some of the relationships might change over time – but they could not change too fast, or the psychological concepts would lose their grip.

There is of course a difficulty in expressing this non-contingency thesis in terms of the relations that are supposed to hold between psychological states (for example, sensations, pp. 189, 192) and bodily states, which relations might change over time. For such terminology carries the implication of an external relation between distinct states of affairs, which relation is nevertheless said not to be contingent;

and this implication, if it imputes a non-contingent connexion between the *existence* of the states of affairs, raises questions which it seems to me Shoemaker does not adequately consider.

It is worth distinguishing three sorts of non-contingent dependence between distinct states of affairs – sorts of dependence which in *themselves* are not sufficient to establish a non-contingent connexion of existence. First, it is of course possible that distinct states of affairs A and B may be joined under a concept, as the established correlation between the insertion of sharp objects into tyres and the deflation of those tyres is brought under the concept 'puncture'. It would be tedious to labour the point that while the usefulness, and no doubt the existence, of the concept depends on the existence of the correlation, the existence of the concept does nothing to guarantee the continuation of the correlation.

Second, it may be that the *identification* of A depends on the *identification* of B. This is the sort of relation that Strawson is particularly concerned with in *Individuals*. Such identification dependence is not the same as ontological dependence and does not entail it; thus while Strawson is no doubt right in saying that the identification of atomic and sub-atomic particles (and hence of states of affairs in which they figure) depends on the identification of macroscopic items and the states of affairs that obtain with them, this does not mean that there could not be a world which contained atomic, but not macroscopic, items. Nor does Strawson suppose that it does. In the case of persons, however, whose identification as the bearers of psychological predicates depends on their bodily identification, some closer (though not, in Strawson's views, absolute) dependence is advanced. This must be for a special reason, the reason being, it would seem, that in order to be a person one must be able to identify oneself. I shall come back to this point.

Third, A and B may be connected by the relationship introduced in the argument schema considered at the beginning of these comments, that A must obtain if anyone is to know of the existence of B; or (differently) that a correlation between A and B must obtain for one to know anything at all. It seems to be a relationship of this type that Shoemaker has in mind in claiming that the general relations between psychological and bodily states of affairs are not contingent. For he argues that a general breakdown of such relationships would make it impossible for us to employ psychological concepts about others, and in particular to establish that the relationship had broken down; and moreover that one could not do this in one's own case either. He writes (pp. 189–90), 'The claim that one can imagine what it would be like for [a breakdown in these relationships] to become in one's own case the rule rather than the exception is, I think, equivalent to the claim that we could *establish* [his emphasis] that this had occurred in one's own case.' He then urges that one could not establish this; for while one knows what it would be like for it to *seem* that this had occurred generally, one could not *establish* it as true, since this would depend on memory, and one would have insufficient reason to believe one's memory. This last consideration seems to me – at least if the phenomenon in question went on long enough – to be dubiously consistent with another thesis of Shoemaker's (which I shall not discuss), that it is a necessary truth that most of one's confident memory claims are correct. But it is rather the first part of the argument that I want to consider here. It is extremely unclear *why* the claim that the collapse of a certain correlation is imaginable in my own case should be equated with the claim that it would be possible for me to *establish* this collapse; and indeed a general application of this principle would seem almost tantamount to an *a priori* disproof of the possibility of madness.

Thus I do not think that the impossibility of establishing the breakdown could merely by itself establish the impossibility of the breakdown: it is this latter that the alleged non-contingency of the relationships would naturally be taken to imply. What further premiss might be forthcoming to help bridge the gap? A possible line of search for a premiss could go very roughly as follows.

In the case of Strawson on persons, it was suggested that the evident gap which obtains in general between identification-dependence and existence-dependence might be bridged for persons by the consideration that persons must (in general) be able to identify themselves; one can get from 'A's must be identified if B's are to be identified' to 'A's must exist if B's are to exist' once one grants that B's, in order to exist, must be identified (it is assumed that A's, in order to be identified, must exist). Thus:

$$
\begin{array}{r}
Id\ \mathrm{B} \rightarrow Id\ \mathrm{A} \\
\mathrm{Ex\ B} \rightarrow Id\ \mathrm{B} \\
\therefore \mathrm{Ex\ B} \rightarrow Id\ \mathrm{A} \\
Id\ \mathrm{A} \rightarrow \mathrm{Ex\ A} \\
\hline
\therefore \mathrm{Ex\ B} \rightarrow \mathrm{Ex\ A}
\end{array}
$$

Starting now from some premiss to the effect that psychophysical correlations must obtain if mental states are to be *known*, an argument similar to the last one could lead one to a conclusion connecting the existence of mental and physical states if one added that the existence of mental states involved their being known. For if the existence of mental states involves their being known, and their being known involves their correlation (in general) with physical states, then any mental states there are must (in general) be correlated with physical states; which is, more or less, Shoemaker's conclusion.

To make good this line of argument, it will be necessary to give some plausible content to the relation I have blocked in with the opaque phrase 'Mental states, in order to exist, have to be known.' Clearly this must refer (in the first instance, at least) to knowledge by their subject; the thesis might be taken to entail such particular conclusions as 'A creature which has a sensation must know what sensation it has.' This thesis appears to be false – unless knowing what sensation it has is just reduced to having that sensation. Animals constitute a sufficient counter-example. The thesis might, however, be restricted, without danger to its general intention, to humans and other similar concept users (if any).

I am not sure, however, whether Shoemaker would want the thesis, even so restricted: he brings mental states involved in perception within the orbit, apparently of sensations, certainly of the sorts of mental states he is concerned with, and he valuably makes the point that the natural sort of judgement that goes with perception is, for example, 'There is a table' rather than 'I see a table.' Still less, presumably, would the subject be involved in making judgements about the sensations that he has; and Shoemaker does not seem to have given us anything to show that in order to make perceptual judgements a concept user has to be *able* to make judgements about sensations involved in perception.

Let us leave this, then, and restrict the thesis further to such things as pains. The claim will be, minimally, that a concept-using subject must know that he has a pain if he has one. Then the question arises of how secure our hold is on the other required premiss, that a pre-condition of such knowledge lies in the psychophysical correlations.

It might be thought that the premiss had been provided elsewhere, in the argument against the sceptic about pains: for that seemed to imply that the concept *pain* yoked together those phenomena on the strength of which third-person ascriptions are made and those sensations which the subject has when he sincerely makes first-person claims – that is, it rests on the psychophysical correlation. The argument against the sceptic did not, I suggest, knock the sceptic flat. But its materials might prove useful here. For the concept under which the subject brings his sensation in knowing that he is in pain is *pain*; and this concept involves the psychophysical correlation.

Now the fact that the concept is of this nature does not in itself show the required non-contingency of the correlation: for, in itself, it might be merely a version of the 'puncture' phenomenon, the first kind of superficially non-contingent connexion distinguished above. Although we have a concept our use of which rests on a connexion between sensations and behaviour, nevertheless the connexion might break. If the non-contingency thesis means what I take Shoemaker to mean by it – namely, that there is a non-contingent connexion of the *existence* of sensations and behaviour with regard to such things as pains – then its defender will, on the present construction of the argument, have to show both of the following:

a Pain sensations, in order to be known, have to be brought under a concept which rests on a psychophysical correlation.

b If pain sensations exist, then they must be known.

Shoemaker short-circuits the discussion of such arguments by employing his very close association between meaning and knowledge, some aspects of which I have tried to note. But if no more detailed justification is given, and if in particular we are not given reasons why in connexion with psychological concepts there obtains something which, unless we are idealists, we do not believe to obtain elsewhere – namely, that the conditions of our employing concepts to describe a state of affairs are equally conditions of that state of affairs existing – then the argument to the non-contingency thesis would seem to rest merely on the uninviting argument schema which I introduced at the beginning.

9
Deciding to believe

When the subject of belief is proposed for philosophical discussion, one may tend to think of such things as religious and moral beliefs, belief in the sense of conviction of an ideological or practical character. Indeed, many of the most interesting questions in the philosophy of belief are concerned with beliefs of this type. However, this is not in fact what I shall be talking about, though what I say will, I hope, have some relevance to issues that arise in those areas. I wish to start with the question of what it is to believe something, and then go on from that to discuss (rather briefly) how far, if at all, believing something can be related to decision and will. In order to discuss this, I am not going to take religious and moral beliefs, but cases of more straightforward factual belief; the sort of belief one has when one just believes that it is raining, or believes that somebody over there is one's father, or believes that the substance in front of one is salt.

I shall be talking about belief as a psychological state. The word 'belief', of course, can stand equally for the state of somebody who believes something, and for what he believes. And we can talk about beliefs in an impersonal way, when we talk about certain propositions which people believe or might believe. But my principal concern will be with belief as a psychological state: I shall be talking about people believing things.

The ultimate focus of my remarks is going to be on the relations between belief and decision and certain puzzles that arise about the relation between these two ideas. But before we can get into a position to discuss the questions that concern the relations between belief and decision, we must first ask one or two things about what belief is. I shall begin by stating five characteristics – as I take them – of belief. This will not be very accurate; and each of the five things that I am going to mention as a characteristic of belief can itself give rise to a good bit of dispute and philosophical consideration. In the course of mentioning the five features, it will be necessary to mention things which may seem problematic or completely platitudinous.

The first of these features is something which can be roughly summarised as this: beliefs aim at truth. When I say that beliefs aim at truth, I have particularly in mind three things. First: that truth and falsehood are a dimension of an assessment of beliefs as opposed to many other psychological states or dispositions. Thus if somebody just has a habit of a certain kind, or merely has some disposition to action of some kind, it is not appropriate to ask whether this habit of his is true or false, nor does that habit or disposition relate to something which can be called true or false. However, when somebody believes something, then he believes something which can be assessed as true or false, and his belief, in terms of the content of what he believes, is true or false. If a man recognises that what he has been believing is false, he thereby abandons the belief he had. And this leads us to the second feature under this heading: to believe that *p* is to believe that *p* is true. To believe that so and so is one and the same as to believe that that thing is true. This is the second point under the heading of 'beliefs aim at truth'.

The third point, closely connected with these, is: to say 'I believe that *p*' itself carries, in general, a claim that *p* is true. To say 'I believe that *p*' conveys the message that *p* is the case. It is a way, though perhaps a somewhat qualified way, of asserting that *p* is true. This is connected with the fact that to say 'I believe that *p*, but *p* is not true', 'I believe that it is raining but it is not raining' constitutes a paradox, which was famously pointed out by G. E. Moore. This is a paradox but it is not a formal self-contradiction. If it were, then in general '*x* believes that *p* but *p* is false', would also be a self-contradiction. But this is obviously not so. Thus I can, without any paradox at all, say 'Jones believes that *p* but *p* is false'; it is only in the first person, when I say 'I believe that *p* but *p* is false', that the paradox arises. The paradox is connected with the fact that I assert these two things; it is connected with this, that 'I believe that *p*' carries an implied claim to the truth of *p*.

This trio of points constitutes the first of the features of belief I want to mention, that which I vaguely summed up by saying 'beliefs aim at truth'.

The second feature of belief is that the most straightforward, basic, simple, elementary expression of a belief is an assertion. That is, the most straightforward way of expressing my belief that *p*, is to make a certain assertion. And I think the following is an important point: the assertion that I make, which is the most straightforward or elementary expression of my belief that *p*, is the assertion *that p*, not the assertion 'I believe that *p*.' The most elementary and straightforward expression of the belief that it is raining is to say 'it is raining', not to say 'I believe that it's raining.' 'I believe that it's raining' does a rather special job. As a matter of fact, it does a variety of special jobs.[1] In some cases, it makes what is very like an autobiographical remark; but very often in our discourse it does a special job of expressing the belief that *p*, or asserting that *p*, in a rather qualified way. On the whole, if somebody says to me, 'Where is the railroad station?' and I say 'I believe that it's three blocks down there and to the right', he will have slightly less confidence in my utterances than if I just say 'It's three blocks down there and to the right.' We have a near parallel to this in the field of action, in the contrast between saying 'I will do so and so' and saying 'I intend to do so and so.' The direct or primitive expression of an intention to do so and so, is not saying 'I intend to do so and so'; it is saying 'I *will* do so and so.'

This is not to deny that beliefs can be ascribed to non-language-using animals. There are reasons, however, for saying that these are beliefs in a somewhat impoverished sense. There are many interesting questions in this field; I shall refer briefly to one of them. There is a certain conventionality about the ascription of something like a belief to an animal. Suppose that we present to a rabbit or some similar animal, something that looks like the mask of a fox; and that when the animal notices this object it displays characteristic fear behaviour. We might say in this case that the rabbit had *taken* what it was presented with for a fox. We probably would not use the rather pompous phrase of saying that the rabbit *believed* that it was a fox, though even this might not be in every case entirely unnatural. In the case of animals whose behaviour is, in our terms, more obviously sophisticated, and especially in the case of animals such as dogs which perform a very special rôle for humanity as being things on which we project an enormous amount of anthropomorphic apparatus – in those cases the word 'belief' may come more happily to hand. In any case, we do say about animals that they take things for things, and that they recognise things as things; and in at least certain cases even that they *believe* that something is something. The puzzle about this is: where does this *concept* come from, which, as it were, we pretend the animal is using? We don't think that in an effective sense the animal has the *concept* 'fox'. We have some idea what it is for a human being to have a concept 'fox'; we have a different idea of what it is for him to have the more general concept, for instance, 'predator'. If we were faced with the question: did the

[1] It is important to notice this point. It is even more important not to suppose that discussions of 'I believe that *p*' provide the main highway to an understanding of belief. That they do not, follows from this point itself.

rabbit think that it was a fox, or did the rabbit merely think it was a predator that was in front of it? we have some difficulty in deciding this question, indeed, in knowing how to set about deciding this question.

There is an interesting sideline to this. Suppose there is a dog whose master is the President of the United States; a certain figure comes to the door, and this dog wakes up and pricks up his ears when he hears the person crossing the step – we say 'this dog took the person who was coming up the drive for his master'. If this dog's master was the President of the United States, we would hardly say that the dog had taken this figure for the President of the United States. Is this because it is a better shot to say that the dog has got the concept 'master' than it is to say that the dog has got the concept 'President of the United States'? Why? The concept 'master' is as much a concept that embodies elaborate knowledge about human conventions, society, and so forth as does the concept 'President of the United States'. There seems to be as much conventionality or artificiality in ascribing to a dog the concept 'master' as there is in ascribing to a dog the concept 'President of the United States'. So why are we happier to say that a dog takes a certain figure for his master than we are to say that the dog takes a certain figure for the President of the United States? I think the answer to this has something to do with the fact, not that the dog really has got an effective concept 'master', which would be an absurd notion, but that so much of the dog's behaviour is in fact conditioned by situations which involve somebody's being his master, whereas very little of the dog's behaviour is conditioned by situations which essentially involve somebody's being President of the United States. That is, the concept 'master' gets into our description of the dog's recognition or quasi-thought or belief because this is a concept we want to use in the course of explaining a great deal of the dog's behaviour. It is something on those lines, I think, which is going to justify the introduction of certain concepts into an animal's quasi-thoughts or beliefs, and the refusal to introduce other concepts into an animal's quasi-thoughts or beliefs. In the case of human beings, however, the situation is not just like this, because we have other tests for what concepts the human being in fact has.

This, then, was the second feature of belief: that the most straightforward expression of a belief is an assertion, but this does not prevent our using concepts of belief or something rather like belief with regard to animals which are incapable of making assertions and do not possess a language – although we will have to warn ourselves that such beliefs, recognitions and so on, are going to be ascribed to animals in an impoverished and (I think I have said enough to suggest), a somewhat conventionalised sense.[2]

The third feature of belief is that although the most straightforward, simple, and elementary expression of a belief by a language-using creature is an assertion, the assertion of *p* is neither a necessary nor, and this is the point I want to emphasise, a sufficient condition of having the belief that *p*. It is not a necessary condition, because I can have beliefs which I do not express, which I shall not utter. In fact it is very plausible to say that most people most of the time have a very large number of beliefs which they are not expressing, never have expressed, and never will express. The point, however, that I want to emphasise is the converse, namely that it is possible for someone to assert that *p* and try to bring it about that others think that *p* and think that he believes that *p*, although he does not; that is to say, assertion can be insincere.

The fact that assertion can be insincere, which is an extremely important fact about assertion, shows, what in any case is obvious, that belief cannot be defined as acceptance, at least if 'acceptance' is taken as the name of an action which we can overtly perform. If you take 'accepting' to be something like accepting an invitation – that is, somebody comes up to me and says 'Will you come to my party tomorrow?' and I accept it if I say something like 'Yes, I will'; then in that sense of 'accepting', 'acceptance' is the name of something like a speech-act, and belief cannot be equated with acceptance in such a sense. Suppose somebody comes up to me and says, 'Do you accept that *p*?'; 'Do you accept that such and such is true?' If I just say 'Yes', then in a speech-act sense of accepting that proposition, in that sense I will have accepted; just like the speech-act of accepting an invitation. But, of course, that is not a sufficient condition of my believing that *p*, because this acceptance may have been insincere. Belief lies at the level of what makes my acceptance sincere or insincere; it does not lie at the level of those acceptances themselves. So we have a picture of belief as of the internal state which my overt assertions may represent or misrepresent. Similarly, statements of intention or promises can be sincere or insincere because they do or

[2] I do not think that to say that a psychological concept is applied to other animals in an 'impoverished' sense either merely follows from the fact that they lack a language, or is in itself in the least explanatory. Some psychological concepts, like some concepts of action, apply *straightforwardly* to animals. The claim of 'impoverishment' or 'conventionality' has to be made good by special considerations, such as those concerning the choice of concepts figuring in that application.

do not represent an internal state of intention. Where the expression of a belief is the typical one of an assertion, that assertion itself can be called insincere just in that case in which the man does really believe what he is asserting. This then is the third point; that assertion is not a necessary condition of belief, nor is it a sufficient condition, since assertion can be insincere.

The fourth point is that factual beliefs can be based on evidence. This can mean more than one thing. The weakest sense of this is that the content of a given belief can be probabilified or supported by certain evidential propositions. If I just say that the belief that ancient Crete was occupied by Greek-speaking persons at a certain date is based on, or supported by, the evidence of such and such excavations, I am not, in saying this, talking about any particular person's beliefs: I am talking about a certain proposition which concerns the history of Crete and saying that that proposition is in fact supported by certain evidence which exists. Let us turn from this to a case in which we are referring to a particular person's belief. In saying that his belief is based on particular evidence, we would mean not just that he has the belief and can defend it with the evidence, but that he has the belief just because he has the evidence. This says that if he ceased to believe the evidence, then, other things being equal, he would cease to have that belief. In this case, something that is true of him, namely, that he believes that *p*, depends upon something else being true of him, namely, that he believes these evidential propositions. In this sense of somebody's actual belief being based upon his belief in certain evidential propositions, we have a statement of the form 'A believes that *p* because he believes that *q*'; and such statements are very often true of most of us.

Where the connexion between *p* and *q* is a rational connexion, that is to say, *q* really is some sort of evidence for *p*, then we can also say '*p* because *q*'; if a man says to me 'Why *p*, why do you believe that *p*?' I can rightly say 'because *q*'. Of course there are other cases in which A believes that *p* because he believes that *q*, which are not cases of rational connexion, or even supposed rational connexion, at all. It is just a fact about him that he believes the one thing because he believes the other, by some kind of irrational association. In this case he cannot rightly say '*p* because *q*', that is, claim a rational connexion between the two propositions. Here we have a case where he believes one thing because he believes another, and that is a pure causal connexion. The point I want to make is that where the connexion is rational – that is, not only does he believe that *p* because he believes that *q*, but we, and he, can also say '*p* because *q*', – that does not stop the 'because' in 'A believes that *p* because he believes that *q*' from being causal. The fact that there is a rational connexion between *p* and *q* does not mean that there is not a causal connexion between A's believing *p* and his believing *q*. We tend to bring out the mere causal connexion between his beliefs in the irrational cases because in those cases there is nothing but a causal connexion between them. But that does not mean that in the case in which the man has one belief rationally grounded on another it is *not* the case that there is a causal connexion between his believing the one thing and his believing the other; in fact I think it is, in general, true that when A believes that *p* because he believes that *q*, this 'because' is a causal 'because'. It is a 'because' of causal explanation, the explanation of how one of his states is causally connected with another.

We do have a genuine and systematic difficulty in the philosophy of mind in filling in the content of that causal 'because', and this is mainly because we have a very shadowy model of the kind of internal state belief is. However, this can be no particular objection to causal connexions between beliefs in the case of evidential connexion; because there are many other cases in which we must invoke a causal connexion between such internal states while we still have only a shadowy notion of what that causal connexion consists in. The most obvious case of this is the case of remembering things that one has experienced in the past. Suppose we say concerning a certain man that he remembers being lost in the park when he was five. What are the necessary conditions for its being the case that he remembers being lost in the park when he was five? The first is that he should, in fact, have been lost in the park when he was five and have experienced that at that time. The second is that he should now know that he was lost in the park, and have some further knowledge of that experience. That is not enough. Suppose it were the case that he was lost in the park when he was five but everything he now knows about it he was told by his mother a few years ago. Then it would not be the case that he remembered being lost in the park when he was five. The further condition which makes it the case that he does remember being lost in the park is that he now knows about it because he experienced it.[3] This necessary condition of event-memory appeals to exactly that kind of indeterminate causal 'because' which we need in the case of one belief being based upon another, of a man's believing that *p* because he believes that *q*.

[3] On this see Martin and Deutscher, 'Remembering', *Philosophical Review*, LXXV (1966).

People sometimes argue against the idea that we can have a causal connexion here, on the following ground. It cannot be the case that in rational thought I arrive at one belief causally because I have another belief, since then it would be a perpetual miracle that the laws of nature worked in such a way that we were caused to have beliefs by rational considerations. Granted the different sort of fact that *q* actually supported *p*, that *q* was evidence for *p*, does it not seem a happy accident or even miraculous that when I believe that *q* it comes about that I believe that *p*? This objection is basically an example of what Wisdom has called 'metaphysical double vision', the mistake of taking the same facts twice over and then finding the relation between them mysterious. There are not two facts, first that men are rational creatures who hold beliefs on rational grounds, and second that they have beliefs which quite often cause others in ways which express their rational connexions. On the view in question, the emergence of creatures who are capable of rational thought just is the emergence of creatures who are capable of having beliefs which are so related. Some may think it a miracle that any such creatures have emerged, but if it is, it is at least not *another* miracle that the required causal connexions obtain in them: if the causal connexions broke down, they would just cease to be rational creatures – and since very many of the beliefs which are held by rational creatures could be held only by rational creatures, they would cease to be capable of holding these beliefs at all.

Not every belief that I have which is *based*, is based on *evidence*. There are some beliefs that I have which are not (relative to the probability of their being true) random or arbitrary, and which are very proper beliefs to have, but which are not based on further evidence; that is, are not based on other beliefs that I have. Indeed, there is a very good reason why it cannot be the case that every belief which one has is based on another belief that one has – namely, one could never stop (or start). Quite evidently there are non-random beliefs which are not based on further evidence. The most notable examples of these, of course, are perceptual beliefs, beliefs that I gain by using my senses around the environment.

In the case of human perception, we have something which we found lacking in the earlier discussion of animals' 'beliefs'. We can understand what it is for somebody to acquire a belief from his environment, and we have a kind of guarantee that the terms in which we describe the cause, that is, the environment which gave rise to his belief, can match the concepts that he uses in describing the environment and therefore, by the same token, in expressing his beliefs. The very condition of having a shared experience, having a shared language and having a common perceived environment which we can know to be such, is this: we share concepts which simultaneously enable us to express our beliefs about our environment, to describe that environment, and to describe other people's perception of the environment. Therefore we get a match between our descriptions of the environment which causes another person's belief, and the concepts which he himself uses in expressing the belief and in describing the environment. This avoids the essentially conventional element which we met in the case of animals, the kind of arbitrariness about which concepts one uses in describing their recognitions or beliefs. In the case of a human being we have his own assertions, his own conceptual apparatus, which will make clear how he sees the world. The cause and the effect are described alike from the resources of a common language.

So much for the causality of beliefs; this was the fourth feature of beliefs. Beliefs can be based upon evidence. It is sometimes true that a man believes that *p* because he believes that *q*. I take that to be a causal 'because', and have tried to dispose of at least one objection to thinking that it is so. The fifth, and last point about the nature of belief (and this is something which I shall mention without elaborating at all), is that belief is in many ways an *explanatory* notion; we can, in particular, explain what a man does by saying what he believes. It is important that one cannot explain a man's actions in terms of his beliefs without making an assumption about what his projects are, just as one cannot infer from his actions what his projects are without making assumptions about his beliefs. The trio: project, belief and action, go together. Granted that I know his projects and beliefs, I may be able to predict his actions. Granted that I know his actions and his projects, I may be able to infer his beliefs. And granted that I know his actions and his beliefs I may be able to infer his projects. But I do need basically to know, or to be able to assume, two out of the three in order to be able to get the third. A standard example of this is: I see a man walking with a determined and heavy step onto a certain bridge. We say that it shows he believes that the bridge is safe, but this, of course, is only relative to a project which it is very reasonable to assume that he has, namely to avoid getting drowned. If this were a man who surprisingly had the project of falling in the river, then his walking with firm step onto this bridge would not necessarily manifest the belief that the bridge was safe. This is a fairly obvious point. It is in terms of the trio of project, belief, and action that we offer our explanations.

These, then, are the five characteristics or features of belief that I have wanted to emphasise.

Now I want to consider a certain machine which satisfies, more or less, three of the conditions which I have mentioned: the first, second, and the fourth conditions. In a weak sense, it produces assertions. That is to say, it produces print-out, or, if you like, it has a speech synthesiser in it – though this would be unnecessary luxury. In any case, it produces messages which express propostions, and it has a device which distinguishes between propositions which it asserts, as opposed, for instance, to propositions which it is prepared to hypothesise in the course of an argument. It comes out with something which roughly, it 'claims to be true'. These things that it comes out with can be assessed for truth or falsehood; and so derivatively can be the states of the machine, which issue in these assertions. Further, the states which go with some of these assertions are based in an appropriate way on other states, and the machine arrives at some of these states from others. It goes through a causal process which is at least something like inference. We can add the fact that it gathers information from the environment; it has various sensory bits and pieces which acquire information about the environment and these get represented in the inner states of the machine, which may eventually issue in appropriate assertions.

Now this machine, I claim, would not manifest belief; its states would not be beliefs. They would be instances of a much impoverished notion which I shall call a '*B* state'. Why would a *B* state fall short of the state of a belief? I claim the essential reason for this is that this machine would not offer any satisfaction of the third condition in the list I earlier gave, namely, that it be possible to make insincere assertions, to assert something other than what you believe. In the case of this machine there is a direct route from the state that it is in to what it prints out; or if something goes wrong on this route, it goes mechanically wrong, that is, if something interrupts the connexion between the normal inner state for asserting that *p* and its asserting that *p*, and it comes out with something else, this is merely a case of breakdown. It is not a case of insincere assertion, of its trying to get you to believe that *p* when really all the time it itself believes that not-*p*: we have not yet given it any way of doing that. The fact that we have not yet given it any way of doing that has, I think, deeply impoverished the concept of belief, as applied to this machine. It also, of course, means that when I said this machine made assertions, I should have actually put that in heavy scare-quotes; 'assertion' itself has got to be understood in an impoverished sense here, because our very concept of assertion is tied to the notion of deciding to say something which does or does not mirror what you believe. 'Assertion' in the case of this machine just means, bringing out something in an assertoric mode, without putting qualifications around it.

It is, however, a notable feature of this machine that it could have true *B*-states which were non-accidentally arrived at, that is, which were not randomly turned out but were the product of the environment, the programming and so on; and these might be called 'knowledge'. We could say of this machine that it knows whether so and so is the case, that it knows when the aircraft leaves, that it knows where somebody left something, that it knows where it is itself, that it knows where certain buildings are in the town. I would claim in fact that the use of the word 'know' about this machine is not far away from a lot of uses we make of the word 'know' about human beings, whereas a use of 'believe' to refer to the *B*-states that this machine is in, is quite a long way away from the way in which we use the word 'believe'. There might be *some* machine to which we could properly ascribe beliefs; the point is that a machine to which we properly ascribed knowledge could be a lot more primitive than one to which we properly ascribed beliefs.

This goes against what is a rather deep prejudice in philosophy, that knowledge must be at least as grand as belief, that what knowledge is, is belief plus quite a lot; in particular, belief together with truth and good reasons. This approach seems to me largely mistaken. It is encouraged by concentrating on a very particular situation which academic writings about knowledge are notably fond of, that which might be called the *examiner* situation: the situation in which I know that *p* is true, this other man has asserted that *p* is true, and I ask the question whether this other man really knows it, or merely believes it. I am represented as checking on someone else's credentials for something about which I know already. That of course encourages the idea that knowledge is belief plus reasons and so forth. But this is far from our standard situation with regard to knowledge; our standard situation with regard to knowledge (in relation to other persons) is rather that of trying to find somebody who knows what we don't know; that is, to find somebody who is a source of reliable information about something. In this sense the machine could certainly know something. Our standard question is not 'Does Jones know that *p*?' Our standard question is rather 'Who knows whether *p*?'

As a matter of fact, even with 'Jones knows that *p*', we do not have to have all this elaborate exercise of reasons. Consider the following situation. They are engaged in this illicit love affair; she comes running in, and says 'He knows'. Her lover says: 'You mean he believes it? Well we know it's true. Now has he got good reasons for what he thinks?' She says, 'I think he just picked it up from the gossip next door.' Would her lover then be right in saying 'In that case, he doesn't know'? This would be absurd, basically, because 'he knows' here means 'he's found out', and not that he has very well grounded true beliefs. 'He's found out', however, does express more than 'he's guessed'. What 'he's found out' means is, very roughly, that he has acquired a true belief by an information-chain which starts somewhere near the facts themselves.

In his case, of course, we can speak of a belief. The point is that reflection on this and other common uses of 'know' suggests that much of the point of the concept of knowledge could be preserved if it were applied to things such as our machine which had, not beliefs, but something less.

With regard to the *B*-states, there could be false *B*-states that the machine was in; accidentally or randomly true *B*-states; and non-accidentally true *B*-states, that is *B*-states which were true and which came about in ways which were connected with the fact that they were true, and these last we could call knowledge. But for belief, full-blown belief, we need the possibility of deliberate reticence, not saying what I believe, and of insincerity, saying something other than what I believe. So in a sense we need the will; for it is only with the ability to decide to assert either what I believe or what I do not believe, the ability to decide to speak rather than to remain silent about something, that we get that dimension which is essential to belief, as opposed to the more primitive state, the *B*-state, which we can ascribe to the machine which satisfies the elementary conditions.

From the notion of what belief is, then, we arrive at one connexion between belief and decision, namely, the connexion between full-blown belief and the decision to say or not to say what I believe, the decision to use words to express or not to express what I believe. This is, however, a decision with regard to what we say and do; it is not the decision to believe something. Thus far, belief is connected with decision because belief is connected with the decision to say. It is not the case that belief is connected with any decision to believe. We have not got anything like that yet. Indeed, from what has already been said it seems that we have some rather good reasons for saying that there is not much room for deciding to believe. We might well think that beliefs were things which we, as it were, found we had (to put it very crudely), although we could decide whether to express these or not. In general one feels that this must be on the right track.

It fits in with the picture offered by Hume of belief as a passive phenomenon, something that happens to us. But there is something very peculiar about Hume's account; he seems to think that it is just a contingent fact about belief that it is something that happens to us. He says, in effect: There are some things you can decide and some things you cannot, and that just means that some things happen to respond to the will while others do not. It will be a blank contingent fact if belief does not respond to the will. Now we must agree that there are cases of what we may call contingent limitations on the will. For instance, suppose somebody says that he cannot blush at will. What would it be to blush at will? You could put yourself in a situation which you would guess would make you blush. That is getting yourself to blush – by a route – but it could not possibly count as blushing at will. Consider next the man who brings it about that he blushes by thinking of an embarrassing scene. That is getting a bit nearer to blushing at will, but is perhaps best described as making oneself blush at will. The best candidate of all would be somebody who could just blush in much the way that one can hold one's breath. I do not know whether people can do that, but if they cannot, it will be a contingent fact that they cannot.

Belief cannot be like that; it is not a contingent fact that I cannot bring it about, just like that, that I believe something, as it is a contingent fact that I cannot bring it about, just like that, that I'm blushing. Why is this? One reason is connected with the characteristic of beliefs that they aim at truth. If I could acquire a belief at will, I could acquire it whether it was true or not; moreover I would know that I could acquire it whether it was true or not. If in full consciousness I could will to acquire a 'belief' irrespective of its truth, it is unclear that before the event I could seriously think of it as a belief, i.e. as something purporting to represent reality. At the very least, there must be a restriction on what is the case after the event; since I could not then, in full consciousness, regard this as a belief of mine, i.e. something I take to be true, and also know that I acquired it at will. With regard to no belief could I know – or, if all this is to be done in full consciousness, even suspect – that I had acquired it at will. But if I can acquire beliefs at will, I must know that I am able to do this; and could I know that I was capable of this feat, if with regard to every feat of this kind which I had performed I necessarily had to believe that it had not taken place?

Another reason stems from our considerations about perceptual belief: a very central idea with regard to empirical belief is that of coming to believe that *p* because it is so, that is, the relation between a man's perceptual environment, his perceptions, and the beliefs that result. Unless a concept satisfies the demands of that notion, namely that we can understand the idea that he comes to believe that *p* because it is so and because his perceptual organs are working, it will not be the concept of empirical belief; it will hardly even be that more impoverished notion which I have mentioned, the *B*-state. But a state that could be produced at will would not satisfy these demands, because there would be no regular connexion between the environment, the perceptions and what the man came out with, which is a necessary condition of a belief or even of a *B*-state.

However, even if it is granted that there is something necessarily bizarre about the idea of believing at will, just like that, it may be said that there is room for the application of decision to belief by more roundabout routes. For we all know that there are causal factors, unconnected with truth, which can produce belief: hypnotism, drugs, all sorts of things could bring it about that I believe that *p*. Suppose a man wanted to believe that *p* and knew that if he went to a hypnotist or a man who gave him certain drugs he would end up believing that *p*. Why could he not use this more roundabout method, granted that he cannot get himself into a state of believing just by lifting himself up by his own shoe straps; why could he not bring it about that he believes that *p* by adopting the policy of going to the hypnotist, the drug man or whatever? Well, in some cases he could and in some cases he could not; I am going to say something about the two sorts of cases. I am not going to discuss the issue of self-deception. The issue of self-deception is an important and complex issue in the philosophy of mind which gives rise to a large number of problems; of course it is true that people can deceive themselves into believing things that they know are false. But I am not going to discuss self-deception; what I am going to raise is rather this question: Why, if we're going to bring it about that we believe something in this kind of way, do we have to use self-deception; that is, what, if anything, is wrong with the idea of a conscious project to make myself believe what I want to believe?

The first thing we have to do is to distinguish between two senses or two applications of the notion of 'wanting to believe' something. I am going to distinguish these under the terms 'truth-centred motives' and 'non-truth-centred motives'. Suppose a man's son has apparently been killed in an accident. It is not absolutely certain he has, but there is very strong evidence that his son was drowned at sea. This man very much wants to believe that his son is alive. Somebody might say: If he wants to believe that his son is alive and this hypnotist can bring it about that he believes that his son is alive, then why should he not adopt the conscious project of going to the hypnotist and getting the hypnotist to make him believe this; then he will have got what he wants – after all, what he wants is to believe that his son is alive, and this is the state the hypnotist will have produced in him. But there is one sense – I think the more plausible one – of 'he wants to believe that his son is alive' in which this means *he wants his son to be alive* – what he essentially wants is the *truth* of his belief. This is what I call a truth-centred motive. The man with this sort of motive cannot conceivably consciously adopt this project, and we can immediately see why the project for him, is incoherent. For what he wants is something about the world, something about his son, namely, that he be alive, and he knows perfectly well that no amount of drugs, hypnotism and so on applied to himself is going to bring that about. So in the case of the 'truth-centred motives', where *wanting to believe* means *wanting it to be the case*, we can see perfectly clearly why this sort of project is impossible and incoherent.

However, he might have a different sort of motive, a non-truth-centred motive. This would be the case if he said, 'Well, of course what I would like best of all is for my son to be alive; but I cannot change the world in this respect. The point is, though that even if my son isn't alive, I want, I need to believe that he is, because I am so intolerably miserable knowing that he isn't.' Or again a man may want to believe something not caring a damn about the truth of it but because it is fashionable or comfortable or in accordance with the demands of social conformity to believe that thing. Might not such a man, wanting to believe this thing, set out to use the machinery of drugs, hypnotism, or whatever to bring it about that he did? In this case the project does not seem evidently incoherent in the way in which the project was incoherent for the man with the truth-centred motive. What it is, is very deeply irrational, and I think that most of us would have a very strong impulse against engaging in a project of this kind however uncomfortable these truths were which we were having to live with. Why? What is the source of our very strong internalised objection to this kind of project?

I will raise one or two questions which may assist in the discussion of this. First, is the project of trying to get yourself to believe something because it is more comfortable fundamentally different or not from the project (more familiar, and, it might seem, more acceptable) of trying to forget something because it is uncomfortable? That is, if I just wanted to forget what was disagreeable, would this be very different in principle from the project of actually trying to believe something which is untrue? Is the project of trying to forget the true morally or psychologically different from the project of trying to get oneself to believe the false? If so, why? Is one of them easier than the other? If so why? I would add to that question the suggestion that there is almost certainly a genuine asymmetry here, tied in to the asymmetry that while every belief I have ought ideally to be true, it is not the case that every truth ought ideally to be something I believe: belief aims at truth, knowledge does not similarly aim at completeness.

Perhaps, further, one objection to the projects of believing what is false is that there is no end to the amount you have to pull down. It is like a revolutionary movement trying to extirpate the last remains of the *ancien régime*. The man gets rid of this belief about his son, and then there is some belief which strongly implies that his son is dead, and that has to be got rid of. Then there is another belief which could lead his thoughts in the undesired direction, and that has to be got rid of. It might be that a project of this kind tended in the end to involve total destruction of the world of reality, to lead to paranoia. Perhaps this is one reason why we have a strongly internalised objection to it. If we are not going to destroy all the evidence – all consciousness of the evidence – we have to have a project for steering ourselves through the world so as to avoid the embarrassing evidence. That sort of project is the project of the man who is deceiving himself, and he must really know what is true; for if he did not really know what was true, he would not be able to steer around the contrary and conflicting evidence. Whether we should or should not say that he also believes what he really knows to be true, is one of the problems that surround self-deception. But at least the project that leads to that condition, the project of self-deception, is something different from the blank projects of belief-inducement which we were considering.

10
Imperative inference

I shall argue that there is not in general anything that can be called *imperative inference.* I do admit that there are certain logical relations between imperatives: these may be summed up in the fact that two imperatives may be said to be inconsistent, if and only if it is logically impossible that they should both be obeyed. What I deny is that this fact enables us in general to apply the notion of inference to imperatives.

By 'an inference' I mean a sequence of sentences of the form '*A*, *B*, . ., so *C*', such that (*a*) each of the sentences is actually used for its primary logical purpose – that is to say, where '*A*' is an indicative sentence, '*A*' is used to make a statement or assertion, and where '*A*' is an imperative sentence, it is used to issue a command or order, tell someone what to do, etc.; (*b*) the final sentence is used to make a statement or issue a command which is *arrived at* or *concluded* from the previous statements or commands in virtue of a logical rule. This is not meant to be more than a very vague characterisation of an inference; to carry the characterisation further would involve anticipating some of the discussion that follows. One point, however, is important. I do suppose that every inference could in principle be conducted by someone. In connexion with formal logic in general such a point is not made; but this is only, I take it, because it does not need to be made. I shall at any rate take it for granted that if inferences could not be conducted and patterns of inference put to use, by individual speakers or thinkers, the notion of inference would lose its content and be of no use to us. (I omit from this general point any reference to inferences with an infinite number of premisses, which raise different issues of no concern to us here.)

I shall consider only the case in which *A*'s uttering an imperative to *B* constitutes his ordering or commanding *B* to do something, and I shall indeed use 'imperative', 'command' and 'order' more or less interchangeably. Correspondingly, I shall speak of *obedience* to imperatives. There are, of course, uses of imperatives other than those of giving commands or orders, and what I say will apply less directly, at least, to some of these other uses. However, it seems obvious that the use of imperatives to give orders or commands is the basic use of imperatives,[1] and if my criticism of the idea of inference in this connexion is correct, radical doubts about the idea of imperative inference in general would seem to follow.

I shall take as example an imperative inference supposedly modelled on the valid truth-functional schema:

(*D*1) *p* or *q*; not *p*; so *q*.

Does the schema

(*D*2) do *x* or do *y*; do not do *x*; so do *y*

represent a form of inference? The first premiss of this supposed inference, 'do *x* or do *y*', expresses an imperative the force of which would also be expressed by the words 'do *x* or *y*': there is nothing but a stylistic difference between the two.

What is the function of such an imperative? One function it has, as opposed to the simple imperatives 'do *x*' or 'do *y*', is to give the recipient of the command a choice of what he is to do – it allows him some latitude in its obedience. We might put this by saying that such a command *permits* the agent not to do *x*, so long as he does *y*, and permits him not to do *y*, so long as he does *x*. Thus the notion of such a command introduces the notion of permission – permission implicitly given or admitted by the commander. However, this is not all that is to be said about the *permissive presuppositions* (as I shall term them) of this command. For it is clear that the conditional permissions already identified, viz.

I permit you not to do *x*, if you do *y*

and

I permit you not to do *y*, if you do *x*

would not in fact constitute genuine permissions unless *y* and *x*, respectively, were themselves permitted: since the formula

I permit you to do *x* if you do *y*, but I do not permit you to do *y*

does not confer or admit any permission at all. Thus it follows that the permissive presuppositions of the disjunctive command include permission to do *x* and *y* themselves.

This point can in any case be reached by a more direct route. It is

[1] This seems to be tacitly conceded by Geach in his reply to this paper (which followed it in *Analysis Supplement* 1963). Although he emphasises the use of imperatives in *counsel* (p. 39), his explanation of the importance of inconsistency between imperatives turns on their use in commands: 'we wish the commands we give to be obeyed' (p. 37). That this is in general true indeed follows from the idea of a command; it is less obvious that it follows in a parallel way from the idea of counsel or advice that we wish our advice to be taken. Don't we leave that to the person we are advising?

in general a presupposition of the command 'do x' that x is permitted – where this means, of course, permitted so far as the present activity of commanding is concerned, since it is evidently possible that someone should command something which he admits to be not permitted by some other authority or standard. The formula

do x, but I do not permit you to do x

is self-defeating in a way parallel to, though not identical with, the way in which 'p, but I do not believe that p' is self-defeating. Granted this, we should be able to construct for any given command its set of permissive presuppositions. We can see that the presuppositions of the disjunctive command 'do x or y' must include permission to do x, and permission to do y; but not, of course, permission to do both x and y, since there are many cases in which such a command is used with exclusive force, where the commander would not countenance joint performance of both the actions mentioned, or where joint performance would be impossible.

If we admit these permissive presuppositions of the disjunctive command, we can see an objection to construing the schema ($D2$) as anything that could be called a pattern of inference. For the first premiss presupposes permission to do x, and permission to do y; but the second premiss, 'do not do x', obviously has the force of denying permission to do x. Thus the speaker implicitly gives or admits something with his first utterance, which he withdraws with his second; and this can be construed only as the speaker *changing his mind*, or going back on what he first said. This destroys any resemblance of this sequence of commands to an inference; it is essential to the idea of an inference of q from a set of premisses P that in reaching q, the speaker should not go back on or change his mind about any of the members of P – the form of an inference is '*given* P, q'.

The same point can be seen if we consider a yet simpler inference which holds truth-functionally for statements, and which might be expected to hold for imperatives: the inference

p; so p or q.

Could we admit as an inference the sequence

do x; so do x or y ?

I suggest not, for reasons similar to those already considered.[2] One function of the command 'do x' is to withhold permission not to do x; the formula

do x, but I permit you not to do x

[2] (Additional note 1972). I should have mentioned the original discussion of this paradox by Alf Ross, *Theoria*, VII (1941), pp. 53–71.

is again, self-defeating or paradoxical. But the effect of the disjunctive command, here the conclusion of the supposed inference, is (as already argued) to give permission not to do *x*, on a certain condition, viz. the doing of *y*. So the permissive presuppositions of (respectively) the premiss and the conclusion of the supposed inference are

I do not permit you not to do *x*

I permit you not to do *x*, if you do *y*

and here again we encounter an inconsistency, only interpretable as a change of mind: the change of mind from giving the agent no leeway in respect of the non-performance of *x*, to giving him some leeway.

I suggest, therefore, that when we examine the function of disjunctive commands in terms of their permissive presuppositions, we find that the successive utterance of the commands involved in the supposed inferences has a cancelling effect, the effect of withdrawing what has already been said; and that this feature is incompatible with construing such a sequence as an inference.

But, it may be objected, does the last step follow? Even if it be granted that there are permissive presuppositions which are incompatible in the way described, does this fact destroy the inferential character of the sequence? Are there not certain presuppositions or implications of the premisses even of statement inferences which are in parallel ways inconsistent, but which nevertheless do not destroy either the validity or the inferential character of the inference? We may consider the disjunctive statement schema (*D*1). Here we might say that the assertion of the first premiss standardly implied or presupposed that the speaker did not know whether not-*p* was true or not, since if he did he could not sincerely leave open, as he does, the disjunction between *p* and *q*. But the assertion of the second premiss does imply or presuppose that he knows, or at least believes, that not-*p* is true. So here again we have two conflicting presuppositions; but they evidently do not destroy the inference.

In reply to this objection, I think it might first be questioned whether the assertion of '*p* or *q*' does imply or presuppose ignorance about the truth-value of not-*p*. But this I shall leave; a more basic consideration is that even if this were true, it would not matter. Even granted these presuppositions about knowledge, the statement sequence would be in a quite different situation from the command sequence. For the movement from the presupposition of the assertion of the first premiss of (*D*1) to the presupposition of the assertion of the second would be merely the movement from ignorance to knowledge, and such a movement, so far from upsetting the consistency of a set of premisses in an inference, is built into the very notion of inference. We move from ignorance to knowledge by acquiring more truths; and adding one truth (or supposed truth) to another is just one thing that can be involved in accumulating a set of premisses.

The essential differences from commands in these respects come out if we consider the notion[3] that statements of fact stand in a converse relation to the world compared to commands and other forms of practical discourse. To put it very roughly, our aim is to model our statements of fact to the world, and they attain their 'fulfilment value' – i.e. truth – by being correctly so modelled. With commands, however, the aim is that the world should be modelled to them, and they obtain their fulfilment value – they are obeyed – by changes in the world being made in accordance with them. Statements of fact are changed to fit the world; the world is changed to fit commands. It is changed, of course, not by any magical means, but by the intervention of human agents who understand commands and (if the commands are successful) act in accordance with them.

From this distinction there follow two related ways in which a *sequence* of commands differs from a *sequence* of statements. The first way follows merely from the converse relation to the world of the two sorts of utterance. What commands are appropriate depends basically on the will of the commander: it is up to him, at each stage, to decide what changes he wants initiated by means of his commands. What he wants may be more or less determinate: he may, for instance, be content with either x or y being done, or he may want precisely y to be done and not x. If he moves from the first to the second, he has changed his mind about what he wants: if y was what he wanted in the first place, it was, after all, open to him to command just that. With statements of fact, what statement is appropriate at each stage does not depend on what the speaker wants, and if he moves from a less determinate statement to a more determinate one, this does not imply change of mind parallel to that in the case of commands. There is indeed a sense of 'change of mind' in which a speaker's changing his mind upsets a statement-inference – if he omits or withdraws a premiss already admitted. The difference is that with commands, *any* revision of what the commander requires, permits etc. in respect of a given set of actions counts equally as a change of mind: it will be a change in what he wants, and what he wants is all that matters.

[3] Suggested by G. E. M. Anscombe in *Intention* (Oxford: Blackwell, 1957), § 32; cf. Bernard Mayo, 'Rule-Making and Rule-Breaking', *Analysis* 15.1 (1954), p. 19.

The second way in which the two sorts of sequence differ follows from the fact that commands are carried out by the agency of other human beings. A command having been given, the onus passes to the agent, to do what is required; in the simplest situation, when the command has been given, the agent (assuming that he obeys it) just *goes off* and does the action. If a commander first gives a disjunctive command, and then moves to the negation of a disjunct, he is in effect calling the agent back, and starting again. It is significant that he may actually be too late, the agent having already obeyed the disjunct which is later negated: in this case the commander will be disappointed, though his first command has been obeyed, and this is a good illustration of his change of mind. But the same basic point applies, even if he is not too late, the performance of the actions mentioned in the disjuncts lying at some point in the future: here the agent has been 'wound up' in one way by the disjunctive command (for instance, to choose between the disjuncts) and to move to the new command involves 'unwinding' him and starting again.

It is interesting here to compare the command 'do x or y' with the warning or preparatory statement 'I am going to command you to do x or to do y'. This latter indeed prepares the agent for a later command, e.g. 'don't do x, do y', and it not only can be, but must be, followed by some such command. But it is not itself a command. 'Do x or y' is a command, but for that very reason does not prepare the agent for some later and more determinate command: it precisely *unprepares* him for any such thing, by leaving him with a choice of his own between x and y.

The disjunctive statement 'p or q' is in one way more like the preparatory warning than it is like the disjunctive command: it allows the speaker to add 'and I may be able to tell you later which is true'. On the other hand, it does not *require* him to provide more determinate information later; and it is, of course, itself as much a statement as any statement that follows it, while the warning is not a command like the command that follows it. The essential difference between statements and commands in relation to their hearers is that once a command has been given, the situation is, as it were, cut off: the hearer, if he is to obey, goes and acts. But with statements, the hearer can always come back for more, and less determinate information can always be, though it need not be, followed by more determinate information.

These considerations show, I think, why a sequence of imperatives with conflicting presuppositions should be regarded as essentially *discontinuous*, as involving a change of mind on the part of the speaker which prevents the set of imperatives being cumulatively assembled into anything that could be called a set of premisses. But the cumulative assembly of premisses is a necessary condition of there being an inference; hence we cannot call a sequence of imperatives of this kind an *inference*.

But, it may be said, the most that this shows is that there is no imperative inference on the part of the speaker. But is this not to ignore another, and perhaps more obvious, possibility? For certainly there is a logical relation between the imperatives 'do *x* or do *y*' and 'don't do *x*': the logical relation which consists in the impossibility of obeying both save by doing *y*. Now even if the successive production of these imperatives by one speaker would constitute, as I have argued, a change of mind, there could easily be a situation in which they were uttered to an agent who was disposed to obey both: e.g. by two different authorities, both of whom he wished to obey. Indeed, they could be uttered by one and the same, mind-changing, authority, and the agent be disposed to obey both. This being so, would it not be a feat of logical inference for the agent to recognise that *y* was what he should do?

It would: the point, however, is that it would not be a feat of *imperative* inference, i.e. an inference expressible by the sequence 'do *x* or *y*, don't do *x*' etc. This is for the extremely simple reason that imperatives are uttered by those who give commands, not by those who obey them. The only inference that the agent could carry out would be in some form such as: 'I must do *x* or *y*; I must not do *x*; so I must do *y*', and this is a deontic inference, not an imperative one. It may illuminate this point to imagine an agent listening to a wireless set which transmitted various imperatives, from various sources, all of which he was disposed to obey. We can imagine the agent saying to himself, as the wireless goes on, 'do *x* or *y* – don't do *x* – ': then – addressing himself – '. . . do *y*'. This scene might seem to embody an imperative inference. But it does not in fact. A sufficient reason for this – leaving aside all the difficulties involved in interpreting the supposed conclusion of the inference, the imperative addressed by the agent to himself – is that the imperatives which form the supposed premisses are not being used by the agent, but quoted. He is just following the voices on the wireless, and his inferential process, fully expanded, would be of the form: 'I must do whatever the wireless tells me: it tells me "do *x*", so I must do *x*', etc. – after which, he can add the deontic premisses together and draw the deontic conclusion, as above.

It appears, then, that sequences of imperatives cannot be construed as inferences conducted either by the commander or by the agent. But every inference can be conceived of as possibly conducted by someone. I conclude that, while imperatives have some logical relations, there is not in general anything that can be called imperative inference.

ADDITIONAL NOTE (1972)

This article attracted a certain amount of criticism; for a helpful account, with comments, of work on this and related topics, see Jonathan Bennett's review in *Journal of Symbolic Logic*, Vol. 35 (1970), pp. 314–18. Although I now think that the article runs together too briskly a number of different considerations and is in important respects unclear, I remain unrepentant about its general upshot, and have yet to see an entirely convincing account of how imperative inference is possible – though there are increasing numbers of systems perhaps designed to show what a formalisation of it would be like if it were possible.

One of the most careful replies came from Professor Hare,[1] and I should like to add some comments on his criticism – more particularly because his main points have been accepted by Bennett, and also in order to try to put my claim more clearly than I succeeded in doing before.

Hare's central idea is that the 'permissive presuppositions', as I called them, of disjunctive commands are not entailments but rather in the nature of the 'conversational implicatures' discussed by H. P. Grice (*PASS* 1961): they represent conclusions which it is reasonable for hearers to draw in virtue of very general conventions about the relevance, pointfulness, adequacy etc. of what is said. As such (and unlike logical entailments), they can, in special circumstances, be explicitly waived or 'cancelled'; and Hare gives an example, as he claims, of such a cancellation with respect to a disjunctive command. I shall discuss the example at the end of these remarks. Hare's point is that if the permissive presuppositions are of a Gricean character, then reference to them will help to explain why the 'inferences' I discuss are peculiar as speech-act performances in standard circumstances, but will not support any attack on their logical respectability as inferences.

So far as the examples under discussion go, it is only with regard

[1] 'Some Alleged Differences between Imperatives and Indicatives', *Mind*, LXXVI (1967); reprinted in his *Practical Inferences* (London: Macmillan, 1971). Page references here are to the latter.

to the special permissive presuppositions of the disjunctive commands that Hare takes the Gricean line. Some permissive relatives of simple commands he regards as *entailed*: 'Although there might be further argument about this, I propose to take it that "Post the letter" *entails* "You may not refrain from posting the letter"' (p. 27, his emphasis; and see p. 31 for negative commands). It is not altogether easy to construe Hare's view, since he moves between different formulations of what kind of thing is entailed or 'conversationally implicated' by what: important issues lurk here about content and speech acts, and I shall come back to some of them.

Further difficulties lie in the interpretation that Hare gives to entailment for commands and permissions. The passage just quoted continues: 'Another way of putting this is to say that "Post the letter" is logically inconsistent with "You may refrain from posting the letter" . . . two commands, or a command and a permission, are logically inconsistent if the statement that one is going to be acted on is inconsistent with the statement that the other is going to be acted on . . .' Thus Hare extends his standard semantics of commands to permissions. The first thing to be noted is that the logical relations of permission-statements are not based, as in the most natural interpretations of deontic logic, in considerations of what permissions (forbiddings etc) are *in force*, but in whether they are *acted on*: and granted that they are to be linked by entailment to commands, and the logic of commands is thus interpreted, there is indeed no alternative. But then there is a question about what 'acted on' means in connexion with a permission. The example just quoted, which can be expressed as

(i) Do x! *entails* not-*P* (not-x),

and that on p. 31, which can be expressed as

(ii) Do not do x! *entails* not-*P*(x),

involve non-permissions, construed as forbiddings, and to *act on* them is construed as refraining from what is non-permitted. Similarly, if not at once so obviously, to *act on* '*P*(x)' is construed as doing x, as emerges from the claim that 'do x!' is inconsistent with '*P*(not-x)'; relatedly, '*P*(x)' and 'not-*P*(x)' are implicitly regarded as contradictories. But from these interpretations it follows that '*P*(x)' and '*P*(not-x)' are inconsistent with one another (since it is logically impossible to *act on* both of them). From that, further, it follows that of every contradictory pair of actions, one is forbidden; and, consequently, that the other is obligatory. Hence the category of the permitted falls out altogether. I conclude from that, that this interpretation of permission cannot be correct, and, since Hare must need it for entailments with commands interpreted as he interprets them, he should give up his admittedly tentative support of (i) and (ii).

One gets a further view of the oddness of Hare's model if one considers the contraposition of (i) or (ii). If one accepts double negation and the equivalence of 'Do not do *x*!' with 'Do not-*x*!', one gets e.g.

(ii)′ *P*(*x*) *entails* do *x*!

Now it may well be that Hare would reject (ii)′ on the strength of special restrictions on imperative logic. But merely on the strength of the 'acting on' interpretation, (ii)′ is correct; and that fact in itself casts the gravest doubts on the acceptability of the model.

What follows? Hare obviously thinks that if his tentative introduction of entailment in the simple case is mistaken, then so much the worse for my view: if all 'permissive presuppositions' are 'implicatures', then *a fortiori* the relations I discuss are not strictly logical, and the case against imperative inference collapses. But this is a confusion. I did not claim that permissive presuppositions were entailments – I in fact compared 'do *x* but I do not permit you to do *x*' to the self-defeatingness of '*p* but I do not believe that *p*' – nor does my point rest on their being entailments. It might do so, if I were arguing that these imperative 'inferences' were invalid: the claim, however, is not that, but that they are not inferences at all.

The fact that we are not dealing with entailments does not necessarily mean, however, that what we have is a kind of implication which can (like Grice's implicatures as used by Hare) straightforwardly be *cancelled*. Cancellation is possible with one sort of implication which I mentioned, in order to contrast it with the permissive case, viz. the *epistemic* implication of the assertion of 'either *p* or *q*': the normal implication of this, that the speaker does not know which obtains, is certainly cancellable, as when he adds 'and I know which, but I am not telling you'. It is not like this with the relation between commanding and permitting. The implication of my saying to someone 'do *x*', that I permit him to do *x* and do not permit him not to, is not cancellable: 'do *x* but I permit you not to' remains obstinately paradoxical.

The reason for this stems from two, interrelated, considerations. First, if I take an utterance by a given speaker on a given occasion as conveying a command[2] to a given agent to do a certain thing,

[2] This over-extended use of 'command' requires the same indulgence as was asked for in the original article.

I cannot also take it as conveying a permission (relative to the same set of institutions, interests, etc.) not to do that thing, since those two communicatory intentions cannot be intelligibly combined. The second point is that, the facts of the English language being what they are, the utterance of sentences of the forms 'do x' and 'I permit you not to do x' or 'you may refrain from doing x' cannot in general and without a special scenario be understood as doing other, respectively, than conveying such a command and permission. Taking these two consideration together, one is licensed to say that it is a property of the English *sentence*-forms 'do x but I permit you not to do x' or 'do x but you may refrain from doing x' that they are paradoxical: meaning by that, that without a special scenario, the utterance of a sentence of either of these forms cannot be understood except as *per impossibile* the joint performance of two speech-acts which cannot be jointly performed – hence the utterance cannot be understood.

What we have here is neither entailment nor cancellable implicature. Spelled out in these terms, my claims that certain commands have certain permissive presuppositions are to be construed in terms of what an utterer is to be taken as having permitted if an utterance of his is to be taken as the commanding of a certain thing. When, further, certain imperative forms of words are said to be associated with certain permissive presuppositions, this is to be construed via the consideration that utterances of those forms of words cannot, without extra scenario, be understood as other than the kinds of commanding in question.

The claim that there is no such thing as imperative inference is to be construed in these terms (indeed, that it is to be understood in a way which involves the notion of a speech-act follows from clause (*a*) of my original definition of an inference). The claim can be spelled out: there are no sets of imperative sentences S1 and S2 such that all of the following are satisfied – (i) the utterance of the members of S1 and S2 on some occasion constitute the giving of a sequence of commands; (ii) a sequence of commands, C, constituted by the utterance of the members of S1, forms a set of premisses; (iii) commands constituted by the utterance of the members of S2 are arrived at or concluded from C.

I see no confusion of sentence and speech-act levels in that, as is objected to the controversy in general by Bar-Hillel.[3] Nor do I think that a notion of inference quite independent of speech-act considerations will serve adequately to characterise the interesting question

[3] *Analysis* 26, pp. 79–82.

here, as perhaps is suggested by Bar-Hillel in his rather vague plea for formalised, or at least normalised, language in the discussion of these issues. The notion of imperative inference is the notion of something which is used as an imperative – paradigmatically, to give a command – inferred from something which is used as an imperative; short of something which embodies, or can yield, that notion, we do not yet have distinctively imperative inference. In particular, we are not given the notion by a system which *merely* exploits the fact, admitted by all, that incompatibility can obtain between imperatives; a system which merely exploited that fact could allow us to infer e.g. from the fact that one imperative had been obeyed to the fact that another necessarily had not, but that does not provide any imperative inference at all, only a special application of indicative inference.[4]

My denial that there is such a thing as imperative inference does not necessarily mean that in no sense can there be such a thing as a 'logic of imperatives'; for perhaps it is enough for a logic of imperatives, in some sense, that there is inference about imperatives. Of course, that sense may be depressingly weak; and it may be that a lot of the interest in imperative logics in fact depends on the supposition that there is such a thing as imperative inference.

To return to Hare's criticism: once the issues have been disembarrassed of the simple opposition between entailment and Gricean 'implicature', the questions are whether Hare has shown that I was wrong about the permissions which I claimed were implicit in the giving of a disjunctive command, and, even if so, whether the sequence of commands he offers in such a case can yet be seen as constituting an inference. The situation in Hare's example is that out of several roads to a destination, the commander intends a driver to take one of two, via *B* or *C*; and, before they divide, to call for further orders. He says (p. 32): 'Go via C or *B*; I am not saying which at the moment; and I am not authorising you yet to go via C', and he tells him to get further orders later. Now, I do not of course deny that the commander's words are perfectly intelligible, nor that the driver can be clear what he is to do. The question is, how much insight these facts give us into disjunctive commands and imperative inference; I suggest, very little, as can be shown independently of any views that Hare contests.

What is meant by 'I am not authorising you yet to go via *C*'? What is being discussed is permissive presupposition, and the point

[4] This point incidentally answers Geach's objection (*loc. cit*) that unobvious incompatibility can be discovered only by inference.

of the example is to show that these, being of Gricean character, can be cancelled or waived in such a case; so I take it that the remark about authorisation, if relevant, can be taken to mean something like 'I do not permit you (yet) to go via *C*'. But there is nothing special about *C* – the point is that neither route is yet 'authorised'. So, equally, the commander can say 'I do not permit you (yet) to go via *B*'. But putting those together, we have, it seems – using obvious abbreviations – not-*P*(*C*) *and* not-*P*(*B*), which must be inconsistent with 'do *B* or *C*' even on Hare's own account of the matter. Does the 'yet' make all the difference? Surely not. For all it gives us is that, as of now, it is not yet the case that *P*(B) (though it may be later), and, as of now, it is not yet the case that *P*(C) (though it may be later). Now putting these together does not, of course give us: as of now, it is not yet the case that *P*(B) and *P*(C), though it may be later. But putting them together surely *does* give us: as of now, not-*P*(B) and as of now, not-*P*(C). If, as is entailed by Hare's own view, commanding the driver to do (*B* or C) implies that *P*(*B* or C); and if, as of now, not-*P*(*B*), and, as of now, not-*P*(C); then, surely, *as of now* he is not commanded to do (B or C).

This machinery is essentially too crude to explicate adequately the force of the communication quoted by Hare. But if Hare were right, it would be adequate, since the case is meant to be a simple counter-example to what I claimed. The machinery is certainly adequate to show that if it is that, then it is by the same token a counter-example to what anyone, including Hare, is disposed to say about the relations between commanding and permitting.

Even apart from that, Hare fails adequately to answer the puzzle about the *hearer* carrying out an *imperative* inference. I agreed originally that a man assailed by a set of imperatives might reason about how to obey them all or as many as possible, but I claimed that this would be a deontic and not an imperative inference. Hare pictures the man who conducts the inference as concluding 'that he is to go via Berwick' (p. 32). That is to say, – if 'I am to go via Berwick' is an imperative – the theory of imperative inference turns out once more to depend on the deeply suspect notion of the self-addressed imperative.[5] But, in any case, why should 'I am to . . .' be thought of as an imperative? Hare's chief reason seems to be (pp.

[5] See D. F. Pears, 'Predicting and Deciding', British Academy Lecture 1964, reprinted in Strawson, ed. *Studies in Thought and Action* (Oxford University Press, 1968); Hare, *Wanting: Some Pitfalls*, in Binkley, Bronaugh and Marras, eds. *Agent, Action and Reason* (Oxford: Blackwell, 1971), pp. 81 *seq*, and Pear's comments, *ibid*., pp. 108 *seq*.

33–4) that 'You are to go . . .' and 'Go . . .' are, in certain contexts, not very different. That is, on more than one ground, a very weak reason. If there really is imperative inference, why cannot we have what are indisputably imperatives making a more convincing appearance in what are indisputably inferences?

11
Ethical consistency

I shall not attempt any discussion of ethical consistency in general. I shall consider one question that is near the centre of that topic: the nature of moral conflict. I shall bring out some characteristics of moral conflict that have bearing, as I think, on logical or philosophical questions about the structure of moral thought and language. I shall centre my remarks about moral conflict on certain comparisons between this sort of conflict, conflicts of beliefs, and conflicts of desires; I shall start, in fact, by considering the latter two sorts of conflict, that of beliefs very briefly, that of desires at rather greater length, since it is both more pertinent and more complicated.

Some of what I have to say may seem too psychological. In one respect, I make no apology for this; in another, I do. I do not, in as much as I think that a neglect of moral psychology and in particular of the rôle of emotion in morality has distorted and made unrealistic a good deal of recent discussion; having disposed of emotivism as a theory of the moral judgement, philosophers have perhaps tended to put the emotions on one side as at most contingent, and therefore philosophically uninteresting, concomitants to other things which are regarded as alone essential. This must surely be wrong: to me, at least, the question of what emotions a man feels in various circumstances seems to have a good deal to do, for instance, with whether he is an admirable human being or not. I do apologise, however, for employing in the following discussion considerations about emotion (in particular, *regret*) in a way which is certainly less clear than I should like.

1 It is possible for a man to hold inconsistent beliefs, in the strong sense that the statements which would adequately express his beliefs involve a logical contradiction. This possibility, however, I shall not be concerned with, my interest being rather in the different case of a man who holds two beliefs which are not inconsistent in this sense, but which for some empirical reason cannot both be true. Such beliefs I shall call 'conflicting'. Thus a man might believe that a certain person was a Minister who took office in October 1964 and also that that person was a member of the Conservative Party. This case will be different from that of inconsistent beliefs, of course, only if the man is ignorant of the further information which reveals the two

beliefs as conflicting, viz. that no such Minister is a Conservative. If he is then given this information, and believes it, then either he becomes conscious of the conflict between his original beliefs[1] or, if he retains all three beliefs (for instance, because he has not 'put them together'), then he is in the situation of having actually inconsistent beliefs. This shows a necessary condition of beliefs conflicting: that if a pair of beliefs conflict, then (*a*) they are consistent and (*b*) there is a true factual belief which, if added to the original pair, will produce a set that is inconsistent.

2 What is normally called conflict of *desires* has, in many central cases, a feature analogous to what I have been calling conflict of beliefs: that the clash between the desires arises from some contingent matter of fact. This is a matter of fact that makes it impossible for both the desires to be satisfied; but we can consistently imagine a state of affairs in which they could both be satisfied. The contingent root of the conflict may, indeed, be disguised by a use of language that suggests logical impossibility of the desires being jointly satisfied; thus a man who was thirsty and lazy, who was seated comfortably, and whose drinks were elsewhere, might perhaps represent his difficulty to himself as his both wanting to remain seated and wanting to get up. But to put it this way is for him to hide the roots of his difficulty under the difficulty itself; the second element in the conflict has been so described as to reveal the obstacle to the first, and not its own real object. The sudden appearance of help, or the discovery of drinks within arm's reach, would make all plain.

While many cases of conflict of desires are of this contingent character, it would be artificial or worse to try to force all cases into this mould, and to demand for every situation of conflict an answer to the question 'what conceivable change in the contingent facts of the world would make it possible for both desires to be satisfied?' Some cases involving difficulties with space and time, for instance, are likely to prove recalcitrant: can one isolate the relevant contingency in the situation of an Australian torn between spending Christmas in Christmassy surroundings in Austria, and spending it back home in the familiar Christmas heat of his birthplace?

A more fundamental difficulty arises with conflicts of desire and aversion towards one and the same object. Such conflicts can be represented as conflicts of two desires: in the most general case, the desire to have and the desire not to have the object, where 'have' is

[1] I shall in the rest of this paper generally use the phrase 'conflict of beliefs' for the situation in which a man has become conscious that his beliefs conflict.

a variable expression which gets a determinate content from the context and from the nature of the object in question.[2] There are indeed other cases in which an aversion to x does not merely take the form of a desire *not to have* x (to avoid it, reject it, to be elsewhere, etc.), but rather the form of a desire that x *should not exist* – in particular, a desire to destroy it. These latter cases are certainly different from the former (aversion here involves advancing rather than retreating), but I shall leave these, and concentrate on the former type. Conflicts of desire and aversion in this sense differ from the conflicts mentioned earlier, in that the most direct characterisation of the desires – 'I want to have x' and 'I want not to have x' – do not admit an imaginable contingent change which would allow both the desires to be satisfied, the descriptions of the situations that would satisfy the two desires being logically incompatible. However, there is in many cases something else that can be imagined which is just as good: the removal from the object of the disadvantageous features which are the ground of the aversion or (as I shall call aversions which are merely desires *not to have*) negative desire. This imaginable change would eliminate the conflict, not indeed by satisfying, but by eliminating, the negative desire.

This might be thought to be cheating, since any conflict of desires can be imagined away by imagining away one of the desires. There is a distinction, however, in that the situation imagined without the negative desire involves no loss of utility: no greater utility can be attached to a situation in which a purely negative desire is satisfied, than to one in which the grounds of it were never present at all. This does not apply to desires in general (and probably not to the more active, destructive, type of aversion distinguished before). Admittedly, there has been a vexed problem in this region from antiquity on, but (to take the extreme case) it does seem implausible to claim that there is no difference of utility to be found between the lives of two men, one of whom has no desires at all, the other many desires, all of which are satisfied.

Thus it seems that for many cases of conflict of desire and aversion towards one object, the basis of the conflict is still, though in a slightly different way, contingent, the contingency consisting in the co-existence of the desirable and the undesirable features of the object. Not all cases, however, will yield to this treatment, since there may be various difficulties in representing the desirable and undesirable features as only contingently co-existing. The limiting case

[2] For a discussion of a similar notion, see A. Kenny, *Action, Emotion and Will* (London: Routledge & Kegan Paul, 1963), Ch. 5.

in this direction is that in which the two sets of features are identical (the case of ambivalence) – though this will almost certainly involve the other, destructive, form of aversion.

This schematic discussion of conflicts between desires is meant to apply only to non-moral desires; that is to say, to cases where the answer to the question 'why do you want x?' does not involve expressing any moral attitude. If this limitation is removed, and moral desires are considered, a much larger class of non-contingently based conflicts comes into view, since it is evidently the case that a moral desire and a non-moral desire which are in conflict may be directed towards exactly the same features of the situation.[3] Leaving moral desires out of it, however, I think we find that a very large range of conflicts of desires have what I have called a contingent basis. Our desires that conflict are standardly like beliefs that conflict, not like beliefs that are inconsistent; as with conflicting beliefs it is the world, not logic, that makes it impossible for them both to be true, so with most conflicting desires, it is the world, not logic, that makes it impossible for them both to be satisfied.

3 There are a number of interesting contrasts between situations of conflict with beliefs and with desires; I shall consider two.

(*a*) If I discover that two of my beliefs conflict, at least one of them, by that very fact, will tend to be weakened; but the discovery that two desires conflict has no tendency, in itself, to weaken either of them. This is for the following reason: while satisfaction is related to desire to some extent as truth is related to belief, the discovery that two desires cannot both be satisfied is not related to those desires as the discovery that two beliefs cannot both be true is related to those beliefs. To believe that p is to believe that p is true, so the discovery that two of my beliefs cannot both be true is itself a step on the way to my not holding at least one of them; whereas the desire that I should have such-and-such, and the belief that I will have it, are obviously not so related.

(*b*) Suppose the conflict ends in a decision, and, in the case of desire, action; in the simplest case, I decide that one of the conflicting

[3] Plato, incidentally, seems to have thought that all conflicts that did not involve a moral or similar motivation had a contingent basis. The argument of *Republic* IV which issues in the doctrine of the divisions of the soul bases the distinction between the rational and epithymetic parts on conflicts of desire and aversion directed towards the same object in the same respects. But not all conflicts establish different parts of the soul: the epithymetic part can be in conflict with itself. These latter conflicts, therefore, cannot be of desires directed towards the same object in the same respects; that is to say, purely epithymetic conflicts have a contingent basis.

beliefs is true and not the other, or I satisfy one of the desires and not the other. The rejected belief cannot substantially survive this point, because to decide that a belief is untrue *is* to abandon, i.e. no longer to have, that belief. (Of course, there are qualifications to be made here: it is possible to say 'I know that it is untrue, but I can't help still believing it.' But it is essential to the concept of belief that such cases are secondary, even peculiar.) A rejected desire, however, can, if not survive the point of decision, at least reappear on the other side of it on one or another guise. It may reappear, for instance, as a general desire for something of the same sort as the object rejected in the decision; or as a desire for another particular object of the same sort; or – and this is the case that will concern us most – if there are no substitutes, the opportunity for satisfying that desire having irrevocably gone, it may reappear in the form of a *regret* for what was missed.

It may be said that the rejection of a belief may also involve regret. This is indeed true, and in more than one way: if I have to abandon a belief, I may regret this either because it was a belief of mine (as when a scientist or a historian loses a pet theory), or – quite differently – because it would have been more agreeable if the world had been as, when I had the belief, I thought it was (as when a father is finally forced to abandon the belief that his son survived the sinking of the ship). Thus there are various regrets possible for the loss of beliefs. But this is not enough to reinstate a parallelism between beliefs and desires in this respect. For the regret that can attach to an abandoned belief is never sufficiently explained just by the fact that the man did have the belief; to explain this sort of regret, one has to introduce something else – and this is, precisely, a desire, a desire for the belief to be true. That a man regrets the falsification of his belief that *p* shows not just that he believed that *p*, but that he wanted to believe that *p*: where 'wanting to believe that *p*' can have different sorts of application, corresponding to the sorts of regret already distinguished. That a man regrets not having been able to satisfy a desire, is sufficiently explained by the fact that he had that desire.

4 I now turn to moral conflict. I shall discuss this in terms of *ought*, not because *ought* necessarily figures in the expression of every moral conflict, which is certainly not true, but because it presents the most puzzling problems. By 'moral conflict' I mean only cases in which there is a conflict between two moral judgements that a man is disposed to make relevant to deciding what to do; that is to say, I shall be considering what has traditionally, though mis-

leadingly, been called 'conflict of obligations', and not, for instance, conflicts between a moral judgement and a non-moral desire, though these, too, could naturally enough be called 'moral conflicts'. I shall further omit any discussion of the possibility (if it exists) that a man should hold moral principles or general moral views which are intrinsically inconsistent with one another, in the sense that there could be no conceivable world in which anyone could act in accordance with both of them; as might be the case, for instance, with a man who thought both that he ought not to go in for any blood-sport (as such) and that he ought to go in for foxhunting (as such). I doubt whether there are any interesting questions that are peculiar to this possibility. I shall confine myself, then, to cases in which the moral conflict has a contingent basis, to use a phrase that has already occurred in the discussion of conflicts of desires.

Some real analogy, moreover, with those situations emerges if one considers two basic forms that the moral conflict can take. One is that in which it seems that I ought to do each of two things, but I cannot do both. The other is that in which something which (it seems) I ought to do in respect of certain of its features also has other features in respect of which (it seems) I ought not to do it. This latter bears an analogy to the case of desire and aversion directed towards the same object. These descriptions are of course abstract and rather artificial; it may be awkward to express in many cases the grounds of the *ought* or *ought not* in terms of features of the thing I ought or ought not to do, as suggested in the general description. I only hope that the simplification achieved by this compensates for the distortions.

The two situations, then, come to this: in the first, it seems that I ought to do *a* and that I ought to do *b*, but I cannot do both *a* and *b*; in the second, it seems that I ought to do *c* and that I ought not to do *c*. To many ethical theorists it has seemed that actually to accept these seeming conclusions would involve some sort of logical inconsistency. For Ross, it was of course such situations that called for the concept of *prima facie* obligations: two of these are present in each of these situations, of which at most one in each case can constitute an actual obligation. On Hare's views, such situations call (in some logical sense) for a revision or qualification of at least one of the moral principles that give rise, in their application, to the conflicting *ought*'s. It is the view, common to these and to other theorists, that there is a logical inconsistency of some sort involved here, that is the ultimate topic of this paper.

5 I want to postpone, however, the more formal sorts of consideration for a while, and try to bring out one or two features of what

these situations are, or can be, like. The way I shall do this is to extend further the comparison I sketched earlier, between conflicts of beliefs and conflicts of desires. If we think of it in these terms, I think it emerges that there are certain important respects in which these moral conflicts are more like conflicts of desires than they are like conflicts of beliefs.

(*a*) The discovery that my factual beliefs conflict *eo ipso* tends to weaken one or more of the beliefs; not so, with desires; not so, I think, with one's conflicting convictions about what one ought to do. This comes out in the fact that conflicts of *ought*'s, like conflicts of desires, can readily have the character of a struggle, whereas conflicts of beliefs scarcely can, unless the man not only believes these things, but wants to believe them. It is of course true that there are situations in which, either because of some practical concern connected with the beliefs, or from an intellectual curiosity, one may get deeply involved with a conflict of beliefs, and something rather like a struggle may result: possibly including the feature, not uncommon in the moral cases, that the more one concentrates on the dilemma, the more pressing the claims of each side become. But there is still a difference, which can be put like this: in the belief case my concern to get things straight is a concern both to find the right belief (whichever it may be) and to be disembarrassed of the false belief (whichever it may be), whereas in the moral case my concern is not in the same way to find the right item and be rid of the other. I may wish that the facts had been otherwise, or that I had never got into the situation; I may even, in a certain frame of mind, wish that I did not have the moral views I have. But granted that it is all as it is, I do not think in terms of banishing error. I think, if constructively at all, in terms of acting for the best, and this is a frame of mind that *acknowledges* the presence of both the two *ought*'s.

(*b*) If I eventually choose for one side of the conflict rather than the other, this is a possible ground of regret – as with desires, although the regret, naturally, is a different sort of regret. As with desires, if the occasion is irreparably past, there may be room for nothing but regret. But it is also possible (again like desires) that the moral impulse that had to be abandoned in the choice may find a new object, and I may try, for instance, to 'make up' to people involved for the claim that was neglected. These states of mind do not depend, it seems to me, on whether I am convinced that in the choice I made I acted for the best; I can be convinced of this, yet have these regrets, ineffectual or possibly effective, for what I did not do.

It may be said that if I am convinced that I acted for the best; if, further, the question is not the different one of self-reproach for having got into the conflict-situation in the first place; then it is merely irrational to have any regrets. The weight of this comment depends on what it is supposed to imply. Taken most naturally, it implies that these reactions are a bad thing, which a fully admirable moral agent (taken, presumably, to be rational) would not display. In this sense, the comment seems to me to be just false. Such reactions do not appear to me to be necessarily a bad thing, nor an agent who displays them *pro tanto* less admirable than one who does not. But I do not have to rest much on my thinking that this is so; only on the claim that it is not inconsistent with the nature of morality to think that this is so. This modest claim seems to me undeniable. The notion of an admirable moral agent cannot be all that remote from that of a decent human being, and decent human beings are disposed in some situations of conflict to have the sort of reactions I am talking about.

Some light, though necessarily a very angled one, is shed on this point by the most extreme cases of moral conflict, tragic cases. One peculiarity of these is that the notion of 'acting for the best' may very well lose its content. Agamemnon at Aulis may have said 'May it be well',[4] but he is neither convinced nor convincing. The agonies that a man will experience after acting in full consciousness of such a situation are not to be traced to a persistent doubt that he may not have chosen the better thing; but, for instance, to a clear conviction that he has not done the better thing because there was no better thing to be done. It may, on the other hand, even be the case that by some not utterly irrational criteria of 'the better thing', he is convinced that he did the better thing: rational men no doubt pointed out to Agamemnon his responsibilities as a commander, the many people involved, the considerations of honour, and so forth. If he accepted all this, and acted accordingly: it would seem a glib moralist who said, as some sort of criticism, that he must be irrational to lie awake at night, having killed his daughter. And he lies awake, not because of a doubt, but because of a certainty. Some may say that the mythology of Agamemnon and his choice is nothing to us, because we do not move in a world in which irrational gods order men to kill their own children. But there is no need of irrational gods, to give rise to tragic situations.

Perhaps, however, it might be conceded that men may have regrets in these situations; it might even be conceded that a fully admirable

[4] Aeschylus, *Agamemnon* 217.

moral agent would, on occasion, have such regrets; nevertheless (it may be said) this is not to be connected directly with the structure of the moral conflict. The man may have regrets because he has had to do something distressing or appalling or which in some way goes against the grain, but this is not the same as having regrets because he thinks that he has done something that he ought not to have done, or not done something that he ought to have done – and it is only the latter that can be relevant to the interpretation of the moral conflict. This point might be put, in terms which I hope will be recognisable, by saying that regrets may be experienced in terms of purely *natural* motivations, and these are not to be confused, whether by the theorist or by a rational moral agent, with *moral* motivations, i.e. motivations that spring from thinking that a certain course of action is one that one ought to take.

There are three things I should like to say about this point. First, if it does concede that a fully admirable moral agent might be expected to experience such regrets on occasion, then it concedes that the notion of such an agent involves his having certain natural motivations as well as moral ones. This concession is surely correct, but it is unclear that it is allowed for in many ethical theories. Apart from this, however, there are two other points that go further. The sharp distinction that this argument demands between these natural and moral motivations is unrealistic. Are we really to think that if a man (*a*) thinks that he ought not to cause needless suffering and (*b*) is distressed by the fact or prospect of his causing needless suffering, then (*a*) and (*b*) are just two separate facts about him? Surely (*b*) can be one expression of (*a*), and (*a*) one root of (*b*)? And there are other possible connexions between (*a*) and (*b*) besides these. If such connexions are admitted, then it may well appear absurdly unrealistic to try to prise apart a man's feeling regrets about what he has done and his thinking that what he has done is something that he ought not to have done, or constituted a failure to do what he ought to have done. This is not, of course, to say that it is impossible for moral thoughts of this type, and emotional reactions or motivations of this type, to occur without each other; this is clearly possible. But it does not follow from this that if a man does both have moral thoughts about a course of action and certain feelings of these types related to it, then these items have to be clearly and distinctly separable one from another. If a man in general thinks that he ought not to do a certain thing, and is distressed by the thought of doing that thing; then if he does it, and is distressed at what he has done, this distress will probably have the shape of his thinking that in doing that thing, he has done something that he ought not to have done.

The second point of criticism here is that even if the sharp distinction between natural and moral motivations were granted, it would not, in the matter of regrets, cover all the cases. It will have even the appearance of explaining the cases only where the man can be thought to have a ground of regret or distress independently of his moral opinions about the situation. Thus if he has caused pain, in the course of acting (as he sincerely supposes) for the best, it might be said that any regret or distress he feels about having caused the pain is independent of his views of whether in doing this, he did something that he ought not to have done: he is just naturally distressed by the thought of having caused pain. I have already said that I find this account unrealistic, even for such cases. But there are other cases in which it could not possibly be sustained. A man may, for instance, feel regret because he has broken a promise in the course of acting (as he sincerely supposes) for the best; and his regret at having broken the promise must surely arise *via* a moral thought. Here we seem just to get back to the claim that such regret in such circumstances would be irrational, and to the previous answer that if this claim is intended pejoratively, it will not stand up. A tendency to feel regrets, particularly creative regrets, at having broken a promise even in the course of acting for the best might well be considered a reassuring sign that an agent took his promises seriously. At this point, the objector might say that he still thinks the regrets irrational, but that he does not intend 'irrational' pejoratively: we must rather admit that an admirable moral agent is one who on occasion is irrational. This, of course, is a new position: it may well be correct.

6 It seems to me a fundamental criticism of many ethical theories that their accounts of moral conflict and its resolution do not do justice to the facts of regret and related considerations: basically because they eliminate from the scene the *ought* that is not acted upon. A structure appropriate to conflicts of belief is projected on to the moral case; one by which the conflict is basically adventitious, and a resolution of it disembarrasses one of a mistaken view which for a while confused the situation. Such an approach must be inherent in purely cognitive accounts of the matter; since it is just a question of which of the conflicting *ought* statements is true, and they cannot both be true, to decide correctly for one of them must be to be rid of error with respect to the other – an occasion, if for any feelings, then for such feelings as relief (at escaping mistake), self-congratulation (for having got the right answer), or possibly self-criticism (for having

so nearly been misled). Ross – whom unfairly I shall mention without discussing in detail – makes a valiant attempt to get nearer to the facts than this, with his doctrine that the *prima facie* obligations are not just *seeming* obligations, but more in the nature of a claim, which can generate residual obligations if not fulfilled.[5] But it remains obscure how all this is supposed to be so within the general structure of his theory; a claim, on these views, must surely be a claim for consideration as the only thing that matters, a duty, and if a course of action has failed to make good this claim in a situation of conflict, how can it maintain in that situation some residual influence on my moral thought?

A related inadequacy on this issue emerges also, I think, in certain prescriptivist theories. Hare, for instance, holds that when I encounter a situation of conflict, what I have to do is modify one or both of the moral principles that I hold, which, in conjunction with the facts of the case, generated the conflict. The view has at least the merit of not representing the conflict as entirely adventitious, a mere misfortune that befalls my moral faculties. But the picture that it offers still seems inadequate to one's view of the situation *ex post facto*. It explains the origin of the conflict as my having come to the situation insufficiently prepared, as it were, because I had too simple a set of moral principles; and it pictures me as emerging from the situation better prepared, since I have now modified them – I can face a recurrence of the same situation without qualms, since next time it will not present me with a conflict. This is inadequate on two counts. First, the only focus that it provides for retrospective regret is that I arrived unprepared, and not that I did not do the thing rejected in the eventual choice. Second, there must surely be something wrong with the consequence that, granted I do not go back on the choice I make on this occasion, no similar situation later can possibly present me with a conflict. This may be a not unsuitable description of *some* cases, since one thing I may learn from such experiences is that some moral principle or view that I held was too naïve or *simpliste*. But even among lessons, this is not the only one that may be learned. I may rather learn that I ought not to get into situations of this kind – and this lesson seems to imply very much the opposite of the previous one, since my reason for avoiding such situations in the

[5] Cf. *The Foundations of Ethics* (Oxford: The Clarendon Press, 1938), pp. 84 *seq.* The passage is full of signs of unease; he uses, for instance, the unhappy expression 'the most right of the acts open to us', a strong indication that he is trying to have it both ways at once. Most of the difficulties, too, are wrapped up in the multiply ambiguous phrase 'laws stating the tendencies of actions to be obligatory in virtue of this characteristic or of that' (p. 86).

future is that I have learned that in them both *ought*'s *do* apply. In extreme cases, again, it may be that there is no lesson to be learned at all, at least of this practical kind.

7 So far I have been largely looking at moral conflict in itself; but this last point has brought us to the question of avoiding moral conflict, and this is something that I should like to discuss a little further. It involves, once more, but in a different aspect, the relations between conflict and rationality. Here the comparison with beliefs and desires is once more relevant. In the case of beliefs, we have already seen how it follows from the nature of beliefs that a conflict presents a problem, since conflicting beliefs cannot both be true, and the aim of beliefs is to be true. A rational man in this respect is one who (no doubt among other things) so conducts himself that this aim is likely to be realised. In the case of desires, again, there is something in the nature of desires that explains why a conflict essentially presents a problem: desires, obviously enough, aim at satisfaction, and conflicting desires cannot both be satisfied. Corresponding to this there will be a notion of practical rationality, by which a man will be rational who (no doubt among other things) takes thought to prevent the frustration of his desires. There are, however, two sides to such a policy: there is a question, not only of how he satisfies the desires he has, but of what desires he has. There is such a thing as abandoning or discouraging a desire which in conjunction with others leads to frustration, and this a rational man will sometimes do. This aspect of practical rationality can be exaggerated, as in certain moralities (some well known in antiquity) which avoid frustration of desire by reducing desire to a minimum: this can lead to the result that, in pursuit of a coherent life, a man misses out on the more elementary requirement of having a life at all. That this is the type of criticism appropriate to this activity is important: it illustrates the sense in which a man's policy for organising his desires is *pro tanto* up to him, even though some ways a man may take of doing this constitute a disservice to himself, or may be seen as, in some rather deeper way, unadmirable.

There are partial parallels to these points in the sphere of belief. I said just now that a rational man in this sphere was (at least) one who pursued as effectively as possible truth in his beliefs. This condition, in the limit, could be satisfied by a man whose sole aim was to avoid falsity in his beliefs, and this aim he might pursue by avoiding, so far as possible, belief: by cultivating scepticism, or ignorance (in the sense of never having heard of various issues), and of the second of these, at least, one appropriate criticism might be similar to one in the case of desires, a suggestion of self-impoverishment. There are many other considerations relevant here, of course; but a central point for our present purpose does stand, that from the fact that given truths or a given subject-matter exist, it does not follow that a given man ought to have beliefs about them: though it does follow that if he is to have beliefs about them, there are some beliefs rather than others that he ought to have.

In relation to these points, I think that morality emerges as different from both belief and desire. It is not an option in the moral case that possible conflict should be avoided by way of scepticism, ignorance, or the pursuit of *ataraxia* – in general, by indifference. The notion of a moral claim is of something that I may not ignore: hence it is not up to me to give myself a life free from conflict by withdrawing my interest from such claims.

It is important here to distinguish two different questions, one moral and one logical. On the one hand, there is the question whether extensive moral indifference is morally deplorable, and this is clearly a moral question, and indeed one on which two views are possible: *pas trôp de zèle* could be a moral maxim. That attitude, however, does not involve saying that there are moral claims, but it is often sensible to ignore them; it rather says that there are fewer moral claims than people tend to suppose. Disagreement with this attitude will be moral disagreement, and will involve, among other things, affirming some of the moral claims which the attitude denies. The logical question, on the other hand, is whether the relation of moral indifference and moral conflict is the same as that of desire-indifference and desire-conflict, or, again, belief-indifference and belief-conflict. The answer is clearly 'no'. After experience of these latter sorts of conflict, a man may try to cultivate the appropriate form of indifference while denying nothing about the nature of those conflicts as, at the time, he took them to be. He knows them to have been conflicts in believing the truth or pursuing what he wanted, and, knowing this, he tries to cut down his commitment to believing or desiring things. This may be sad or even dotty, but it is not actually inconsistent. A man who retreats from moral conflict to moral indifference, however, cannot at the same time admit that those conflicts were what, at the time, he took them to be, viz. conflicts of moral claims, since to admit that there exist moral claims in situations of that sort is incompatible with moral indifference towards those situations.

The avoidance of moral conflict, then, emerges in two ways as something for which one is not merely free to devise a policy.

A moral observer cannot regard another agent as free to restructure his moral outlook so as to withdraw moral involvement from the situations that produce conflict; and the agent himself cannot try such a policy, either, so long as he regards the conflicts he has experienced as conflicts with a genuine moral basis. Putting this together with other points that I have tried to make earlier in this paper, I reach the conclusion that a moral conflict shares with a conflict of desires, but not with a conflict of beliefs, the feature that to end it in decision is not necessarily to eliminate one of the conflicting items: the item that was not acted upon may, for instance, persist as regret, which may (though it does not always) receive some constructive expression. Moral conflicts do not share with conflicts of desire (nor yet with conflicts of belief) the feature that there is a general freedom to adopt a policy to try to eliminate their occurrence.

It may well be, then, that moral conflicts are in two different senses ineliminable. In a particular case, it may be that neither of the *ought*'s is eliminable. Further, the tendency of such conflicts to occur may itself be ineliminable, since, first, the agent cannot feel himself free to reconstruct his moral thought in a policy to eliminate them; and, second, while there are *some* cases in which the situation was his own fault, and the correct conclusion for him to draw was that he ought not to get into situations of that type, it cannot be believed that all genuine conflict situations are of that type.

Moral conflicts are neither systematically avoidable, nor all soluble without remainder.

8 If we accept these conclusions, what consequences follow for the logic of moral thought? How, in particular, is moral conflict related to logical inconsistency? What I have to say is less satisfactory than I should like; but I hope that it may help a little.

We are concerned with conflicts that have a contingent basis, with conflict *via* the facts. We distinguished earlier two types of case: that in which it seems that I ought to do *a* and that I ought to do *b*, but I cannot do both; and that in which it seems that I ought to do *c* in respect of some considerations, and ought not to do *c* in respect of others. To elicit something that looks like logical inconsistency here obviously requires in the first sort of case extra premisses, while extra premisses are at least not obviously required in the second case. In the second case, the two conclusions 'I ought to do *c*' and 'I ought not to do *c*' already wear the form of logical inconsistency. In the first case, the pair 'I ought to do *a*' and 'I ought to do *b*' do not wear it at all. This is not surprising, since the conflict arises not from these two alone, but from these together with the statement that I cannot do both *a* and *b*. How do these three together acquire the form of logical inconsistency? The most natural account is that which invokes two further premisses or rules: that *ought* implies *can*, and that 'I ought to do *a*' and 'I ought to do *b*' together imply 'I ought to do *a* and *b*' (which I shall call the *agglomeration principle*). Using these, the conflict can be represented in the following form:

(i) I ought to do *a*
(ii) I ought to do *b*
(iii) I cannot do *a* and *b*.

From (i) and (ii), by agglomeration

(iv) I ought to do *a* and *b*;

from (iii) by '*ought* implies *can*' used contrapositively,

(v) It is not the case that I ought to do *a* and *b*.

This produces a contradiction; and since one limb of it (v), has been proved by a valid inference from an undisputed premiss, we accept this limb, and then use the agglomeration principle contrapositively to unseat one or other of (i) and (ii).

This formulation does not, of course, produce an inconsistency of the *ought–ought not* type, but of the *ought–not ought* type, i.e. a genuine *contradiction*. It might be suggested, however, that there is a way in which we could, and perhaps should, reduce cases of this first type to the *ought–ought not* kind, i.e. to the pattern of the second type of case. We might say that 'I ought to do *b*', together with the empirical statement that doing *a* excludes doing *b*, jointly yield the conclusion that I ought to do something which, if I do *a*, I shall not do; hence that I ought to refrain from doing *a*; hence that I ought not to do *a*. This, with the original statement that I ought to do *a*, produces the *ought–ought not* form of inconsistency. A similar inference can also be used, of course, to establish that I ought not to do *b*, a conclusion which can be similarly joined to the original statement that I ought to do *b*. To explore this suggestion thoroughly would involve an extensive journey on the troubled waters of deontic logic; but I think that there are two considerations that suggest that it is not to be preferred to the formulation that I advanced earlier. The first is that the principle on which it rests looks less than compelling in purely logical terms: it involves the substitution of extensional equivalences in a modal context, and while this might possibly fare better with *ought* than it does elsewhere, it would be rash to embrace it straight off. Second, it suffers from much the same defect as was noticed much earlier with a parallel situation with conflicts of desires: it conceals the real roots of the conflict. The formulation with '*ought* implies *can*' does not do this, and offers a more realistic picture of how the situation is.

Indeed, so far from trying to assimilate the first type of case to the second, I am now going to suggest that it will be better to assimilate the second to the first, as now interpreted. For while 'I ought to do *c*' and 'I ought not to do *c*' do indeed wear the form of logical inconsistency, the blank occurrence of this form itself depends to some extent on our having left out the real roots of the conflict – the considerations or aspects that lead to the conflicting judgements. Because of this, it conceals the element that is in common between the two types of case: that in both, the conflict arises from a contingent impossibility. To take Agamemnon's case as example, the basic *ought*'s that apply to the situation are presumably that he ought to discharge his responsibilities as a commander, further the expedition, and so forth; and that he ought not to kill his daughter. Between these two there is no inherent inconsistency. The conflict comes, once more, in the step to action: that as things are, there is no way of doing the first without doing the second. This should encourage us, I think, to recast it all in a more artificial, but perhaps more illuminating way, and say that here again there is a double *ought*: the first, to further the expedition, the second, to refrain from the killing; and that as things are he cannot discharge both.

Seen in this way, it seems that the main weight of the problem descends on to '*ought* implies *can*' and its application to these cases; and from now on I shall consider both types together in this light. Now much could be said about '*ought* implies *can*', which is not a totally luminous principle, but I shall forgo any general discussion of it. I shall accept, in fact, one of its main applications to this problem, namely that from the fact that I cannot do both *a* and *b* it follows contrapositively that it is not the case that I ought to do both *a* and *b*. This is surely sound, but it does not dispose of the logical problems: for no agent, conscious of the situation of conflict, in fact thinks that he ought to do *both* of the things. What he thinks is that he ought to do *each* of them; and this is properly paralleled at the level of 'can' by the fact that while he cannot do both of the things, it is true of each of the things, taken separately, that he can do it.

If we want to emphasise the distinction between 'each' and 'both' here, we shall have to look again at the principle of agglomeration, since it is this that leads us from 'each' to 'both'. Now there are certainly many characterisations of actions in the general field of evaluation for which agglomeration does not hold, and for which what holds of each action taken separately does not hold for both taken together: thus it may be *desirable*, or *advisable*, or *sensible*, or *prudent*, to do *a*, and again desirable or advisable etc. to do *b*, but not desirable etc. to do both *a* and *b*. The same holds, obviously enough, for what a man wants; thus marrying Susan and marrying Joan may be things each of which Tom wants to do, but he certainly does not want to do both. Now the mere existence of such cases is obviously not enough to persuade anyone to give up agglomeration for *ought*, since he might reasonably argue that *ought* is different in this respect; though it is worth noting that anyone who is disposed to say that the sorts of characterisations of actions that I just mentioned are evaluative *because they entail 'ought'-statements* will be under some pressure to reconsider the agglomerative properties of *ought*. I do not want to claim, however, that I have some knock-down disproof of the agglomeration principle; I want to claim only that it is not a self-evident datum of the logic of *ought*, and that if a more realistic picture of moral thought emerges from abandoning it, we should have no qualms in abandoning it. We can in fact see the problem the other way round: the very fact that there can be two things, each of which I ought to do and each of which I can do, but of which I cannot do both, shows the weakness of the agglomeration principle.

Let us then try suspending the agglomeration principle, and see what results follow for the logical reconstruction of moral conflict. It is not immediately clear how '*ought* implies *can*' will now bear on the issue. On the one hand, we have the statement that I cannot do both *a* and *b*, which indeed disproves that I ought to do both *a* and *b*, but this is uninteresting: the statement it disproves is one that I am not disposed to make in its own right, and which does not follow (on the present assumptions) from those that I am disposed to make. On the other hand, we have the two *ought* statements and their associated 'can' statements, each of which, taken separately, I can assert. But this is not enough for the conflict, which precisely depends on the fact that I cannot go on taking the two sets separately. What we need here, to test the effect of '*ought* implies *can*', is a way of applying to each side the fact that I cannot satisfy both sides. Language provides such a way very readily, in a form which is in fact the most natural to use in such deliberations:

(i) If I do *b*, I will not be able to do *a*;
(ii) If I do *a*, I will not be able to do *b*.

Now (i) and (ii) appear to be genuine conditional statements; with suitable adjustment of tenses, they admit both of contraposition and of use in *modus ponens*. They are thus not like the curious non-conditional cases discussed by Austin.[6]

Consider now two apparently valid applications of '*ought* implies *can*':

(iii) If I will not be able to do *a*, it will not be the case that I ought to do *a*;

(iv) If I will not be able to do *b*, it will not be the case that I ought to do *b*.

Join (iii) and (iv) to (i) and (ii) respectively, and one reaches by transitivity:

(v) If I do *b*, it will not be the case that I ought to do *a*;

(vi) If I do *a*, it will not be the case that I ought to do *b*.

At first glance (v) and (vi) appear to offer a very surprising and reassuring result: that whichever of *a* and *b* I do, I shall get off the moral hook with respect to the other. This must surely be too good to be true; and suspicion that this is so must turn to certainty when one considers that the previous argument would apply just as well if the conflict between *a* and *b* were not a conflict between two *ought*'s at all, but, say, a conflict between an *ought* and some gross inclination; the argument depends solely on the fact that *a* and *b* are empirically incompatible. This shows that the reassuring interpretation of (v) and (vi) must be wrong. There is a correct interpretation, which reveals (v) and (vi) as saying something true but less interesting: (taking (v) as example), that if I do *b*, it will then not be correct to say that I ought (then) to do *a*. And this is correct, since *a* will *then* not be a course of action open to me. It does not follow from this that I cannot correctly say then that I *ought to have done a*; nor yet that I was wrong in thinking earlier that *a* was something I ought to do. It seems, then, that if we waive the agglomeration principle, and just consider a natural way of applying to each course of action the consideration that I cannot do both it and the other one, we do not get an application of *ought* implies *can* that necessarily cancels out one or other of the original *ought*'s regarded retrospectively. And this seems to me what we should want.

As I have tried to argue throughout, it is surely falsifying of moral thought to represent its logic as demanding that in a conflict situation one of the conflicting *ought*'s must be totally rejected. One must, certainly, be rejected in the sense that not both can be acted upon; and this gives a (fairly weak) sense to saying that they are incompatible. But this does not mean they do not both (actually) *apply* to

[6] *Ifs and Cans*, reprinted in his *Philosophical Papers* (Oxford: The Clarendon Press, 1961).

the situation; or that I was in some way mistaken in thinking that these were both things that I ought to do. I may continue to think this retrospectively, and hence have regrets; and I may even do this when I have found some moral reason for acting on one in preference to the other. For while there are some cases in which finding a moral reason for preference *does* cancel one of the *ought*'s, this is not always so. I may use some emergency provision, of a utilitarian kind for example, which deals with the conflict of choice, and gives me a way of 'acting for the best'; but this is not the same as to revise or reconsider the reasons for the original *ought*'s, nor does it provide me with the reflexion 'If I had thought of that in the first place, there need have been no conflict.' It seems to me impossible, then, to rest content with a logical picture which makes it a necessary consequence of conflict that one *ought* must be totally rejected in the sense that one becomes convinced that it did not actually apply. The condition of moving away from such a picture appears to be, at least within the limits of argument imposed by my rather crude use of *ought* implies *can*, the rejection of the agglomeration principle.

I have left until last what may seem to some the most obvious objection to my general line of argument. I have to act in the conflict; I can choose one course rather than the other; I can think about which to choose. In thinking about this, or asking another's advice on it, the question I may characteristically ask is 'what ought I to do?' The answer to this question, from myself or another, cannot be 'both', but must rather be (for instance) 'I (or you) ought to do *a*.' This (it will be said) just shows that to choose in a moral conflict, or at least to choose as a result of such deliberation, is to give up one of the *ought*'s completely, to arrive at the conclusion that it does not apply; and that it cannot be, as I have been arguing that it may be, to decide not to act on it, while agreeing that it applies.

This objection rests squarely on identifying the *ought* that occurs in statements of moral principle, and in the sorts of moral judgements about particular situations that we have been considering, with the *ought* that occurs in the deliberative question 'what ought I to do?' and in answers to this question, given by myself or another. I think it can be shown that this identification is a mistake, and on grounds independent of the immediate issue. For suppose I am in a situation in which I think that I ought (morally) to do *a*, and would merely very much like to do *b*, and cannot do both. Here, too, I can presumably ask the deliberative question 'what ought I to do?' and get an answer to it. If this question meant 'Of which course of action is it the case that I ought (morally) to do it?', the answer is so patent that the question could not be worth asking: indeed, it would not be a deliberative question at all. But the deliberative question can be worth asking, and I can, moreover, intelligibly arrive at a decision, or receive advice, in answer to it which is offensive to morality. To identify the two *ought*'s in this sort of case commits one to the necessary supremacy of the moral; it is not surprising if theories that tend to assimilate the two end up with the Socratic paradox. Indeed, one is led on this thesis not only to the supremacy, but to the ubiquity, of the moral; since the deliberative question can be asked and answered, presumably, in a situation where neither course of action involves originally a moral *ought*.

An answer to the deliberative question, by myself or another, can of course be supported by moral reasons, as by other sorts; but its rôle as a deliberative *ought* remains the same, and this rôle is not tied to morality. This remains so even in the case in which both the candidates for action that I am considering involve moral *ought*'s. This, if not already clear, is revealed by the following possibility. I think that I ought to do *a* and that I ought to do *b*, and I ask of two friends 'what ought I to do?'. One says 'You ought to do *a*', and gives such-and-such moral reasons. The other says 'You ought to do neither: you ought to go to the pictures and give morality a rest.' The sense of *ought* in these two answers is the same: they are both answers to the unambiguous question that I asked.

All this makes clear, I think, that if I am confronted with two conflicting *ought*'s, and the answer to the deliberative question by myself or another *coincides* with one of the original *ought*'s, it does not represent a mere *iteration* of it. The decision or advice is decision or advice to act on that one; not a re-assertion of that one with an implicit denial of the other. This distinction may also clear up what may seem troubling on my approach, that a man who has had a moral conflict, has acted (as he supposes) for the best, yet has the sorts of regrets that I have discussed about the rejected course of action, would not most naturally express himself with respect to that course of action by saying 'I ought to have done the other'. This is because the standard function of such an expression in this sort of situation would be to suggest a deliberative mistake, and to imply that if he had the decision over again he would make it differently. That he cannot most naturally say this in the imagined case does not mean that he cannot think of the rejected action as something which, in a different sense, he ought to have done; that is to say, as something of which he was not wrong at the time in thinking that he ought to do it.

In fact, of course, it is not even true that *the* deliberative question is 'what ought I to do?'. It may well be, for instance, 'what am I to do?'; and that question, and the answers to it – such as 'do *a*', or 'if I were you, I should . . .' – do not even make it look as though decision or advice to act on one of the *ought*'s in a moral conflict necessarily involves deciding that the other one had no application.

12

Consistency and realism

This paper approaches the subject of consistency by trying to establish certain differences between the rôle of consistency with respect to assertions, and its rôle (and that, of course, of inconsistency) in discourse other than assertions: the example I treat in some detail is that of imperatives. The thesis I advance here is that while 'consistent' and 'inconsistent' apply to imperatives all right, the consequences and significance of this are different and less fundamental than with assertions. I try to make a similar point, briefly, about rules. The later part of the paper tries to sketch, I fear very vaguely, a direction for explaining the differences brought out in the first part; this involves taking seriously the platitude that assertions are concerned with truth. This leads me to realism; having merely arrived at it, I stop, except for some considerations about ethics which I hope may suggest that the direction I have taken is at least a direction. So 'Consistency' is the name of the subject, and 'Realism' the name of a problem; I hope the discussion of the subject will suggest that there is that problem, where I think it is.

I shall start with some considerations about consistency and inconsistency between imperatives. This is, in a number of respects, a well-worn subject; I shall rely on this fact to the extent of passing lightly over some issues which demand, and have received, more precise treatment. Thus I shall speak fairly generally of people issuing or uttering imperatives, and of people obeying imperatives, and these phrases will stand duty for more determinate and precise expressions appropriate to various contexts, such as 'giving orders', 'issuing commands', etc. I shall also not bother too much about the cross-over of logical and grammatical considerations implicit in the term 'imperative' itself.[1] My use of the term will, however, be confined to what Hofstadter and McKinsey[2] called 'directives', i.e., second-person single-tense forms addressed to an agent: I shall not be concerned with optatives, etc.

It is a familiar idea that consistency and inconsistency between

[1] I shall demand a similar, and greater, charity towards my use of 'indicative'.
[2] *Philosophy of Science*, 1939, pp. 446 *seq.*

imperatives be understood in terms of the possibility of obedience to them, where 'obedience' must be understood in an etiolated sense, equivalent to 'corresponding action': the necessity for a minimal interpretation of 'obedience' in this connexion is particularly clear if one considers the requirement – which presumably exists if anything is to be done with the notion of contradiction in these terms – that of two contradictory commands, one must be obeyed. The joint-obedience model is thought to provide a direct link between imperative logic and standard propositional logic; at least with respect to consistency – how much further one might go, e.g., in the construction of patterns of imperative *inference*, is a further question, which I shall not be concerned with here.[3]

The direct link is achieved if the joint-obedience model is spelled out in the following way: that corresponding to any imperative 'do x', there is an indicative statement, 'x is done', which might be called its 'obedience-statement'; and we may say that two imperatives are inconsistent if their obedience-statements are inconsistent, and that otherwise they are consistent. However, this test for the consistency of imperatives will not work unless further work is done on the interpretation of the obedience-statements: the highly indeterminate form of statement, 'x is done', will not by itself work as the indicative correlate of a particular imperative 'do x', as uttered to a particular agent in a particular context. The normal response to this difficulty is to regard the identity of the agent addressed, the time-limits of compliance with the imperative, and other such matters, as analogous to context-dependent references in the case of inexplicit indicative statements; and one, though presumably not the only, way of exploiting this analogy is to spell out these context-dependent matters in the content of the imperative, so that it reveals the agent it is aimed at, the required time of action, and so forth, its obedience-statement being correspondingly determinate. This device is central to the phrastic-neustic model (to use the terms introduced by Hare).

The phrastic-neustic model, however, may be intended to go further in the direction of assimilating imperative and indicative consistency than what I have so far outlined. The programme I have indicated is that of defining imperative consistency in terms of indicative consistency, by means of associating with any set of imperatives a set of corresponding indicatives, for which the notion of inconsistency is taken as independently given. The phrastic-neustic model, however, may seem to imply something stronger than this,[4] namely

[3] See Imperative Inference (pp. 152–65).

[4] Cf. Hare: *The Language of Morals* (Oxford: The Clarendon Press, 1964), p. 28;

that the application of 'consistent' and, again, 'inconsistent', to imperatives and to indicatives is straightforwardly univocal; since consistency and inconsistency hold between phrastics, and phrastics are what imperatives and indicatives have in common. This idea, at first glance, may appear attractive: if, for instance, the phrastic is identified with a proposition or Fregean *thought*, and the indicative neustic with an assertion sign – for consistency and inconsistency evidently obtain between propositions independently of whether they are asserted. But it is at most doubtful whether an indicative neustic can be identified with an assertion sign; and, in any case, consistency and inconsistency cannot hold between bare phrastics.

The question whether the indicative neustic can be identified with an assertion sign would be answered in the negative if there were examples in which analysis demanded the presence of an indicative neustic in some unasserted component of a complex statement (or command). It might seem that there were obviously such examples, since in e.g.,

(i) If it rains, put your coat on

the antecedent is evidently unasserted, and at the same time seems indisputably indicative. It might seem essential to representing the sense of (i) that an indicative neustic appear in the antecedent, and an imperative one in the consequent; in which case, of course, the indicative neustic cannot be an assertion sign, nor can an imperative neustic be the parallel thing for commands, i.e., that which makes what it is attached to into an actual command. Yet such an analysis may not in fact be essential, and there may indeed be reasons against it. For the example

(ii) If you go out, put your coat on

equally gives at first glance the impression of indicativeness in its antecedent; yet it is an important point, as Dummett[5] has pointed out, that someone could be counted as having obeyed (ii) by refraining from going out (if e.g., he was unable to find his coat). This point gives a motive for analysing (ii) by merely attaching an imperative neustic to the whole conditional; and it may be argued that this is the correct treatment for all such conditionals, the cases (such as (i)) in which the antecedent refers to a state of affairs not in the agent's

also his 'Imperative Sentences', *Mind*, lvii (1949), pp. 33–4. [Note 1972: To distinguish mood and assertion-sign, Hare has now introduced a more elaborate apparatus. See 'Meaning and Speech Acts', in *Practical Inferences* (London Macmillan, 1971), esp. pp. 89 *seq.*]

[5] 'Truth', PAS, LIX (1958/9) p. 150. Reprinted in G. Pitcher ed. *Truth* (New York: Prentice-Hall, 1964).

power being only materially, and not logically different: it is merely that here there is not, as a matter of fact, a way of obeying such imperatives which consists in falsifying the antecedent.

The important point here, as Dummett says, is whether a distinction can be drawn between a conditional command and a command of the material conditional, as (in his view) a distinction can be drawn between a conditional bet and a bet on the material conditional. Dummett argues that in the case of commands as we normally use them this distinction cannot be drawn. His argument for this, however, rests on using notions of obedience and disobedience which are more substantial than those being considered here: this comes out in his linking of disobedience with punishment, whereas mere *lack of conforming action* is not necessarily linked to punishment – it may not have been the agent's fault. At the same time, these more substantial notions seem artificially rigorous, allowing only the incurring or escaping of punishment as the relevant matters. It is this that encourages Dummett to rule out, for our ordinary practice, the notion of a conditional command in the sense of one with which the question of obedience or disobedience does not come up if the antecedent is not fulfilled. But surely there are commands of which this is true; and surely we do have conditional imperatives in other, non-command, contexts – if the instructions on the machine say something of the form 'if *p*, then do *x*', and the circumstances referred to in '*p*' do not come about, there is no question of my having followed or failed to follow this instruction. If so, and we do attend realistically to substantial notions of obedience, following, etc., then there are genuinely conditional imperatives, and the indicative neustic will not be an assertion sign, nor the imperative neustic the corresponding thing for imperatives. With the etiolated sense of 'obedience', however, these everyday notions cannot be appealed to, at least directly, and so long as we confine ourselves to that sense, it is not clear how the question under discussion can be determined.

However all this may be, the main point here, that consistency and inconsistency do not hold between bare phrastics, seems obvious on independent grounds. It seems, indeed, boringly obvious, since

(iii) Smith will sweep the yard this afternoon.

is inconsistent with

(iv) Smith will not sweep the yard this afternoon,

while, in contrast,

(v) Smith, sweep the yard this afternoon

is in no sense inconsistent with (iv). The most extreme logical discomfort that could arise with the combination of (iv) and (v) would be a certain pragmatic embarrassment if (iv) were asserted to, or in the evident presence of, Smith; but this would be a long way short of what is wrong with the joint assertion of (iii) and (iv), and in any case is beside the point, since there is nothing in (iv) – unlike (v) – to determine to whom it is uttered. But now (iii) and (v) are phrastically equivalent, so, since one of them is inconsistent with (iv) and the other is not, inconsistency (and hence consistency) cannot be a relation between bare phrastics.

It might be replied that inconsistency is not well-defined for the relations between imperatives and indicatives, but nevertheless it remains true that inconsistency between different imperatives, and again between different indicatives, consists in inconsistency between their phrastics. But I am not sure that this restriction would be acceptable to many who want to use the phrastic-neustic model; and in any case, on this showing, I am not sure that much remains of the position (which, I said, might suggest itself from the phrastic-neustic analysis) that the application of 'consistent' and 'inconsistent' to imperatives and to indicatives is straightforwardly univocal. There seems little, except the acceptance of the phrastic-neustic analysis, to distinguish this revised position from the weaker position that I started by considering, that a notion of consistency for imperatives can be defined from the notion of consistency for indicatives. This latter is the position that I shall have in mind for the rest of the discussion.

It seems to me basically correct, in the sense that it adequately represents such notions of consistency and inconsistency between imperatives as we have. It allows us, for instance, – or at least with a little tinkering it will allow us – to represent a distinction between imperatives which are logically inconsistent and imperatives which are empirically inconsistent or, as we might put it, merely conflict; the distinction turning on whether it is logically necessary or merely empirically the case that the imperatives in question cannot all be obeyed. This distinction is presumably one that we don't mind being able to make.

But if this account is, as I suppose, basically the correct account of such notions of imperative consistency as we have, I think it follows that the *significance* of consistency and inconsistency with respect to imperatives stands on a radically different footing from their significance with respect to indicatives. This is what I shall now try to show. Consider two situations: (1) speakers A and B make respectively statements *P* and not-*P*; all present agree that these are inconsistent, i.e., cannot both be true. (2) A and B utter respectively imperatives 'do *x*' and 'do not do *x*', to the same agent with respect to the same situation; all present agree that these are inconsistent, i.e., cannot both be obeyed. Though situations (1) and (2) are parallel to the extent mentioned, there are evident and important asymmetries between them.

The first and most obvious asymmetry concerns the relation between, on the one hand, inconsistency and the recognition of inconsistency, and, on the other hand, the rôle of agreement and disagreement of third parties with A or B. The asymmetry stems from the platitude that a statement of inconsistency, whether between statements or between imperatives, is itself a statement and not an imperative. The consistency in situation (1) or (2) being noted, some third party C may make his contribution, in the form of agreement with either A or B. In (1), he will express agreement with (say) B by saying (basically) that B's assertion is the one that has the thing that A's and B's assertions cannot both have – truth. But in (2) he certainly cannot express agreement with B by something exactly parallel to this; for what would be parallel with reference to the notion of inconsistency would seem to be a statement to the effect that B's is the imperative that will be obeyed, and this remark has obviously enough a quite different point and effect in (2) from those possessed by a remark in (1) claiming that B's assertion is true. With respect to point and effect, what it is like in (1) is not the remark that B's assertion is true, but the remark that B's assertion is the one that will be believed.

If he is to express agreement with B's imperative in (2), he will himself have to use an imperative, and say (to the same agent) something like 'do not do *x*', or 'obey "do not do *x*"'. But now there is an obvious asymmetry with the indicative case. In (1), we have the same expression '... is true' that figures both in the expression of agreement and in the statement of inconsistency, and in the same sense. This is not unimportant, since it is what licenses the argument

(I) It is impossible that both A's assertion is true and
B's is;
A's assertion is true;
So B's assertion is not.

Such an argument can be put to good use, on occasion; for it might be the case (though perhaps not in as simple a case as (1)) that I was more certain initially that A's assertion was true than that B's assertion was false, and it was only in the light of recognising the inconsistency that I saw that in agreeing with A I must disagree with B. But the sequence

(II) It is impossible that both A's imperative be obeyed and B's be obeyed;
Obey A's imperative;
So do not obey B's,

if it is any sort of argument at all, is certainly not parallel to (I), since its first premiss, being indicative, must be of quite a different character from its second one, which is imperative; certainly no consistent parallelism to 'is true' in (I) has been achieved. If one starts from the idea that the parallel to 'is true' for agreement in imperative cases is 'obey', the parallel to (I) would seem to be

(III) Do not (ever?) obey both A's imperative and B's;
Obey A's imperative;
So, etc.,

and in this the first premiss fails to express inconsistency between the two imperatives altogether.

If we cannot parallel for imperatives the occurrence, with indicatives, of 'is true' both in statements of inconsistency and in expressions of agreement, it follows that we cannot parallel the use of 'inconsistent' as itself an expression of disagreement or, as we might more naturally say, rejection. Consider the situation, different from the ones so far considered, in which one man jointly asserts (presumably at some distance from one another) both *P* and not-*P*; since his compound assertion is inconsistent, it is not true, and to say that it is inconsistent is, *inter alia*, to reject it as not true. Consideration of logical connexions between his remarks may further lead us, using other premisses and a reductive style of argument, to reject as untrue some other particular assertion of his. Thus the pointing out of inconsistency, the rejection of the inconsistent, and the rejection of logically associated assertions not themselves inconsistent are all of a piece in indicative discourse. But this will not be so with imperative discourse. For if one man utters inconsistent imperatives, to point out that they are inconsistent will be a totally different kind of thing from rejecting any particular imperative in the sense of 'reject' corresponding to the 'agreement' we have been discussing, viz., telling someone not to obey it. What, once more, would be all of a piece with *that* would be to tell someone not to obey the compound, inconsistent, imperative (cf. the first premiss of (III) above); and that both fails to state, or in any way to reveal, that what is wrong with the imperative is that it is inconsistent, and also is a patently supererogatory activity in any case. I shall leave this point here for the moment. I shall now go on to a second type of asymmetry between the cases.

In situation (1), it might be that, at least up to the point where the inconsistency of their assertions comes out, both A and B thought that they had the best possible reasons for asserting what they did assert. The expression 'reasons for asserting . . .' is of course ambiguous, covering at least three different things: (a) Granted that I believe that *P*, and that my aim is to be sincere, i.e., to assert, if anything, what I believe, my *reason for asserting P* may be taken as my reason for asserting *P* rather than remaining silent on the question. (*b*) I may regard the question as open whether I should or should not mislead others as to my belief, i.e., whether I should speak sincerely; here my *reason for asserting P* may be taken as my reason for asserting *P* rather than something else (e.g., not-*P*) on the question, whether I believe *P* or not. (*c*) Granted that I believe that *P*, and sincerely assert it, my *reason for asserting P* may be taken as my reason for taking *P* to be the content of a true assertion on the question, i.e. (in effect) my reason for believing *P*. Now if two speakers make inconsistent assertions, it might nevertheless remain the case that each had the best possible reasons in senses (*a*) and (*b*) for asserting what he did assert; the question of whether B, for the best possible reasons, comes out with what he believes has no tendency to weaken A's best possible reasons for coming out with what he believes (sense (*a*)), and with sense (*b*), while it may be the case that A's reasons for asserting what he did may be upset by B's contradicting him – e.g., he decided to lie precisely on the calculation that B would not dare to contradict him – this is not necessarily so: thus equally he may have decided to lie in the knowledge that B would contradict him. When we get to sense (*c*), however, it does look as though there may be some sense in which it is impossible for the reasons that A and B have for asserting what they did to be in each case the best possible reasons; just because their assertions cannot both be true, so that the reasons for at least one of the assertions cannot ultimately be as good as all that. This does not mean, of course, that the mere fact that someone else asserts something inconsistent with what I have asserted must make me revise or even reconsider the reasons for my own assertion; I may just be convinced that he is mistaken. The suggestion is rather that, whatever the actual reactions of the speakers to the situation, there must in fact be something wrong with the reasons of at least one of them. This is lamentably rough; but to try to refine it would involve a discussion too elaborate for the present context. I hope that there is enough in what I have said to support a contrast with imperatives that I shall mention later.

Turning back now to imperatives, and considering the notion of a man's having good reason for uttering an imperative, one sees first that the distinctions, drawn in the case of indicative assertions, of different senses of 'reason for asserting' have little parallel; though there are some rudimentary points of analogy. The distinction between (*a*) and (*c*), for instance, which is clear and basic with assertions – for it never just follows from the fact that I believe something that I should now assert it – scarcely exists with imperatives: if there are good reasons against coming out with a particular imperative, then there is not in general a clear sense in which nevertheless the imperative might be appropriate to the situation. There are indeed some cases in which something like this arises; that, for instance, in which I am strongly tempted to say to some tedious person 'shut up and push off', but refrain from this on grounds of politeness, deference, prudence or whatever. Here one has something which is rather like *thinking* an imperative but not saying it. But one cannot generalise such cases, for the reasons that bear on coming out with the imperative in such cases form a continuum with the reasons that bear on whether it would be (apart from those first reasons) an appropriate thing to come out with. Consider for instance the difference between the tedious person being important and influential, and the tedious person being vulnerable and pathetic; in the second case, the reasons against coming out with such an imperative begin to move in towards being reasons against even (as it were) entertaining it.

Again, it is not easy to find any real analogy for the issues raised by sense (*b*) with assertion; this because the notion of sincerity has no clear footing with imperatives. Certainly the consideration of whether I *want* the agent addressed to do a certain thing is not the consideration we are looking for here; we cannot say that the analogy for imperatives to speaking 'contrary to my mind' in assertion is telling somebody to do something which I do not want him to do. For in any ordinary sense of 'want', one might suppose that it could be A's duty to tell B to do something which A does not *want* him to do. A better candidate would be the consideration of whether the speaker *means* the agent to do the act in question. For this seems to have something to do with whether the speaker means what he says, when he says 'do x', and this is not unlike the question of whether, in the sense relevant to sincerity, a speaker means what he says when he says e.g., 'I was not in Paris last week.' But while a man who makes an insincere assertion does not in one sense mean what he says, there is of course another sense in which he does – i.e., he intends his words to be taken in their usual sense. In the case of indicative assertion there is an absolutely general distinction between these two things. But it is not clear that in the case of imperatives any such general distinction can be mounted.

There are indeed some cases to which something like this distinction applies. Thus if I tell someone whom I know to be counter-suggestible, not to do something, with the intention that he should do it, I might be said not to mean what I say, though I mean my words to be taken in their usual sense. This might be called an 'insincere order'. But it provides no parallel to insincere assertion in general; depending as it does on a known peculiarity of the hearer, it most resembles in the field of assertion the case of modifying the assertions I make to a man whom I know never to believe what I say, and this is a case so special that it runs counter to the general point and practice of even insincere assertion.

Less eccentric than this are cases in which the speaker is not fully identified with an order that he gives, and thus might be said not fully to mean the agent to carry it out. Thus Wotan's order to Brünnhilde, not to defend Siegmund; an order which, discerning his deeper desire, she disobeyed. It is essential to the situation, however, that Wotan is divided, between his aspirations for Siegmund's race, and the moral requirements pressed on him by Fricka; and that while Brünnhilde has certainly done what in one sense he wanted, and even – perhaps – what in one sense he intended,[6] she has nevertheless 'willed against his will' and has to be punished for so doing. Such a case provides suggestive parallels to cases of half-belief and divided mind with assertion. What we still seem to lack, however, is any general parallel to *straightforward* cases of insincere assertion, and hence for the issues raised by sense (*b*) of 'reasons for asserting'.

Now there certainly are such things as reasons for uttering a certain imperative, or for not uttering it. They are of various types: one's duty, one's position, one's wants, one's feelings towards the agent, and many others. But if the previous line of argument has been correct, there is no systematic way of sorting these out so as to reveal basically different sorts of relations of them to the imperative,

[6] Wagner makes Brünnhilde at one point say that Wotan in giving his order was 'estranged' from his own intention: '*Als Fricka den eig'nen Sinn dir entfremdet: da ihrem Sinn du dich fügtest, warst du selber dir Feind.*' She is speaking in her own defence. Wotan, more straightforwardly, says, '*So tatest du was so gern zu tun ich begehrt*': *Die Walküre*, Act 3, Scene 3, a passage which makes the psychological situation extremely convincing.

as can be done in the case of assertions. There is just an assemblage of different sorts of reasons, appropriate to different sorts of case. This makes the notion of 'the best possible reason' for coming out with an imperative a pretty indeterminate notion. But let us assume that we can give the notion application; I would suggest that this much at least is clear about it, that two people could have each the best possible reasons for coming out with imperatives which were inconsistent with each other. Nor need a spectator or the agent involved be led to the thought that there must be something amiss with the reasons on one side or the other. There seems here to be an evident disanalogy with assertions, even allowing for the very sketchy form of the contrary principle that I have advanced about assertions. Put extremely crudely, the point comes to this: when two people come out with inconsistent assertions, there must be something wrong; when two people come out with inconsistent imperatives, there need be nothing wrong – that is just how things have worked out.

This ties up with some of what was said in the earlier part of my argument. We saw there that in the case of assertions, to note an inconsistency and to agree with one side of it rather than the other is all logically of a piece: 'is true', 'is false', work homogeneously throughout. Whereas with imperatives, to note an inconsistency and to agree with one side are two quite different sorts of activity. We now see a further point. In the assertion case, to opt for *A*'s assertion and to reject *B*'s involves an implicit invitation to *B* to reconsider: both in the sense of withdrawing his remark, and in the sense of reviewing his reasons. For even in the case where I just happen to know that A is right, though A's actual reasons are poor, while *B* is wrong for rather good reasons, there must still be some way in which *B*'s reasons are defective. With imperatives, it is not so; the most that my siding with A implies is that if the agent takes my line, B will not secure obedience, which is no criticism of his *relation* to the situation or of whatever reasons he has for uttering his imperative.

I would suggest, then, that imperatives supply an area – no doubt, the clearest area – in which, although we can apply the notion of inconsistency all right, what goes with the notion of inconsistency is very different, and much slighter, than what goes with it in the case of assertions. In particular, the idea that the occurrence of inconsistent utterances indicates that something has gone wrong is well-founded with assertions, but – so far at least – this does not seem to be so with imperatives. If this is true, the next question must be: what is it about imperatives that makes this the case?

We can take up this question by considering first the suggestion that it is not in fact anything about imperatives as such: it is at most something about imperatives from different sources. For while it might imply no criticism of either *A*'s or *B*'s situation that they utter severally inconsistent imperatives, surely it would be a criticism of *A* if he did, or of some system if it yielded such imperatives? One might suggest that it is a condition of rational statement-making and of rational order-giving alike that any one person engaged in these activities should observe consistency. Now it is of course true that an order-giver is not going to be much use to himself or anyone else if he produces (at least frequently) inconsistent orders; indeed, if he does this too often, one may begin to wonder whether he is giving orders at all, or meaning his imperatives in their usual sense. Here there is a point of similarity. But I shall now try to show that dis-analogies that we have noticed between indicatives and imperatives in the intra-personal case extend also to this one-person, or system, case in such a way as to make the basis of the aim of consistency different in the two cases.

There are two main points. The first goes back to the considerations about reasons. A man may have the best possible reasons for issuing each of two inconsistent imperatives to an agent. He will probably refrain from doing so, and opt for one rather than the other, or for some third imperative. But his recognition of the fact that he cannot for any good purpose come out with both does not in itself have any effect of making him reconsider the reasons he had for wanting to utter them in the first place. It is like any other practical choice, where one can't have everything; and the question of whether a man should school himself not to be disposed to issue such imperatives is rather like the question of whether a man should school himself not to have conflicting desires – or at least, it would be if it were a real question, and not a very artificial one. His problem is just that he has aims of obedience-securing which conflict; to what extent he feels obliged to sort these out is an application of the general question of to what extent he feels obliged to sort out conflicting aims. A man, however, who has a disposition to make inconsistent assertions just cannot, once he has recognised the situation, continue to think (if he did so before) that he has the best possible reasons for making both assertions as unqualified and sincere assertions; he has discovered that he has inconsistent beliefs, and the reasons for each of two inconsistent beliefs cannot in the end be the best possible reasons. Of course, I am not denying that it is possible for people to be irrational. But there are logical limits to the degree of irrationality which is compatible with saying that a man is making sincere assertions at all, or having genuine beliefs. There are, indeed, also logical limits, as I have said, to the degree to which a man can utter inconsistent imperatives, and our still say that he is giving orders, meaning what he says, etc. But this is about what he does, not about what lies behind it; the criticism of the conflicting aims that lay behind the utterance of these imperatives is a different sort of criticism.

The second point, which is closely related, arises specifically out of the distinction between the (*a*) and (*c*) senses of 'reasons for asserting', a distinction which we found not systematically paralleled in the case of imperatives. With assertions, we can raise two separate questions, whether A should say it, and whether he should think it. In the case of imperatives, we cannot in general raise these separate questions. This has the consequence that if disposed to issue inconsistent imperatives, I avoid not only the appearance but the substance of logical offence if I merely keep quiet. With assertions, it is not so, for what is most fundamentally wrong about making inconsistent assertions is also wrong about having inconsistent thoughts.

This point, about keeping silence, can be illustrated in another connexion, if we move from simple imperatives to rules. I shall be brief about this; but I hope that what I have to say will be enough to suggest that the differences from assertion with respect to consistency are at least not confined to simple imperatives, but extend more widely. It is certainly basically desirable that a set of rules should not be formally inconsistent, since we can take their general aim to be to secure conforming behaviour, and if they are formally inconsistent there will be a whole dimension of their application in which this will be necessarily frustrated. But what about cases of empirical conflict, where the injunctions of the rules will be inconsistent if and only if some contingent conjunction of circumstances comes about? Suppose some institution has rules of the form 'In all A-cases, *x* shall be done' and 'In all *B*-cases, *x* shall not be done', A and *B* being logically independent, there is obviously a latent possibility of conflict should a case which is both A and *B* present itself. Now this possibility might be ruled out by its being understood, in virtue of the rules themselves, that there *shall be* no such cases. Thus if the club rules say that all ladies on the premises should wear hats, and no hats should be worn in the Smoking Room, we may well be given to understand (possibly by the conjunction of those rules alone) that no ladies should be in the Smoking Room. Differently from this, the rules may be all right because no such case is, independently of the rules, expected to arise: if, within the purview of the rules, there just aren't any Catholic Socialists, it doesn't matter that what is laid down for Catholics is incompatible with what is laid down for Socialists.

Now it may be said that in this latter possibility, though not in the former, the situation is just as with empirical generalisations. For the two statements, 'All *A*'s are *B*'s and 'No *C*'s are *B*'s' can both be true if and only if there is nothing that is both A and C (if the generalisations are not (just) generalisations, but laws, it would presumably be said that we require that there *could* not be such a case). But now with the generalisations if there is in fact such a case, one of the generalisations is false; and if a man comes to know of such a case, and he believes the generalisations, he will have to do something about it; and if he has fairly well-entrenched reasons for believing the generalisations, he may have to do something fairly drastic about it. But if the rule-administrators are confronted with the awkward case, they don't have to do anything about it at all; they may just say that it is a very rare sort of case, unlikely to arise again, and it is not worth changing the rules. It is not just that they make an exception, still less that they implicitly write an exception into the rules (this can be done with the generalisations, though it is often not very satisfactory). They *may* just say nothing about it at all. It is an interesting point that the stronger the reasons they have for having these particular rules, the less drastically they may regard the situation: the pragmatic convenience of keeping the rule outweighs the problems raised by the particular case. Of course, the exceptional case cannot actually conform to both the rules, any more than an agent can obey two inconsistent imperatives; so it might be said that they have actually allowed something to happen contrary to one of the rules, and hence implicitly at least modified the rule. But we are not logically forced to say this, and sometimes it would not be appropriate thing to say.

There are indeed many good reasons, particularly for very institutionalised sets of rules, why they should seek to avoid conflict-cases, and also why those who administer them should in fact make plain decisions in conflict cases and thus implicitly or explicitly modify the rules. But the reasons for consistency in this respect are essentially pragmatic, and can be weighed against other pragmatic considerations. It can be, in some circumstances, the most rational thing to do to ignore a particular difficulty, and keep on with just the rules one had before. It cannot be the rational thing to do with a counter-example to a pair of generalisations, just to overlook it; if at least they are generalisations that one is supposed to believe, and 'overlook' does not merely mean 'save up for consideration later'.

I think that these considerations about rules, and the contrasts between imperatives and indicatives that I have discussed already, serve to bring out a number of requirements that will have to be satisfied by any account of the need for consistency with assertions. The first requirement, by immediate contrast with the rules case, is that any such account must explain why the need for consistency with assertions has no exceptions. In the case of rules, or of imperatives coming from one source, we can see *in general* good reasons for consistency being observed; but these do not eliminate the possibility that it might on occasion be more trouble to change the rules than to put up with the inconsistency, so that we can have an adequate pragmatic justification for staying as we are. No account of the need for consistency with assertions will be adequate which leaves the situation looking merely like this. Another consideration may help to make this clear. It is often suggested that the need for consistency derives from the nature of the act of assertion – that to allow assertion and denial of the same thing would undermine the point of assertion. This is in some sense certainly true; the problem however remains of making it clear why as strong a rule about consistency as we have should follow from the nature of assertion. There is another rule which is equally connected with the nature and presuppositions of assertion: the general requirement of sincerity or truth-telling. But it seems doubtful in the extreme that one could get from these considerations more than a general requirement; one could not get an exceptionless requirement. Indeed, most would presumably hold that a thesis to the effect that there were no justified cases of lying could not be established from anything, since it is incorrect.

It might be said that, contrary to what I am suggesting, there are exceptions to the demand for consistency, even with assertions, and that not every case of inconsistency is objectionable, since there are acceptable utterances of the form '*P* and not-*P*'. But this will not do; for where remarks of this form are acceptable, they are not cases of inconsistent assertion. This is not a vacuous reply, for it is not merely that we do not *say* 'inconsistent assertion' about such remarks, if we are to regard them as acceptable, but that we seek to interpret them, by taking them as saying that something is so in one respect but not in another, or as indicating a border-line case, or as belonging to some fictional discourse, fantasy, etc., etc. The necessity of moving towards such interpretations is an independent consideration that gives content to denying that such cases are simply acceptable instances of inconsistent assertion. Whereas a justifiable lie is straightforwardly an example of insincere assertion or non-truth-telling, i.e., of what is in general forbidden.

The first requirement of an explanation of the need for consistency in assertion is, then, that it should make clear the exceptionless nature of this demand. Another, which emerged from our comparison of imperatives and assertions, is that there is not merely an objection to *coming out with* inconsistent assertions, as is basically the case with imperatives, but even to thinking them. And another requirement, which also emerged from the previous considerations, is that the objection to inconsistency in the discourse of one speaker should be linked up with the fact that something has gone wrong even if inconsistent assertions come from different speakers, a feature again not paralleled with imperatives. I see no way in which these requirements can all be met save by offering an account of the need for consistency that puts the weight squarely on the consideration that the basic aim of assertions is to be true; for it seems only the notion of truth that joins these points, and others implicit in the comparisons we made before, together. (The point about the exceptionless nature of the demand, for instance, comes out in the idea that all the acceptable utterances which are apparently exceptions can be independently explained as having a sense which would allow them to be true, or else as not in fact aiming at truth.)

However, if one is going to rely on the notion of truth in giving the account of assertion and consistency, it will have to be a substantial notion of truth. None of the requirements that I have been discussing will follow from the thesis that assertions basically aim at truth if all that the thesis is taken to mean is that 'true' is the word we use in registering the acceptability of assertions, but do not use in registering the acceptability of e.g., imperatives. In particular, these consequences will not follow if we accept the view that the nature of truth is sufficiently explained by the consideration that in saying '*P* is true' we confirm, re-assert, or express agreement with *P*. This view cannot be correct in any case, since, for instance, it gives no account at all of the occurrence of '*P* is true' in contexts where we are not actually asserting that *P* is true. But there will be a further argument against this type of view if one both accepts the asymmetries that I have been arguing for between assertions and such things as imperatives, and also agrees that these asymmetries, and the particular significance of consistency in connexion with assertions, is to be explained in terms of assertions basically aiming at truth.

For I do not see how on such a theory it could be more than an accident of language that 'is true' signified agreement with *assertions* rather than agreement with anything else. For if all that 'is true' does when applied to an assertion is, roughly, to repeat it, there seems no reason why this expression or one only trivially different from it should not do the same job for imperatives. I have suggested that connexions between assertion, truth, and consistency, make the differences here much more fundamental than such an account could permit.

If what is implied by all this is a substantial notion of truth, the interesting question is what this notion is going to be like, and what sort of account can be given of it. I confess that I have not much idea of how to go on with these questions. But one direction, if a foggy one, may be suggested by a possible answer to a question which I raised earlier, and left: the question of why consistency played a different and (in a sense) less significant rôle with imperatives than with assertions, and whether it was just with imperatives, or with some wider class of utterances, that this contrast obtained. Some considerations about rules suggested that the contrasting class was wider than that of imperatives; after that, I have suggested that the rôle of consistency with assertions requires explanation in terms of a substantial notion of truth. Putting these ideas together, as it were, one reaches the idea that the line on one side of which consistency plays its peculiarly significant rôle is the line between the theoretical and the practical, the line between discourse which (to use a now familiar formula) has to fit the world, and discourse which the world has to fit. With discourse that is practical in these terms, we can see both why there should be applicable notions of consistency, and why consistency should be in various ways a general requirement; but one can also see why the aim of consistency, being basically connected with the *effects* of the discourse, should have essentially pragmatic sorts of justification, should admit of exception, and should be connected with coherence notions of a less logical character, such as the coherence of a man's desires and aims (as we noticed in the case of imperatives). On the other side of the line, we have the basic requirement that a man's words, and his beliefs, should reflect things as they are; and the requirement of consistency, more fundamental and pervasive in this case than the other, seems connected with the possibility of this being so at all. If there is anything in this, the peculiar significance of consistency, and the substantial notion of truth that appears to go with it, will be linked to the idea which may be called 'realism', that there is an independent order of things which it is the concern of this sort of discourse to reflect.

To spell out these lamentably hazy notions would be, if it can be done at all, a large task. I shall not try to set off on that here. I shall end by briefly mentioning one area which may help to illustrate a connexion between the notions I have brought together here, and to suggest that the issues of realism are genuine ones. This is the area of ethics. It is obvious, and agreed by all, that the general run of ethical discourse has some features in common with assertions or descriptive discourse, which are not shared by simple imperatives; one example, to which perhaps less weight is given by some ethical theories than it deserves, is that it is possible for a man to conceal his moral opinion, and to think one thing and say another. These features, together with other and very familiar considerations, notoriously led some philosophers to take the view that moral judgements were assertions reporting moral states of affairs. Such a view, one version of which is represented by Intuitionism, is sometimes labelled Objectivism; but this is a hopeless label for this, as for most other purposes, since, apart from the general confusion which it generates, there seems no reason why a view which held moral judgements to be expressions of rules or applications of rules should not equally be called Objectivist under some conditions, e.g., if it also held that men could all come to accept these rules in the light of rational reflection. The view in question might better be called Ethical Realism; and the Ethical Realist is the one who so much emphasises the claim that moral judgements can be true or false.

This claim of the Ethical Realist is often thought to be vacuous, unless it is taken as equivalent to the highly uninteresting claim that we use the words 'true' and 'false' of moral judgements. But if my general line of argument in this paper is correct, I am not sure that it is vacuous. For a realist view would seem to determine a different view of consistency in ethics from that determined by a non-realist view. Everyone would agree to there being a rôle, and presumably quite an important one, for the notions of consistency and inconsistency with respect to moral judgements and moral thought. But on a realist view, the significance of consistency, and the explanation of it as an aim, are going to come down to the simple point that moral judgements being straightforwardly assertions, two inconsistent moral judgements cannot both be true, and hence (truth being the aim of assertions) cannot both be acceptable: one of them must be rejected; its reasons must be defective; something must be wrong. On a non-realist view, the significance of consistency is going to be different: it is going to turn on such points as that inconsistent moral principles cannot both be put into practice; inconsistent moral decisions cannot both be carried out; inconsistent moral advice cannot be followed, nor injunctions obeyed. It will also involve the important dimension of assessment by which a tendency to produce frequently conflicting moral judgements follows from an incoherence (not purely logical) in one's aims, desires and emotions. Such considerations will reveal a lot of good reasons, of various sorts, for avoiding inconsistency. But they cannot endow that aim with the ultimate kind of significance that it possesses on the realist view. In particular, the non-realist approach may well allow for the possibility that one can be forced to two inconsistent moral judgements about the same situation, each of them backed by the best possible reasons, and each of them firmly demanding acceptance; and while action or advice demands deciding between them, it does not demand – or permit – deciding that either of them was wrong, or only apparently a requirement of the situation. The inconsistency does not necessarily show that something was wrong – except with the situation. Whereas on the realist view, this just could not ultimately be the state of affairs.

If the picture of moral conflict that I have here ascribed to the 'non-realist' is, as I suppose, nearer to the truth;[7] and if the connexions between consistency and realism which I have vaguely gestured towards in the later part of this paper have any substance in them; then one might have some reason for supposing that Ethical Realism is not vacuous, but is false.

ADDITIONAL NOTE (1972)

The two articles *Ethical Consistency* and *Consistency and Realism* leave an important obscurity about the relations between 'inconsistency' and 'conflict', taking the former term (as I generally have done) to relate to the logical impossibility of joint truth of beliefs, joint satisfaction of desires, etc., and the latter to relate to empirical impossibility. The first article pays some attention to difficulties here, in discussing the presentation of *ought*-conflicts, but does it in a way which I now think underestimates the depth of those difficulties. A central question concerns the different ways in which beliefs, desires, practical principles, and moral sentiments are related to

[7] See *Ethical Consistency*, pp. 166–86.

their various verbal expressions – hence, the different ways in which inconsistency in verbal expression may reflect a conflict or opposition in the inner states which are expressed. The relations between logical and non-logical conflict are themselves a major issue.

I hope to deal with this better in a later book, which will also take further the idea that while it is an indisputable ideal for an empirical belief-system to be free from conflict, it is not at all – contrary to what almost all philosophers seem to assume – an indisputable ideal for a personal value-system. That difference has consequences for the virtue of rationality. If 'rationality' entails the project of eliminating, ideally, all conflict, then rationality is a very qualified or partial virtue of a moral outlook or of the person who has it. If 'rationality' is taken to cover more generally the indisputable virtue of thinking intelligently and responsibly about one's desires and commitments, then the problematical issue is to what extent rationality demands consistency and the elimination of conflict, and in what forms.

13

Morality and the emotions

Recent moral philosophy in Britain has not had much to say about the emotions. Its descriptions of the moral agent, its analyses of moral choice and moral judgement, have made free use of such notions as attitude, principle and policy, but have found no essential place for the agent's emotions, except perhaps for recognising them in one of their traditional rôles as possible motives to backsliding, and thus potentially destructive of moral rationality and consistency. Much the same is true when one turns to what has been said about the *objects* of moral judgement: here there is much discussion of what it is to judge favourably or unfavourably actions, decisions, principles, states of affairs, intentions; indeed, men and men's characters. There is less, however, about what a man ought or ought not to feel in certain circumstances, or, more broadly, about the ways in which various emotions may be considered as destructive, mean or hateful, while others appear as creative, generous, admirable, or – merely – such as one would hope for from a decent human being. Considerations like these certainly play a large part in moral thought, except perhaps in that of the most restricted and legalistic kind; but it is my impression that the part they play has not adequately been mirrored in the recent concerns of moral philosophers.

There are a number of reasons for this neglect. Some of the reasons are no doubt of mainly historical or sociological interest, but others are of more direct concern to philosophical theory; and of these, there are two that seem to me particularly significant. The first is connected with questions about language. The second consists in a combination of two things – a rather simple view of the emotions, and a deeply Kantian view of morality. The first part of what I have to say will be about language; this will lead into those other issues, about which I shall try to say something in the latter part.

The first reason for the neglect of the emotions lies in some considerations about language. In these years philosophy has found its way to lie in reflection on language, and moral philosophy in reflection on the language of morality. Now this tendency, in itself, does not exclude much; for the diversity of what can be called 'reflection on language' is equalled by the diversity of what can be called 'the language of morality', and there was no basic reason why a generous approach to the linguistic endeavour should not have embraced those features of our speech about morality that reveal or suggest the parts played by the emotions; such features, as I shall try to show, certainly exist. What has largely inhibited this development is something over and above the linguistic programme itself: this is the preoccupation with the distinction between fact and value. This preoccupation has been inevitable. It has also, in many respects, been valuable. But there is no doubt that some of its consequences have been unfortunate. Since the preoccupation is one with fact and value as such, it has imposed on the linguistic enterprise a concentration on the most general features of moral language, or indeed, yet more widely, of evaluative language. Thus the attention goes to such very general linguistic activities as 'commendation', 'evaluation' and 'prescription', and to such very general terms as 'good', 'right' and 'ought', and the more specific notions in terms of which people a lot of the time think and speak about their own and others' conduct have, with the exception of one or two writers, largely gone by default.

This concentration has helped to push the emotions out of the picture. If you aim to state the most general characteristics and connexions of moral language, you will not find much to say about the emotions; because there are few, if any, *highly general* connexions between the emotions and moral language. It has been all the easier for recent analytical philosophy to accept this truth because of the evident failings of a theory, itself one of the first in the linguistic style, which claimed precisely the contrary. This was emotivism, which offered a connexion between moral language and the emotions as straightforward and as general as could be conceived, in the form of the thesis that the function and nature of moral judgements was to express the emotions of the speaker and to arouse similar emotions in his hearers. This theory not proving very plausible, and the interest in the highly general questions remaining, it was natural enough to look to things quite other than the emotions for the answers. Not that emotivism has ceased to be mentioned. It is mentioned in order to be refuted, and indeed the demolition of emotivism has almost come to take the place in undergraduate exercises that used to be held (as Stephen Spender comically recalls in his autobiography *World Within World*) by the equally mechanical dismembering of Mill's *Utilitarianism*. The emotivist is specially suitable for this rôle of sacrificial victim because he is at once somewhat disreputable (emotivism being regarded as irrationalist) and at the same time embarrassingly likely to be taken for a close relative. But there are things to be learned from emotivism which do not always emerge in the course of the ritual exercises; and it is some of these that I shall now go on to consider. My aim will not be to reconstruct emotivism, but to steal from it; not to rebuild the pagan temple, but to put its ruins to a holier purpose.

Emotivism held that there were two purposes of moral judgements: to express the emotions of the speaker, and to influence the emotions of his hearers. I want to concentrate on the first of these. Now it was clearly the intention of emotivism, in referring to the expression of emotions, to offer a view about the nature of moral judgements, a view of their logical and linguistic character; it was not offering merely an empirical claim to the effect that moral judgements (themselves identified in some other way) always do express the emotions of their utterers. This being so, it must be part of an emotivist thesis that there are some kinds of linguistic rule associating moral judgements with the expression of emotion. What form might such linguistic rules take? Here there are two importantly different possibilities, which must be distinguished. On the one hand, they might be rules about the correct use of certain sentences or forms of words – those forms of words, namely, in uttering which we make a moral judgement; and the rules would state that unless those forms of words were used in expression of emotion, they were being misused. In this form, the rules would be about the correct use of the sentences that we use in making moral judgements, laying it down about those sentences that their correct use lies partly in the expression of emotion. The second possibility is that the linguistic rules should concern not the correct or incorrect use of those sentences, but should rather regulate the application of the expression 'moral judgement'. In this form, the rules would not lay it down that a speaker would be guilty of a misuse of certain sentences if he used them not in expression of his emotions; it would merely lay down that if he did so use them, he would not count as making a moral judgement. In slightly more technical terms, one might say that the first possibility concerns the semantics of a certain class of sentences, while the second possibility concerns the definition of a certain speech-act, the speech-act of *making a moral judgement*. I shall consider these two possibilities in turn.

On the first possibility, that the requirement for expression of emotion actually enters into the semantic rules of sentences employed in moral judgements, it might be wondered whether there are any sentences at all whose use was governed by semantic rules of this type. There certainly are. I shall leave out the case of sentences which also say something explicitly about the speaker's emotional state, e.g.

I am extremely angry with you;

these raise interesting problems about the relations between statement and expression,[1] but they are not likely to provide much direct help in the present question. But consider a sentence like

He has broken his tricycle again, blast him.

Here it seems reasonable to say that the use of this sentence is governed by the requirement that the speaker be expressing irritation, or some feeling of that sort. We encounter here the matter of intonation in utterances of this sort; it is notable that there is a large range of intonations in which the sentence would be inappropriate, and others in which it would be appropriate, and if the latter were employed when the speaker was not irritated, his utterance would be misleading, even deceitful.

In this case, these features of the sentence of course centre on one word, the expletive; and this backs up the account of these features in terms of the semantics of the sentence, for they are features connected with the use of this expression: if someone did not know that the expression worked like this, he would be ignorant of a fact about the English language. That the features centre on this expression makes this example particularly simple in a certain way; the inclusion of the expletive merely adds something to what, without it, would be a straightforward statement of fact. That statement by itself could of course also be made in a manner expressive of irritation, but it does not have to be; the addition of the expletive gives a way of making that same statement of fact which is restricted to cases in which its utterance is to be taken as expressive of irritation. This is the sort of case to which one can straightforwardly apply the old *New Yorker* request: Just Stick to the Facts, Please.

The most primitive type of emotivist theory assimilated moral judgements to this type of utterance: statement of fact plus expletive addition. This, as has been often pointed out, will not do. It is only too obvious that the moral judgement

He did wrong in not going to the appointment

is not necessarily expressive of indignation or any other emotion; though of course a particular utterance of it may be expressive of some emotion, just as a statement of fact may be. Apart from this,

[1] For a helpful discussion of this and related issues, see W. P. Alston, 'Expressing', in Max Black ed., *Philosophy in America* (London: Allen and Unwin, 1965).

expletives are not logically manoeuvrable enough to provide a model for moral, or any other value judgements. To adapt to this question an argument that has been used by J. R. Searle[2] against a more sophisticated thesis, it is notable that you cannot *make conditional* the expressive functions of an expletive. Thus the sentence

> If he has broken his tricycle again, blast him, he'll go without his pocket money

obeys the same sorts of rules as the simpler sentence considered before; it can be appropriately used only by someone who is *already* irritated. But even if I shall be indignant if I believe that he did wrong in not going to his appointment, it is clear that the sentence, uttered when I am still in doubt about the circumstances,

> If he did wrong in not going to the appointment, I shall have something to say to him,

does not express existing indignation, my indignation remaining as hypothetical as the truth of the antecedent. A similar point can be shown with negation. If A asks

> Has he broken his tricycle again, blast him?

and *B* replies

> No, he has not broken his tricycle again, blast him

either *B* is himself irritated, or (just possibly) he is sarcastically *quoting* A's expletive.

The same consideration can be applied to cases more sophisticated than the simple occurrence of expletives. If my infatuated friend says

> Lisa looks incomparably lovely tonight

it scarcely seems open to me, even if I wish to disagree with his estimate of Lisa's appearance, to do so by just denying his assertion in its own terms:

> No, she does not look incomparably lovely tonight

would be an odd thing to say, and would have a place, I suspect, only if I were in effect quoting him, as above – and thus being very rude – or possibly, and more interestingly, if I were myself fairly

2 'Meaning and speech-acts', *Philosophical Review* (1962), pp. 423–32. Although the principle of Searle's argument and of mine is the same, the arguments proceed in contrary directions. His point is that there is not a meaning-link between a certain sentence and the performance of a certain speech-act, since the speech-act is not performed when the sentence occurs in contexts other than that of simple assertion. My argument rather suggests that there is a meaning between the expletive and its expressive function, since the expressive function is preserved in such contexts.

infatuated, and disagreeing only about the incomparability of her loveliness tonight; in which case, paradoxically, the denied expressive terms are still doing their expressive job. This resistance to losing their force in conditional, negative, etc., contexts may well be a mark of sentences which *semantically incorporate* the expression of emotion. Those sentences which are used to make moral judgements do not in general have this peculiarity, and the first possibility for a general emotivist link between moral language and the emotions fails.

While this is so, it is not the end even of this part of the story. While those sentences that are used to make moral judgements do not in general semantically incorporate the expression of emotion, it seems clear that some of them do. For instance,

> Of course, he went back on his agreement when he got to the meeting, the little coward

seems to be reserved for use in circumstances where certain emotions, such as contempt, are felt by the speaker. What else does the utterance of this sentence do? First, it states or implies certain facts, as that he made an agreement, and went back on it at the meeting; and second, it imports an explanation, since 'cowardice' is an explanatory notion (the speaker would be taking a different view of what had happened if, equally unamiably, he called the man an 'ambitious little crook'). Is this all? If so, we can analyse the utterance into statement of fact, suggestion of explanation and (something like an) expletive addition: i.e. as merely a slightly more complex example of the 'blast him' sort. But this seems to leave something out, since one would be naturally disposed to think that the original remark also embodied some moral opinion or assessment of the man's behaviour. On the present analysis, it looks as though this function will be borne only by the expletive addition – that is to say we shall be accepting for this case the primitive emotivist account which has been in general rejected. If this is not acceptable, it seems that there should be some way of representing the moral assessment feature independently of the expletive addition; so that the removal of the expletive addition will leave us with a triple core, of stating facts, suggesting explanation and making a moral assessment. If this is so, we should be able in principle to isolate this core without the expletive trimmings – obeying, as it were, an amplified *New Yorker* instruction: Just Stick to the Facts, Explanations and Moral Assessments, Please.

What would the isolated core look like? Here there are difficulties which particularly centre on the expression 'little coward'. While 'coward' is an explanatory term, it is not a very unemotional one; and if 'little' refers to the man's moral, rather than his physical stature, it is not (at least in this collocation) a very unemotional way of making a moral assessment. This phrase seems inextricably linked to the expletive addition, and so cannot appear in the core. The core is, then, going to look something like this:

> As might have been predicted, he went back on his agreement at the meeting through fear; which he ought not to have done (*or* this was a bad thing).

This sentence is supposed to stand in the same relation to its earlier emotional counterpart as 'he broke his tricycle' does to 'he broke his tricycle, blast him'; i.e. in this more complex case, it states the same facts, suggests the same explanation and makes the same moral assessment. All that the replacement sentence has supposedly lost are the expletive additions. But is this in fact so?

It is made a little easier to agree to this by my having introduced a term that is sometimes introduced in this sort of connexion, viz. 'moral *assessment*', since there is a satisfactory sense of 'assessment' in which you and I give the same assessment merely if we are both 'pro' or both 'con' or, perhaps, both 'neutral'. Certainly in the present case both the original sentence and its non-emotional replacement equally reveal the speaker as 'con'. In one sense of the phrase 'moral judgement', the notion of 'same moral judgement' might be adequately modelled on this very skeletal pattern of 'assessment'; this is where 'judgement' is something offered by a judge, one who applies such labels as 'pass' or 'fail', 'first', 'second', 'highly commended' and so forth. In this sense, we might say that the original sentence and its replacement embodied the same moral judgement. But, as has been quite often pointed out, the technical phrase 'moral judgement' has other overtones, being virtually the only survivor into contemporary philosophical vocabulary of that Idealist usage by which beliefs and opinions, roughly, were called 'judgements'. And these overtones have to be preserved if the phrase 'moral judgement' is to have any hope of doing adequate work in its exposed position in moral philosophy; since, in being interested in a person's moral judgement, so called, we are in fact not merely interested in whether he is pro this and con that, whether he grades these men in one order or in another. We are interested in what moral view he takes of the situations, how those situations look to him in the light of his moral outlook.

Could we in this broader sense of 'moral judgement' say – to revert to our example – that the replacement sentence expressed the same moral judgement as the first one? Does it lay before us the same moral view of the situation? Scarcely so. To agree to this would commit us to saying that the contempt (or something like it) that the speaker of the first sentence felt and put into his words was not an integral part of his moral view of the situation; that contempt was an adventitious addition to his low rating of the man's behaviour at the committee, as my irritation is no doubt an adventitious reaction to my learning that Tommy has broken his tricycle again. Something like this *could* be true; but very obviously, it need not be so. Indeed, it is far from clear what content is to be assigned, in the moral connexion, to the bare notion of 'grading low'; this is an idea which seems much more at home in highly structured professional or technical kinds of comparison. In the present case, the mode in which this man's behaviour appeared bad may precisely have been that of its being contemptible; and if the person who made the remark comes not to think of it in those terms, he will cease to take the same moral view as before of this man's behaviour. Where this is so, we may not be able to isolate the moral-judgement content of the utterances from what makes them expressive of emotion.

We shall get back to this area again. Now, however, let me take up what I mentioned earlier as the second line by which an emotivist type of theory might seek to make a direct link between the making of moral judgements, and the expression of emotion. This was the suggestion that the expression of emotion might be logically involved, not in the semantics of certain sentences that people utter, but in the description that we give of their uttering them: that a speaker's expressing emotions should be regarded as a necessary condition of his utterance's counting as the making of a moral judgement. This was the 'speech-act' thesis. I think we shall see that this suggestion, while no less false than the last one, also raises some questions that lead us, by a rather different route, to entanglements of the emotions with moral judgement.

The 'speech-act thesis' takes 'moral judgement', or more precisely 'making or expressing a moral judgement', as the name of a certain type of speech-act; that is to say, as a member of the class that includes also such items as 'giving a warning', 'making a promise', 'stating an intention', 'making an apology', 'expressing regret', 'describing what happened' and so forth. Interest in such speech-acts, promoted by the work of the late J. L. Austin, has been prominent in recent philosophy, not least in moral philosophy, where particularly such linguistic activities as 'commending' have been to the fore. I think that valuable light has been shed by these studies, and that this will continue to be so.

We shall be able to see the possible relations of emotions to the speech-act of making a moral judgement, only if we get clearer about a somewhat complex question, which is the rôle of *sincerity* in different speech-acts. The category of sincerity and insincerity is of fundamental importance for the understanding of linguistic activities; for it is a necessary feature of linguistic behaviour that it can be deliberately inappropriate, designed to mislead, etc. This does not mean, however, that the notions of sincerity and insincerity apply equally to all speech-acts, or in the same way to all. I shall try to distinguish very briefly six different types of case; this will be only a very rough exercise, designed to clear a bit of the undergrowth round our present problem.

1 There are some highly conventionalised speech-acts which cannot be sincere or insincere at all: such as greetings (or at least very simple ones). Just saying 'hello' cannot in itself be done sincerely or insincerely, though certain accompaniments, such as a tone of warm enthusiasm, may admit the notions. Similarly, saying 'How are you?' cannot be insincere, if regarded as a greeting; if regarded as an *expression of concern for the man's health,* it can be.

2 Orders cannot be sincere or insincere. However, there are some associated conditions on the speaker and his situation which get us nearer to the realm of sincerity, without actually reaching it. These concern whether the speaker wants the hearer to do the thing ordered or not; and, differently, whether he means the speaker to do the thing or not.

3 Consider now certain sorts of judgement: grading and (in one sense) commending, as where a man gives his judgement, allocates an order of merit, etc., at a dog show or examination. It could be said (though it would be an unnatural thing to say) that a man does these things 'sincerely' or 'insincerely'; and there is more than one way of doing them 'insincerely' (there are important differences between his having been bribed, and his conscientiously applying official standards which he himself regards as inappropriate). But when he judges or commends insincerely, he really does judge or commend – the act is performed, though 'insincerely'.

4 In this respect, there is a similarity between these acts and that of promising: an insincere promise is quite certainly a promise. Promising, however, has the feature not present in the last case, that the application of 'sincere' and 'insincere' is absolutely clear and well

established – an insincere promise is a promise made without the intention of carrying it out. Yet, one may perhaps repeat, it is quite certainly made: in the phrase 'insincere promise', the word 'insincere' is not what the scholastics called an *alienans*[3] term, that is to say a qualification which weakens or removes the force of the term that it qualifies (as 'bogus', 'imitation', 'pretend', etc.).

5 Equally well established is the application of 'sincere' and 'insincere' to expressions of intention and of belief (which can be regarded together in this connexion). But here it looks as though 'insincere' has a rather different effect: here it does appear to be *alienans*, for an insincere expression of intention is surely not an expression of intention, nor an insincere expression of belief an expression of belief. Perhaps if we are to be accurate, we cannot say anything quite as simple as that; we can indeed speak of the deceiving man, even after we have discovered his deceit, as 'having expressed an intention to . . .', meaning that he used a formula usually taken as an expression of intention, and meant it to be so taken. But, though that may be so, he certainly did not express *his* intentions, nor does the man who misleads us about his beliefs, express *his* belief. This 'his' is perhaps significant. His greetings, his orders, his commendations, his promises are *his*, basically, just in that it is he who utters them; his expressions of intention or belief are *his* not only in this way, but because they are expressions of *his* intentions or *his* beliefs, and these latter lie below the level of the speech-act.

6 Expressions of feeling or emotion are obviously to be regarded in general in the light of what has just been said: he is not expressing his feelings if his remarks are insincere. However, there are at least a few cases in which the steady flow of human pretence has shaped the language, and worn a semantic gap between formula and feeling. 'Expression of regret', for instance, seems to be the name of a type of utterance conventionally identified, and an insincere expression of regret is still an expression of regret. Similarly, perhaps, with expressions of concern. Both, it may be noticed, are among the sorts of items frequently sent by one government to another.

Let me now try to put together what has just been said with the question of moral utterances. There has been a tendency in recent work to assimilate the speech-acts involved in the making of moral utterances – 'making a moral judgement' and so forth – to the sorts of speech-act considered in (2) and (3): the giving of orders, and grading, commending, etc. This assimilation tends to conceal the many

[3] For the use of this term, cf. P. T. Geach, 'Good and evil', *Analysis* 17 (1956), p. 33.

and vital respects in which speech-acts associated with moral utterances belong rather to types (5) and (6). It inclines us to forget that a man who sincerely makes some moral utterance expresses his judgement of the situation, his beliefs about its merits, his moral outlook, his opinion, his feelings on the matter – possibly his intentions. A man who makes an insincere moral utterance does not do these things, but hides his belief and his real feelings. But it is these that chiefly concern us: the moral cast of the man lies below the level of the speech-act.

This is not to say that to concentrate on models in classes (2) and (3) for understanding of moral language necessarily leaves out the notions of sincerity and insincerity. We have already seen that there is some room for them there, if rather less directly than elsewhere; and case (4) – promising – shows that there can be a straightforward use of these terms to qualify speech-acts which, like those others and unlike those grouped in (5), can be expressed by what Austin called an 'explicit performative'.[4] The trouble is not so much that concentration on the models in (2) and (3) displaces the notion of sincerity, as that it misplaces it, and tends to conceal from us the basic, if not simple, truth that one who misleads us about his moral view is, in this respect, like one who misleads us about his factual beliefs or about his feelings – he says something other than what he really thinks or feels.

Consider the grading or commending model (2). We remarked there that a man may grade or commend certain things or persons contrary to his real opinion of their merits, and that could be a form of 'insincerity' (though it need not be: it may not be his job to bring his own opinions into it). But now what does 'his real opinion of their merits' mean? If activities like grading and commending are to be the clue to moral thought, it is *this* that must itself be explained, and presumably explained in terms of grading and commending. Here the line that has been actually pursued, perhaps the only possible one, is that of saying that 'his real opinion of their merits' is to be explained in terms of the gradings or commendations that he gives or would give in accordance with *his own* standards. This in turn has to be explained; and although strenuous efforts have been made to cash this notion merely in terms of systematic action, I myself am convinced that we could not in fact attach much content to it if men did not do such things as express their enthusiasm, admiration, hope, boredom, contempt, dislike, scepticism – that is to say, express views

[4] Neither 'I intend' nor 'I believe' is, of course, an explicit performative. Loose talk about a 'performative' analysis of these expressions (as opposed, presumably, to an 'autobiographical' analysis of them) obscures this obvious fact.

and feelings about the objects or persons that they grade or commend, and not merely go about grading or commending them.

I said earlier that our emotivist suggestion, that the possession of certain emotions might be a necessary condition of performing the speech-act of making a moral judgement, would turn out to be false. We can now see why this is so. First of all, there is certainly a sense of 'expressing a moral judgement' in which an insincere moral judgement is still a moral judgement: the sense in which a man who, quite insincerely and to please an illiberal host, says 'homosexuals ought to be flogged', has expressed the moral judgement that homosexuals ought to be flogged. This sense may encourage the assimilation of 'making a moral judgement' to the types of speech-act (2) and (3), which we have already noticed. But it should not do so. What rather it is like is the sense – noted under (5) – in which a man who insincerely says that he intends to do a certain thing has expressed an intention. In this sense of 'expressing a moral judgement' the emotivist thesis must obviously be false; if one can perform this act without even being sincere, how can it be a necessary condition of performing it that one has feelings appropriate to the content of the judgement?

If we turn now to the notion of a man's expressing *his* moral judgement on a situation, that by which his moral judgement, like his factual and other beliefs, lies below the level of the speech-act; is the presence of appropriate feelings a necessary condition of a man's doing this? This question comes to much, if not exactly, the same as asking: are appropriate feelings a necessary condition of sincerity in expressing a moral judgement in the first sense? To this question, again, the answer seems to be 'no': the facts stand firmly against any simple and general connexion of feelings and sincerity. Thus the general emotivist thesis again fails. Nevertheless, feelings make some contribution to the notion of sincerity: and this in more than one way. I shall now try to consider this contribution.

The first part of the contribution is to be found in this, that there are *some* moral utterances which, if they are to be sincere, must be expressive of emotions or feelings that the speaker has. For instance, there are those moral utterances that are expressed in strong terms. These will include the cases that we were led to before, at the end of our discussion of the first emotivist suggestion, namely those cases in which the moral utterance involves terms that are semantically linked to the emotions. But these will not be the only cases; for it is perfectly possible for a man to express himself on a moral matter in a way which uses no such terms, but makes it perfectly clear that he feels strongly about the matter. He does not have to use expressions like 'little coward', 'outrageous', 'appalling', 'ghastly mess', 'crook', 'disgusting' and so forth, nor yet the vocabulary of ordinary obscenities and swear-words: though it is worth remembering that violent language and obscenities play a larger part in people's remarks in appraisal of human conduct than one would gather from a text-book on moral philosophy. But the speaker, as I said, may not express himself like this; he may just, in few and moderate words, make it clear that he is shocked, disappointed, indignant or (conversely) full of admiration, for instance. It is certainly a condition of his speaking sincerely in all these cases that he should feel those things that we are given to understand he does feel.

It may be said here that this is obvious enough, but that it has nothing particularly to do with the sincerity of moral utterances. It is merely that we are here dealing with those moral utterances which are expressed in terms, or in a manner, expressive of emotion, just as other sorts of utterances may be; and that the link of sincerity and the emotions exists merely in respect of those features, and not in respect of the moral utterance as such. But this objection will have force only if it further claims that we can isolate the content of the moral judgement, as such, from the rest. I have already argued, for the cases where there is a semantic link of what is said to emotion, that this is an unrealistic idea. I think that the new perspective that we now have on the question, from the point of view of sincerity, shows a more general point of the same kind.

It cannot be denied that an intrinsic feature of moral thought are the distinctions between taking a serious view and a less serious view; having strong convictions and less strong convictions, and so forth. It would be a mark of insanity to regard all moral issues as on the same level. Now the man who expresses himself in strong terms, such as we are considering, can usually be taken as indicating that he takes a strong or serious view of the matter in question.[5] This is not inevitably so: sometimes a man may himself be clear, and make it clear to others, that the moral view he is expressing with strong feelings is not a very serious moral view, and that the strong feeling is, for instance, merely personal irritation. But this is certainly a special case; in general, the display of feeling and the moral utterance will be taken together, and the strength of feeling displayed about the matter is generally taken as *one* criterion of the man's having a strong or serious moral view about it.

[5] Some points bearing on this are made by D. Braybrooke, 'How are moral judgements connected with displays of emotion?', *Dialogue*, IV (1965), pp. 206–23.

It is not, of course, *the* criterion, nor an infallible one. Thus it is possible for a man to express strong feelings in his moral remarks about a matter, himself regard the feelings as related to the moral issue, and yet not really take a very serious view of it. It may be, for instance, that his feelings (as we may see, or he may see later) are merely those of hurt pride, or fear, made over for the moment into moral indignation or altruistic upset; in such cases we may speak of self-deception. Again, and differently, his moral reactions may be in general so freely laced with emotion and so little borne out in action or by serious enquiry into the facts that we come to doubt whether he has any serious moral views at all: here we may think in terms of self-indulgent moral frivolity, particularly if the emotion he so generously indulges is indignation. In these cases, what is in a real sense a genuine emotional expression does not guarantee that a strong moral view is really taken. Conversely, it is even possible for a man to give a genuinely strong moral view an insincerely emotional expression: an 'unemotional' practical man, seriously devoted to some moral end, may find it helpful, in persuading others, to lay on a display of anger or sentiment which does not come spontaneously.

These cases, and many others, are commonplaces in the complex relations between the emotions and moral seriousness. While there are these commonplaces, few of them are likely to lie beyond all dispute, since these are obviously matters on which one's views cannot be independent of particular outlooks, values, and even fashions. The charge of insincerity has been exchanged many times in the last two centuries between the practical and the romantic, both in morals and politics, and the notion of sincerity is consequently unsettled in a way which represents sets of perfectly real and very basic divergences – divergences which exist, obviously, not only between but inside individuals.

The variety of cases, however, and the systematic differences in their interpretation, all exist against a background in which there is some connexion taken for granted between strength of feeling displayed on moral issues, and the strength of the moral view taken. This connexion appears to me basic enough for the strength of feeling to be called *a* criterion of taking a strong moral view, rather than saying that there is a mere empirical correlation between them. If it were a mere empirical correlation, we could imagine a world in which people had strong moral views, and strong emotions, and their emotions were not in the least engaged in their morality. Some moral theories certainly involve the conclusion that such a world is conceivable; but I do not think that it is.

The difficulties in such a conception are both psychological and logical. I shall consider just one, logical, difficulty. I shall try to show a point of involvement of the emotions in what may seem an independent criterion of moral sincerity – the only one, I imagine, which is likely to be thought capable of carrying the weight of the concept by itself. This is the criterion of appropriate action. That consistent or appropriate action is the criterion of moral sincerity is an idea that has been constantly stressed in recent discussion. The point I want to make is that the *appropriate action* which is demanded by this conception of moral sincerity is itself something which, often, is not independent of the emotional elements in a man's moral outlook.

It is an essential feature of the action-criterion as it has figured in the discussion of moral sincerity that reference is made to a *class* of appropriate actions; what provides the backing for the sincerity of a particular moral judgement or decision is a disposition on the part of the agent to do a certain type of action in certain types of circumstances. This requirement of generality is imposed for at least three reasons. First, it is only a small class of moral utterances that directly indicate a particular action, performance or non-performance of which by the utterer could constitute a test of his sincerity; those utterances expressing a moral decision in favour of some particular future action by the agent himself (e.g. 'I ought to give back the money'). By contrast with these, judgements about the past, other people's actions, etc., do not point to any relevant particular action on the agent's part; here appeal moves to his disposition to do or refrain from actions similar to those that he is commenting on. Second, it is held that even the cases where some particular action by the speaker is in view call for a general disposition to do things of that sort, if his comment or decision is to count as a moral one: this in virtue of the universalisability requirement on moral judgements. Third, the relevance of a general disposition to the question of attributions of sincerity is also supported by a more general doctrine in the philosophy of mind, that the truth-conditions of the claim that a man was sincere in what he said on a particular occasion are not in general to be found in features of that particular occasion (for instance, in some internal psychological state of the man on that occasion), but to be found rather in some broader pattern into which this occasion fits; this can, though it does not have to, take the form of a general disposition to action of a certain sort. All these considerations need considerable qualification; I shall not try to discuss that here. I shall assume that a general disposition to do actions *of a certain type* is of at least some relevance to the question of a man's sincerity in making a particular moral judgement. The question that concerns us is rather: how is the relevant type of actions determined? What holds together the class of actions?

My suggestion is that, in some cases, the relevant unity in a man's behaviour, the pattern into which his judgements and actions together fit, must be understood in terms of an emotional structure underlying them, and that understanding of this kind may be essential. Thus we may understand a man's particular moral remark as being, if sincere, an expression of compassion. This may then be seen as part of a general current in his behaviour which, taken together, reveals his quality of being a compassionate man; and it may be that it is only in the light of seeing him as a compassionate man that *those* actions, judgements, even gestures, will be naturally taken together at all. It is understanding this set of things as expressions of a certain emotional structure of behaviour that constitutes our understanding them as a set.

A special, but very central, case of this sort of understanding is that which concerns the emotions of remorse or guilt. The relevance of this emotion to moral sincerity is, one would have supposed, obvious; the comparative neglect of this basic moral phenomenon in recent work may be partly explained as a liberal and Utilitarian reaction against the destructive emphasis placed upon it in the more sadistic styles of education. Those uncreative aspects of guilt that motivate the Utilitarian moral objection may indeed at the same time encourage philosophical scepticism about the relevance of the emotion; unproductive self-punishment may be seen as precisely *not* an expression of those principles that ought to have issued in action, but rather as a misdirected substitute for action. In these reactions there may be much that is true. But they neglect the possibly creative aspects of guilt, and overlook that distinction which presents itself in Kleinian psychoanalytical work as that between persecutory and reparative guilt. He who thinks he has done wrong may not just torment himself, he may seek to put things together again. In this rather evident possibility, we not only have in general a connexion between the emotions and the moral life, we also have something that illustrates the point I have been trying to make about the interpretation of a set of actions in terms of an emotional structure. For it is highly probable that the very diverse things that such a man will go on to do and say can be interpreted as one pattern of behaviour only because we understand that the man feels that he has to take reparative action, because we see these activities of his as in various ways expressions of his feeling bad about what he has done or failed to do in the past.

I am suggesting, then, that reference to a man's emotions has a significance for our understanding of his moral sincerity, not as a substitute for, or just an addition to, the considerations drawn from how he acts, but as, on occasion, underlying our understanding of how he acts. But now it may be objected that no such reference to his emotions can ever be essential for the interpretation of his action. For his actions will be relevant to our understanding of his moral outlook and disposition not if they are merely any actions produced by compassion or remorse, but only if they are appropriately done in situations that provide *grounds* for acting in a compassionate manner, or – in the other case – are actions the *reason* for doing which is that they constitute reparative conduct. It is in the light of these grounds and reasons that his conduct is to be viewed; and this makes no essential reference to his emotions. The short answer to this objection is that what is relevant for our understanding of his moral disposition is not whether there are (in our view) grounds or reasons for action of that sort, but whether he takes there to be; whether he sees the situation in a certain light. And there is no reason to suppose that we can necessarily understand him as seeing it in that light without reference to the emotional structure of his thought and action. But this is a very short answer. A more adequate response to the issues presented here can come, I think, only from a more direct confrontation with the nature of the emotions than I have attempted so far.

In what I have said so far I have moved gradually from talking about the sincerity of particular moral judgements to more general considerations about the interpretation of a man's pattern of moral activity. I have progressively tended to discuss the emotions as motives, as states expressed in action; at the same time, I have continued to concentrate on the external point of view, that is to say, on an observer's assessment or understanding of another man's actions and judgements. For the rest of what I have to say, I shall turn the subject round in two dimensions: stop talking about assessments of moral agency and talk rather about moral agency; stop talking about the emotions merely as motives and admit their other aspect, that under which they undoubtedly must be regarded as things that happen to us, to which we are subject, with respect to which we are passive.

That the emotions must be regarded both as productive of action, and also as states to which we are subject, is an important point, which has been stressed by a number of writers.[6] Even in their latter aspect, of course, they are not, as the same writers have pointed out, blank occurrences like certain kinds of bodily sensation; for they have inbuilt – usually, if not inevitably – a reference to an object, and may be said to involve a thought. This helps to explain – or, perhaps, it would be fairer to say, it shows the place at which one would start to explain – how it is that a sane man can, on occasion, control his emotions, and how they can be appropriately directed. Some reports that the cruder moralists have brought back from the weary battleground of Reason and the Emotions seem to suggest that the only known ways of a man's keeping his emotions under control are either to deny them expression when the occasion is not appropriate – here the disciplinary activities of the Will are very important – or else, as a longer-term investment, train himself to have less of them, or to have only those of the more amiable kind. But these pieces of tactical and strategic advice seem to omit the most obvious influence of rational thought or advice on the emotions: that of convincing one that a given object is no proper or appropriate object of that emotion. As the phenomenologists have constantly stressed, to feel a certain emotion towards a given object is to see it in a certain light; it may be wrong, incorrect, inappropriate to see it in that light, and I may become convinced of this. When I am convinced, the emotion may go away; and it is wrong to forget the numbers of cases in which it *does* just go away or turn into something quite different, as when my fear of the impending car journey evaporates on learning that Miss X is not in fact going to be the driver; or my reserve and suspicion towards this man dissolve when something shows that his manner does not mean what it appeared to mean; or my passionate loyalty to the partisan leader suddenly cracks when I am convinced that his actions can only mean betrayal.

Of course, it may be that no thoughts about the object shift the emotion; because they fail to convince (which, notoriously enough, may be a function of the emotion itself) or because, although they in a way convince, the emotional structure persists. The phenomenology, psychology and indeed the logic, of such situations is highly complex and various. But the important point now is this: that when considerations which show the emotion to be inappropriate fail to displace it, this is not because it is an emotion but because it is an irrational emotion.

[6] See, for instance, R. S. Peters, 'Emotions and the category of passivity', *Proceedings of the Aristotelian Society* (1961–2), pp. 116–34; and A. Kenny, *Action, Emotion and Will* (London: Routledge & Kegan Paul, 1963), Ch. 3.

The notions of appropriateness, correctness and so forth in the object of course cry out for examination; and they wear on their front the fact that they are in some part evaluative. What should be feared or hoped for, and so forth, is obviously, to some extent, a matter in which disagreements of value between societies and individuals come out. Equally this is a central matter of moral education. If such education does not revolve round such issues as what to fear, what to be angry about, what – if anything – to despise, where to draw the line between kindness and a stupid sentimentality – I do not know what it is. The phrase 'inculcation of principles' is often used in connexion with moral education. There are indeed areas in which the 'inculcation of principles' is an appropriate phrase for the business of moral education: truth-telling, for example, and the sphere of justice. But more broadly, as Aristotle perceived, we are concerned with something not so aptly called the inculcation of principles, but rather the education of the emotions.

In this, there also lies something important for the question of fact and value. For while, as I have said, in the notion of an appropriate object of an emotion and in the less central issue of what emotions one should feel at all, there is obviously a valuational element that can differ from society to society, there are natural and indeed logical limits to the range of what objects given emotions can take, and what emotions a human being is expected to feel or, alternatively, to dispense with. Reflexion on these limits evidently could not in itself decide the merits of any existing system of human values as against another; for any existing system must exist within these limits. But it opens one way to something which many who feel the force of some distinction between fact and value have nevertheless thought should not and cannot be destroyed by the pressure of that distinction: the possibility of thinking through a moral outlook and reaching its presuppositions, in terms other than those merely of the logical consistency of its principles. It is the points of intersection between the more purely evaluational elements in a moral outlook, and an associated view of human nature, that provide most fruitfully both the sources of understanding, and the focus of criticism. Such a point of intersection will be found quite crucially in the moral significance of the emotions.

It is time, finally, to face up to Kant. For, if one is going to suggest that those things that a man does as the expression of certain emotions, can contribute to our view of him as a moral agent; if, further, one is going to say (as I have perhaps not yet said explicitly, but am very happy to) that one's conception of an admirable human being implies that he should be disposed to certain kinds of emotional response, and not to others; one has to try to answer the very powerful claim of Kant that this is impossible. Nor is this just a claim that turns up in some books sent out from Koenigsberg a long time ago; unless one has been very unusually brought up, it is a claim to be felt in oneself. It is a claim deep enough to make what I can hope to say now very inadequate; but I shall make one or two rather brisk suggestions that may help.

The Kantian objections to the idea that any emotionally governed action by a man can contribute to our assessment of him as a moral agent – or be a contribution, as Kant put it, to his moral worth – are, I think, basically three: that the emotions are too capricious; that they are passively experienced; that a man's proneness to experience them or not is the product of natural causation and (in that sense) fortuitously distributed.

First, they are too capricious. I may feel benevolent towards this man, not towards that, for all sorts of causes or reasons, some lying in my own changing moods. To act in accordance with these promptings is to act irrationally and (possibly) unjustly; but moral action is consistent action, done on principle. This is partly true; but in so far as it is, it tells only against the view that emotional motivation has everything to do with moral worth, not against the view that it has something to do with it. But in any case the point is partly wrong. For, first, it posits a crude view of the emotions themselves; it suggests that there is no way of adjusting one's emotional response in the light of other considerations, of applying some sense of proportion, without abandoning emotional motivation altogether; and this is certainly false, as can be seen from any sane man's attempts to distance and comprehend his emotions in matters which are not directly of moral concern, but are of emotional concern, to him. Moreover, I think – in a contrary direction now – that there is a certain moral woodenness or even insolence in this blank regard for consistency, in any case. It smacks of what I believe Maynard Keynes used to call, with reference to the deliberations of academic bodies, the Principle of Equal Unfairness: that if you can't do a good turn to everybody in a certain situation, you shouldn't do it to anybody. There are indeed human activities and relations in which impartiality and consistency are very much the point. But to raise on these notions a model of all moral relations is, just as Kant said it was, to make us each into a Supreme Legislator; a fantasy which represents, not the moral ideal, but the deification of man.

Next, the emotions are passively experienced, they happen to us

– but moral worth can attach only to what we freely do, to those respects in which we are rationally active. Here there is everything to be said; and I shall not try to take up the most immediate points, that emotionally motivated action can itself be free, if any is, and – against Kant himself – that his account leaves it largely unclear how bad action can be morally assessed. I shall make just two suggestions. The first is that we should not dismiss too hastily the idea that some element of passivity, some sense in which moral impulses prompt us, and courses of action are impressed on us, may itself make a vital contribution to the notion of moral sincerity. There are, after all, some points of resemblance between moral and factual convictions; and I suspect it to be true of moral, as it certainly is of factual, convictions that we cannot take very seriously a profession of them if we are given to understand that the speaker has just *decided* to adopt them. The idea that people decide to adopt their moral principles seems to me a myth, a psychological shadow thrown by a logical distinction; and if someone did claim to have done this, I think one would be justified in doubting either the truth of what he said or the reality of those moral principles. We see a man's genuine convictions as coming from somewhere deeper in him than that; and, by what is only an apparent paradox, what we see as coming from deeper in him, he – that is, the deciding 'he' – may see as coming from outside him. So it is with the emotions.

My second suggestion here is, once more, a moral thought, and a banal one: is it certain that one who receives good treatment from another more appreciates it, thinks the better of the giver, if he knows it to be the result of the application of principle, rather than the product of an emotional response? He may have needed, not the benefits of universal law, but some human gesture. It may be said that this is obviously true enough in many cases, but it has nothing to do with morality; it just shows that people place other sorts of value on human conduct besides moral value. Well, this may be said, and Kant indeed said it, but it leads to an uncomfortable dilemma. Either the recipient *ought* to prefer the ministrations of the moral man to the human gesture, which seems a mildly insane requirement; or, alternatively, if it be admitted that it is perfectly proper and rational of the recipient to have the preference he has, the value of moral men becomes an open question, and we can reasonably entertain the proposal that we should not seek to produce moral men, or very many of them, but rather those, whatever their inconsistencies, who make the human gesture. While there is something in that conclusion, there cannot be anything in it for Kant.

Lastly, Kant urges that men differ very much in their emotional make-up, as a result of many natural factors. As he remarks in a famous and moving passage, some find that the human gesture comes naturally, some do not. To make moral worth, the supreme value achievable by human beings, dependent on such features of character, psychologically determined as they are, would be to make the capacity for moral worth a species of natural advantage; and this is both logically incompatible with the notion of *the moral*, and also in some ultimate sense hideously unfair.

Here it is essential to keep in mind at once two facts about Kant. One is that his work contains the working out to the very end of that thought, a thought which in less thoroughgoing forms marks the greatest difference between moral ideas influenced by Christianity, and those of the ancient world. It is this thought, that moral worth must be separated from any natural advantage whatsoever, which, consistently pursued by Kant, leads to the conclusion that the source of moral thought and action must be located outside the empirically conditioned self. The second fact to be remembered, at the same time, is that Kant's work is in this respect a shattering failure, and the transcendental psychology to which it leads is, where not unintelligible, certainly false. No human characteristic which is relevant to degrees of moral esteem can escape being an empirical characteristic, subject to empirical conditions, psychological history and individual variation, whether it be sensitivity, persistence, imaginativeness, intelligence, good sense; or sympathetic feeling; or strength of will.

Certainly there are very important distinctions between straightforwardly natural advantages, with the sorts of admiration, love and esteem that apply to these, and those characteristics that elicit some more specifically moral reaction. But one cannot attribute to these distinctions that quite ultimate significance which they may have seemed to possess before one grasped the force of Kant's total, if unintended, *reductio ad absurdum*. In the light of that, we can still do much for these distinctions, but we have to do it in a different way, asking, for instance, what the point or significance of moral admiration may be – not just the social significance, but the significance in one's own thought.

Asking that, one may well find reason for thinking that no very adequate conception of moral admiration and its objects will be found in stressing, for instance, characteristics specially associated with monied or academic persons. One might say, reworking in more empirical form Kant's Rousseauesque moral republic, that some more democratic conception should be preferred; and among the relevant sorts of characteristic, the capacity for creative emotional response has the advantage of being, if not equally, at least broadly, distributed.

14
The idea of equality

The idea of equality is used in political discussion both in statements of fact, or what purport to be statements of fact – that men *are* equal – and in statements of political principles or aims – that men *should be* equal, as at present they are not. The two can be, and often are, combined: the aim is then described as that of securing a state of affairs in which men are treated as the equal beings which they in fact already are, but are not already treated as being. In both these uses, the idea of equality notoriously encounters the same difficulty: that on one kind of interpretation the statements in which it figures are much too strong, and on another kind much too weak, and it is hard to find a satisfactory interpretation that lies between the two.[1]

To take first the supposed statement of fact: it has only too often been pointed out that to say that all men are equal in all those characteristics in respect of which it makes sense to say that men are equal or unequal, is a patent falsehood; and even if some more restricted selection is made of these characteristics, the statement does not look much better. Faced with this obvious objection, the defender of the claim that all men are equal is likely to offer a weaker interpretation. It is not, he may say, in their skill, intelligence, strength, or virtue that men are equal, but merely in their being men: it is their common humanity that constitutes their equality. On this interpretation, we should not seek for some special characteristics in respect of which men are equal, but merely remind ourselves that they are all men. Now to this it might be objected that being men is not a respect in which men can strictly speaking be said to be *equal*; but, leaving that aside, there is the more immediate objection that if all that the statement does is to remind us that men are men, it does not do very much, and in particular does less than its proponents in political argument have wanted it to do. What looked like a paradox has turned into a platitude.

I shall suggest in a moment that even in this weak form the statement is not so vacuous as this objection makes it seem; but it must

[1] For an illuminating discussion of this and related questions, see R. Wollheim and I. Berlin, 'Equality', *Proceedings of the Aristotelian Society*, LVI (1955–6), pp. 281 *seq.*

be admitted that when the statement of equality ceases to claim more than is warranted, it rather rapidly reaches the point where it claims less than is interesting. A similar discomfiture tends to overcome the practical maxim of equality. It cannot be the aim of this maxim that all men should be treated alike in all circumstances, or even that they should be treated alike as much as possible. Granted that, however, there is no obvious stopping point before the interpretation which makes the maxim claim only that men should be treated alike in similar circumstances; and since 'circumstances' here must clearly include reference to what a man is, as well as to his purely external situation, this comes very much to saying that for every difference in the way men are treated, some general reason or principle of differentiation must be given. This may well be an important principle; some indeed have seen in it, or in something very like it, an essential element of morality itself. But it can hardly be enough to constitute the principle that was advanced in the name of *equality*. It would be in accordance with this principle, for example, to treat black men differently from others just because they were black, or poor men differently just because they were poor, and this cannot accord with anyone's idea of equality.

In what follows I shall try to advance a number of considerations that can help to save the political notion of equality from these extremes of absurdity and of triviality. These considerations are in fact often employed in political argument, but are usually bundled together into an unanalysed notion of equality in a manner confusing to the advocates, and encouraging to the enemies, of that ideal. These considerations will not enable us to define a distinct third interpretation of the statements which use the notion of equality; it is rather that they enable us, starting with the weak interpretations, to build up something that in practice can have something of the solidity aspired to by the strong interpretations. In this discussion, it will not be necessary all the time to treat separately the supposedly factual application of the notion of equality, and its application in the maxim of action. Though it is sometimes important to distinguish them, and there are clear grounds for doing so, similar considerations often apply to both. The two go significantly together: on the one hand, the point of the supposedly factual assertion is to back up social ideals and programmes of political action; on the other hand – a rather less obvious point, perhaps – those political proposals have their force because they are regarded not as gratuitously egalitarian, aiming at equal treatment for reasons, for instance, of simplicity or tidiness, but as affirming an equality which is believed in some sense already to exist, and to be obscured or neglected by actual social arrangements.

1 *Common humanity.* The factual statement of men's equality was seen, when pressed, to retreat in the direction of merely asserting the equality of men as men; and this was thought to be trivial. It is certainly insufficient, but not, after all, trivial. That all men are human is, if a tautology, a useful one, serving as a reminder that those who belong anatomically to the species *homo sapiens*, and can speak a language, use tools, live in societies, can interbreed despite racial differences, etc., are also alike in certain other respects more likely to be forgotten. These respects are notably the capacity to feel pain, both from immediate physical causes and from various situations represented in perception and in thought; and the capacity to feel affection for others, and the consequences of this, connected with the frustration of this affection, loss of its objects, etc. The assertion that men are alike in the possession of these characteristics is, while indisputable and (it may be) even necessarily true, not trivial. For it is certain that there are political and social arrangements that systematically neglect these characteristics in the case of some groups of men, while being fully aware of them in the case of others; that is to say, they treat certain men as though they did not possess these characteristics, and neglect moral claims that arise from these characteristics and which would be admitted to arise from them.

Here it may be objected that the mere fact that ruling groups in certain societies treat other groups in this way does not mean that they neglect or overlook the characteristics in question. For, it may be suggested, they may well recognise the presence of these characteristics in the worse-treated group, but claim that in the case of that group, the characteristics do not give rise to any moral claim; the group being distinguished from other members of society in virtue of some further characteristic (for instance, by being black), this may be cited as the ground of treating them differently, whether they feel pain, affection, etc., or not.

This objection rests on the assumption, common to much moral philosophy that makes a sharp distinction between fact and value, that the question whether a certain consideration is *relevant* to a moral issue is an evaluative question: to state that a consideration is relevant or irrelevant to a certain moral question is, on this view, itself to commit oneself to a certain kind of moral principle or outlook. Thus, in the case under discussion, to say (as one would naturally say) that the fact that a man is black is, by itself, quite irrelevant to the issue of how he should be treated in respect of welfare, etc., would, on this view, be to commit to oneself to a certain sort of moral principle. This view, taken generally, seems to me quite certainly false. The principle that men should be differentially treated in respect of welfare merely on grounds of their colour is not a special sort of moral principle, but (if anything) a purely arbitrary assertion of will, like that of some Caligulan ruler who decided to execute everyone whose name contained three 'R's.

This point is in fact conceded by those who practise such things as colour discrimination. Few can be found who will explain their practice merely by saying, 'But they're black: and it is my moral principle to treat black men differently from others.' If any reasons are given at all, they will be reasons that seek to correlate the fact of blackness with certain other considerations which are at least candidates for relevance to the question of how a man should be treated: such as insensitivity, brute stupidity, ineducable irresponsibility, etc. Now these reasons are very often rationalisations, and the correlations claimed are either not really believed, or quite irrationally believed, by those who claim them. But this is a different point; the argument concerns what counts as a moral reason, and the rationaliser broadly agrees with others about what counts as such – the trouble with him is that his reasons are dictated by his policies, and not conversely. The Nazis' 'anthropologists' who tried to construct theories of Aryanism were paying, in very poor coin, the homage of irrationality to reason.

The question of relevance in moral reasons will arise again, in a different connexion, in this paper. For the moment its importance is that it gives a force to saying that those who neglect the moral claims of certain men that arise from their human capacity to feel pain, etc., are *overlooking* or *disregarding* those capacities; and are not just operating with a special moral principle, conceding the capacities to these men, but denying the moral claim. Very often, indeed, they have just persuaded themselves that the men in question have those capacities in a lesser degree. Here it is certainly to the point to assert the apparent platitude that these men are also human.

I have discussed this point in connexion with very obvious human characteristics of feeling pain and desiring affection. There are, however, other and less easily definable characteristics universal to humanity, which may all the more be neglected in political and social arrangements. For instance, there seems to be a characteristic which might be called 'a desire for self-respect'; this phrase is perhaps not too happy, in suggesting a particular culturally-limited, bourgeois value, but I mean by it a certain human desire to be identified with what one is doing, to be able to realise purposes of one's own, and not to be the instrument of another's will unless one has willingly accepted such a rôle. This is a very inadequate and in some ways rather empty specification of a human desire; to a better specification, both philosophical reflexion and the evidences of psychology and anthropology would be relevant. Such investigations enable us to understand more deeply, in respect of the desire I have gestured towards and of similar characteristics, what it is to be human; and of what it is to be human, the apparently trivial statement of men's equality as men can serve as a reminder.

2 *Moral capacities.* So far we have considered respects in which men can be counted as all alike, which respects are, in a sense, negative: they concern the capacity to suffer, and certain needs that men have, and these involve men in moral relations as the recipients of certain kinds of treatment. It has certainly been a part, however, of the thought of those who asserted that men were equal, that there were more positive respects in which men were alike; that they were equal in certain things that they could do or achieve, as well as in things that they needed and could suffer. In respect of a whole range of abilities, from weight-lifting to the calculus, the assertion is, as was noted at the beginning, not plausible, and has not often been supposed to be. It has been held, however, that there are certain other abilities, both less open to empirical test and more essential in moral connexions, for which it is true that men are equal. These are certain sorts of moral ability or capacity, the capacity for virtue or achievement of the highest kind of moral worth.

The difficulty with this notion is that of identifying any purely moral capacities. Some human capacities are more relevant to the achievement of a virtuous life than others: intelligence, a capacity for sympathetic understanding, and a measure of resoluteness would generally be agreed to be so. But these capacities can all be displayed in non-moral connexions as well, and in such connexions would naturally be thought to differ from man to man like other natural capacities. That this is the fact of the matter has been accepted by many thinkers, notably, for instance, by Aristotle. But against this acceptance, there is a powerful strain of thought that centres on a feeling of ultimate and outrageous absurdity in the idea that the achievement of the highest kind of moral worth should depend on natural capacities, unequally and fortuitously distributed as they are; and this feeling is backed up by the observation that these natural capacities are not themselves the bearers of the moral worth, since those that have them are as gifted for vice as for virtue.

This strain of thought has found many types of religious expression; but in philosophy it is to be found in its purest form in Kant. Kant's view not only carries to the limit the notion that moral worth cannot depend on contingencies, but also emphasises, in its picture of the Kingdom of Ends, the idea of *respect* which is owed to each man as a rational moral agent – and, since men are equally such agents, is owed equally to all, unlike admiration and similar attitudes, which are commanded unequally by men in proportion to their unequal possession of different kinds of natural excellence. These ideas are intimately connected in Kant, and it is not possible to understand his moral theory unless as much weight is given to what he says about the Kingdom of Ends as is always given to what he says about duty.

The very considerable consistency of Kant's view is bought at what would generally be agreed to be a very high price. The detachment of moral worth from all contingencies is achieved only by making man's characteristic as a moral or rational agent a transcendental characteristic; man's capacity to will freely as a rational agent is not dependent on any empirical capacities he may have – and, in particular, is not dependent on empirical capacities which men may possess unequally – because, in the Kantian view, the capacity to be a rational agent is not itself an empirical capacity at all. Accordingly, the respect owed equally to each man as a member of the Kingdom of Ends is not owed to him in respect of any empirical characteristics that he may possess, but solely in respect of the transcendental characteristic of being a free and rational will. The ground of the respect owed to each man thus emerges in the Kantian theory as a kind of secular analogue of the Christian conception of the respect owed to all men as equally children of God. Though secular, it is equally metaphysical: in neither case is it anything empirical *about* men that constitutes the ground of equal respect.

This transcendental, Kantian conception cannot provide any solid foundation for the notions of equality among men, or of equality of respect owed to them. Apart from the general difficulties of such transcendental conceptions, there is the obstinate fact that the concept of 'moral agent', and the concepts allied to it such as that of responsibility, do and must have an empirical basis. It seems empty to say that all men are equal as moral agents, when the question, for instance, of men's responsibility for their actions is one to which empirical considerations are clearly relevant, and one which moreover receives answers in terms of different degrees of responsibility and different degrees of rational control over action. To hold a man responsible for his actions is presumably the central case of treating him as a moral agent, and if men are not treated as equally responsible, there is not much left to their equality as moral agents.

If, without its transcendental basis, there is not much left to men's equality as moral agents, is there anything left to the notion of the *respect* owed to all men? This notion of 'respect' is both complex and unclear, and I think it needs, and would repay, a good deal of investigation. Some content can, however, be attached to it; even if it is some way away from the ideas of moral agency. There certainly is a distinction, for instance, between regarding a man's life, actions or character from an aesthetic or technical point of view, and regarding them from a point of view which is concerned primarily with what it is *for him* to live that life and do those actions in that character. Thus from the technological point of view, a man who has spent his life in trying to make a certain machine which could not possibly work is merely a failed inventor, and in compiling a catalogue of those whose efforts have contributed to the sum of technical achievement, one must 'write him off': the fact that he devoted himself to this useless task with constant effort and so on, is merely irrelevant. But from a human point of view, it is clearly not irrelevant: we are concerned with him, not merely as 'a failed inventor', but as a man who wanted to be a successful inventor. Again, in professional relations and the world of work, a man operates, and his activities come up for criticism, under a variety of professional or technical titles, such as 'miner' or 'agricultural labourer' or 'junior executive'. The technical or professional attitude is that which regards the man solely under that title, the human approach that which regards him as *a man who has* that title (among others), willingly, unwillingly, through lack of alternatives, with pride, etc.

That men should be regarded from the human point of view, and not merely under these sorts of titles, is part of the content that might be attached to Kant's celebrated injunction 'treat each man as an end in himself, and never as a means only'. But I do not think that this is all that should be seen in this injunction, or all that is concerned in the notion of 'respect'. What is involved in the examples just given could be explained by saying that each man is owed an effort at identification: that he should not be regarded as the surface to which a certain label can be applied, but one should try to see the world (including the label) from his point of view. This injunction will be based on, though not of course fully explained by, the notion that men are conscious beings who necessarily have intentions and purposes and see what they are doing in a certain light. But there seem to be further injunctions connected with the Kantian maxim, and with the notion of 'respect', that go beyond these considerations. There are forms of exploiting men or degrading them which would be thought to be excluded by these notions, but which cannot be excluded merely by considering how the exploited or degraded men see the situation. For it is precisely a mark of extreme exploitation or degradation that those who suffer it do *not* see themselves differently from the way they are seen by the exploiters; either they do not see themselves as anything at all, or they acquiesce passively in the rôle for which they have been cast. Here we evidently need something more than the precept that one should respect and try to understand another man's consciousness of his own activities; it is also that one may not suppress or destroy that consciousness.

All these I must confess to be vague and inconclusive considerations, but we are dealing with a vague notion: one, however, that we possess, and attach value to. To try to put these matters properly in order would be itself to try to reach conclusions about several fundamental questions of moral philosophy. What we must ask here is what these ideas have to do with equality. We started with the notion of men's equality as moral agents. This notion appeared unsatisfactory, for different reasons, in both an empirical and a transcendental interpretation. We then moved, *via* the idea of 'respect', to the different notion of regarding men not merely under professional, social, or technical titles, but with consideration of their own views and purposes. This notion has at least this much to do with equality: that the titles which it urges us to look behind are the conspicuous bearers of social, political, and technical *inequality*, whether they refer to achievement (as in the example of the inventor) or to social rôles (as in the example of work titles). It enjoins us not to let our fundamental attitudes to men be dictated by the criteria of technical success or social position, and not to take them at the value carried by these titles and by the structures in which these titles place them. This does not mean, of course, that the more fundamental view that should be taken of men is in the case of every man the same: on the contrary. But it does mean that each man is owed the effort of understanding, and that in achieving it, each man is to be (as it were) abstracted from certain conspicuous structures of inequality in which we find him.

These injunctions are based on the proposition that men are beings who are necessarily to some extent conscious of themselves and of the world they live in. (I omit here, as throughout the discussion, the clinical cases of people who are mad or mentally defective, who always constitute special exceptions to what is in general true of men.) This proposition does not assert that men are equally conscious of themselves and of their situation. It was precisely one element in the notion of exploitation considered above that such consciousness can be decreased by social action and the environment; we may add that it can similarly be increased. But men are at least potentially conscious, to an indeterminate degree, of their situation and of what I have called their 'titles', are capable of reflectively standing back from the rôles and positions in which they are cast; and this reflective consciousness may be enhanced or diminished by their social condition.

It is this last point that gives these considerations a particular relevance to the political aims of egalitarianism. The mere idea of regarding men from 'the human point of view', while it has a good deal to do with politics, and a certain amount to do with equality, has nothing specially to do with political equality. One could, I think, accept this as an ideal, and yet favour, for instance, some kind of hierarchical society, so long as the hierarchy maintained itself without compulsion, and there was human understanding between the orders. In such a society, each man would indeed have a very conspicuous title which related him to the social structure; but it might be that most people were aware of the human beings behind the titles, and found each other for the most part content, or even proud, to have the titles that they had. I do not know whether anything like this has been true of historical hierarchical societies; but I can see no inconsistency in someone's espousing it as an ideal, as some (influenced in many cases by a sentimental picture of the Middle Ages) have done. Such a person would be one who accepted the notion of 'the human view', the view of each man as something more than his title, as a valuable ideal, but rejected the ideals of political equality.

Once, however, one accepts the further notion that the degree of man's consciousness about such things as his rôle in society is itself in some part the product of social arrangements, and that it can be increased, this ideal of a stable hierarchy must, I think, disappear. For what keeps stable hierarchies together is the idea of necessity, that it is somehow fore-ordained or inevitable that there should be these orders; and this idea of necessity must be eventually undermined by the growth of people's reflective consciousness about their rôle, still more when it is combined with the thought that what they and the others have always thought about their rôles in the social system was the product of the social system itself.

It might be suggested that a certain man who admitted that people's consciousness of their rôles was conditioned in this way might nevertheless believe in the hierarchical ideal: but that in order to preserve the society of his ideal, he would have to make sure that the idea of the conditioning of consciousness did not get around to too many people, and that this consciousness about their rôles did not increase too much. But such a view is really a very different thing from its naive predecessor. Such a man, no longer himself 'immersed' in the system, is beginning to think in terms of compulsion, the deliberate *prevention* of the growth of consciousness, which is a poisonous element absent from the original ideal. Moreover, his attitude (or that of rulers similar to himself) towards the other people in the ideal society must now contain an element of condescension or contempt, since he will be aware that their acceptance of what they suppose to be necessity is a delusion. This is alien to the spirit of human understanding on which the original ideal was based. The hierarchical idealist cannot escape the fact that certain things which can be done decently without self-consciousness can, with self-consciousness, be done only hypocritically. This is why even the rather hazy and very general notions that I have tried to bring together in this section contain some of the grounds of the ideal of political equality.

3 *Equality in unequal circumstances.* The notion of equality is invoked not only in connexions where men are claimed in some sense all to be equal, but in connexions where they are agreed to be unequal, and the question arises of the distribution of, or access to, certain goods to which their inequalities are relevant. It may be objected that the notion of equality is in fact misapplied in these connexions, and that the appropriate ideas are those of fairness or justice, in the sense of what Aristotle called 'distributive justice', where (as Aristotle argued) there is no question of regarding or treating everyone as equal, but solely a question of distributing certain goods in proportion to men's recognised inequalities.

I think it is reasonable to say against this objection that there is some foothold for the notion of equality even in these cases. It is useful here to make a rough distinction between two different types of inequality, inequality of *need* and inequality of *merit*, with a corresponding distinction between goods – on the one hand, goods demanded by the need, and on the other, goods that can be earned by the merit. In the case of needs, such as the need for medical treatment in case of illness, it can be presumed for practical purposes that the persons who have the need actually desire the goods in question, and so the question can indeed be regarded as one of distribution in a simple sense, the satisfaction of an existing desire. In the case of merit, such as for instance the possession of abilities to profit from a university education, there is not the same presumption that everyone who has the merit has the desire for the goods in question, though it may, of course, be the case. Moreover, the good of a university education may be legitimately, even if hopelessly, desired by those who do not possess the merit; while medical treatment or unemployment benefit are either not desired, or not legitimately desired, by those who are not ill or unemployed, i.e. do not have the appropriate need. Hence the distribution of goods in accordance with merit has a competitive aspect lacking in the case of distribution according to need. For these reasons, it is appropriate to speak, in the case of merit, not only of the distribution of the good, but of the distribution of the opportunity of achieving the good. But this, unlike the good itself, can be said to be distributed equally to everybody, and so one does encounter a notion of *general* equality, much vaunted in our society today, the notion of equality of opportunity.

Before considering this notion further, it is worth noticing certain resemblances and differences between the cases of need and of merit. In both cases, we encounter the matter (mentioned before in this paper) of the relevance of reasons. Leaving aside preventive medicine, the proper ground of distribution of medical care is ill health: this is a necessary truth. Now in very many societies, while ill health may work as a necessary condition of receiving treatment, it does not work as a sufficient condition, since such treatment costs money, and not all who are ill have the money; hence the possession of sufficient money becomes in fact an additional necessary condition of actually receiving treatment. Yet more extravagantly, money may work as a sufficient condition by itself, without any medical need, in which case the reasons that actually operate for the receipt of this good are just totally irrelevant to its nature; however, since only a few hypochrondriacs desire treatment when they do not need it, this is, in this case, a marginal phenomenon.

When we have the situation in which, for instance, wealth is a further necessary condition of the receipt of medical treatment, we can once more apply the notions of equality and inequality: not now in connexion with the inequality between the well and the ill, but in connexion with the inequality between the rich ill and the poor ill, since we have straightforwardly the situation of those whose needs are the same not receiving the same treatment, though the needs are the ground of the treatment. This is an irrational state of affairs.

It may be objected that I have neglected an important distinction here. For, it may be said, I have treated the ill health and the possession of money as though they were regarded on the same level, as 'reasons for receiving medical treatment', and this is a muddle. The ill health is, at most, a ground of the *right* to receive medical treatment; whereas the money is, in certain circumstances, the causally necessary condition of securing the right, which is a different thing. There is something in the distinction that this objection suggests: there is a distinction between a man's rights, the reasons why he should be treated in a certain way, and his power to secure those rights, the reasons why he can in fact get what he deserves. But this objection does not make it inappropriate to call the situation of inequality an 'irrational' situation: it just makes it clearer what is meant by so calling it. What is meant is that it is a situation in which reasons are insufficiently *operative*; it is a situation insufficiently controlled by reasons – and hence by reason itself. The same point arises with another form of equality and equal rights, equality before the law. It may be said that in a certain society, men have equal rights to a fair trial, to seek redress from the law for wrongs committed against them, etc. But if a fair trial or redress from the law can be secured in that society only by moneyed and educated persons, to insist that everyone *has* this right, though only these particular persons can *secure* it, rings hollow to the point of cynicism: we are concerned not with the abstract existence of rights, but with the extent to which those rights govern what actually happens.

Thus when we combine the notions of the *relevance* of reasons, and the *operativeness* of reasons, we have a genuine moral weapon, which can be applied in cases of what is appropriately called unequal treatment, even where one is not concerned with the equality of people as a whole. This represents a strengthening of the very weak principle mentioned at the beginning of this paper, that for every difference in the way men are treated, a reason should be given: when one requires further that the reasons should be relevant, and that they should be socially operative, this really says something.

Similar considerations will apply to cases of merit. There is, however, an important difference between the cases of need and merit, in respect of the relevance of reasons. It is a matter of logic that particular sorts of needs constitute a reason for receiving particular sorts of good. It is, however, in general a much more disputable question whether certain sorts of merit constitute a reason for receiving certain sorts of good. For instance, let it be supposed for the sake of argument, that private schools provide a superior type of education, which it is a good thing to receive. It is then objected that access to this type of education is unequally distributed, because of its cost: among children of equal promise or intelligence, only those from wealthy homes will receive it, and, indeed, children of little promise or intelligence will receive it, if from wealthy homes; and this, the objection continues, is irrational.

The defender of the private school system might give two quite different sorts of answer to this objection; besides, that is, the obvious type of answer which merely disputes the facts alleged by the objector. One is the sort of answer already discussed in the case of need: that we may agree, perhaps, that children of promise and intelligence have a right to a superior education, but in actual economic circumstances, this right cannot always be secured. The other is more radical: this would dispute the premiss of the objection that intelligence and promise are, at least by themselves, the grounds for receiving this superior type of education. While perhaps not asserting that wealth itself constitutes the ground, the defender of the system may claim that other characteristics significantly correlated with wealth are such grounds; or, again, that it is the purpose of this sort of school to maintain a tradition of leadership, and the best sort of people to maintain this will be people whose fathers were at such schools. We need not try to pursue such arguments here. The important point is that, while there can indeed be genuine disagreements about what constitutes the relevant sort of merit in such cases, such disagreements must also be disagreements about the nature of the good to be distributed. As such, the disagreements do not occur in a vacuum, nor are they logically free from restrictions. There is only a limited number of reasons for which education could be regarded as a good, and a limited number of purposes which education could rationally be said to serve; and to the limitations on this question, there correspond limitations on the sorts of merit or personal characteristic which could be rationally cited as grounds of access to this good. Here again we encounter a genuine strengthening of the very weak principle that, for differences in the way that people are treated, reasons should be given.

We may return now to the notion of equality of opportunity; understanding this in the normal political sense of equality of opportunity for *everyone in society* to secure certain goods. This notion is introduced into political discussion when there is question of the access to certain goods which, first, even if they are not desired by everyone in society, are desired by large numbers of people in all sections of society (either for themselves, or, as in the case of education, for their children), or would be desired by people in all sections of society if they knew about the goods in question and thought it possible for them to attain them; second, are goods which people may be said to earn or achieve; and third, are goods which not all the people who desire them can have. This third condition covers at least three different cases, however, which it is worth distinguishing. Some desired goods, like positions of prestige, management, etc., are *by their very nature* limited: whenever there are some people who are in command or prestigious positions, there are necessarily others who are not. Other goods are *contingently* limited, in the sense that there are certain conditions of access to them which in fact not everyone satisfies, but there is no intrinsic limit to the numbers who might gain access to it by satisfying the conditions: university education is usually regarded in this light nowadays, as something which requires certain conditions of admission to it which in fact not everyone satisfies, but which an indefinite proportion of people might satisfy. Third, there are goods which are *fortuitously* limited, in the sense that although everyone or large numbers of people satisfy the conditions of access to them, there is just not enough of them to go round; so some more stringent conditions or system of rationing have to be imposed, to govern access in an imperfect situation. A good can, of course, be both contingently and fortuitously limited at once: when, due to shortage of supply, not even the people who are qualified to have it, limited in numbers though they are, can in every case have it. It is particularly worth distinguishing those kinds of limitation, as there can be significant differences of view about the way in which a certain good is limited. While most would now agree that high education is contingently limited, a Platonic view would regard it as necessarily limited.

Now the notion of equality of opportunity might be said to be the notion that a limited good shall in fact be allocated on grounds which do not *a priori* exclude any section of those that desire it. But this formulation is not really very clear. For suppose grammar school education (a good perhaps contingently, and certainly fortuitously, limited) is allocated on grounds of ability as tested at the age of 11; this would normally be advanced as an example of equality of opportunity, as opposed to a system of allocation on grounds of parents' wealth. But does not the criterion of ability exclude *a priori* a certain section of people, viz. those that are not able – just as the other excludes *a priori* those who are not wealthy? Here it will obviously be said that this was not what was meant by *a priori* exclusion: the present argument just equates this with exclusion of anybody, i.e. with the mere existence of some condition that has to be satisfied. What then is *a priori* exclusion? It must mean exclusion on grounds *other* than those appropriate or rational for the good in question. But this still will not do as it stands. For it would follow from this that so long as those allocating grammar school education on grounds of wealth thought that such grounds were appropriate or rational (as they might in one of the ways discussed above in connexion with private schools), they could sincerely describe their system as one of equality of opportunity – which is absurd.

Hence it seems that the notion of equality of opportunity is more complex than it first appeared. It requires not merely that there should be no exclusion from access on grounds other than those appropriate or rational for the good in question, but that the grounds considered appropriate for the good should themselves be such that people from all sections of society have an equal chance of satisfying them. What now is a 'section of society'? Clearly we cannot include under this term sections of the populace identified just by the characteristics which figure in the grounds for allocating the good – since, once more, any grounds at all must exclude some section of the populace. But what about sections identified by characteristics which are *correlated* with the grounds of exclusion? There are important difficulties here: to illustrate this, it may help first to take an imaginary example.

Suppose that in a certain society great prestige is attached to membership of a warrior class, the duties of which require great physical strength. This class has in the past been recruited from certain wealthy families only; but egalitarian reformers achieve a change in the rules, by which warriors are recruited from all sections of the society, on the results of a suitable competition. The effect of this, however, is that the wealthy families still provide virtually all the warriors, because the rest of the populace is so under-nourished by reason of poverty that their physical strength is inferior to that of the wealthy and well nourished. The reformers protest that equality of opportunity has not really been achieved; the wealthy reply that in fact it has, and that the poor now have the opportunity of becoming warriors – it is just bad luck that their characteristics are such that they do not pass the test. 'We are not,' they might say, 'excluding anyone *for* being poor; we exclude people for being weak, and it is unfortunate that those who are poor are also weak.'

This answer would seem to most people feeble, and even cynical. This is for reasons similar to those discussed before in connexion with equality before the law; that the supposed equality of opportunity is quite empty – indeed, one may say that it does not really exist – unless it is made more effective than this. For one knows that it could be made more effective; one knows that there is a causal connexion between being poor and being undernourished, and between being undernourished and being physically weak. One supposes further that something could be done – subject to whatever economic conditions obtain in the imagined society – to alter the distribution of wealth. All this being so, the appeal by the wealthy to the 'bad luck' of the poor must appear as disingenuous.

It seems then that a system of allocation will fall short of equality of opportunity if the allocation of the good in question in fact works out unequally or disproportionately between different sections of society, if the unsuccessful sections are under a disadvantage which could be removed by further reform or social action. This was very clear in the imaginary example that was given, because the causal connexions involved are simple and well known. In actual fact, however, the situations of this type that arise are more complicated, and it is easier to overlook the causal connexions involved. This is particularly so in the case of educational selection, where such slippery concepts as 'intellectual ability' are involved. It is a known fact that the system of selection for grammar schools by the '11+' examination favours children in direct proportion to their social class, the children of professional homes having proportionately greater success than those from working-class homes. We have every reason to suppose that these results are the product, in good part, of environmental factors; and we further know that imaginative social reform, both of the primary educational system and of living conditions, would favourably affect those environmental factors. In these circumstances, this system of educational selection falls short of equality of opportunity.[2]

This line of thought points to a connexion between the idea of equality of opportunity, and the idea of equality of persons, which is stronger than might at first be suspected. We have seen that one is not really offering equality of opportunity to Smith and Jones if one contents oneself with applying the same criteria to Smith and Jones

[2] See on this C. A. R. Crosland, 'Public Schools and English Education', *Encounter* (July 1961).

at, say, the age of 11; what one is doing there is to apply the same criteria to Smith as affected by favourable conditions and to Jones as affected by unfavourable but curable conditions. Here there is a necessary pressure to equal up the conditions: to give Smith and Jones equality of opportunity involves regarding their conditions, where curable, as themselves part of what is done to Smith and Jones, and not part of Smith and Jones themselves. Their identity, for these purposes, does not include their curable environment, which is itself unequal and a contributor of inequality. This abstraction of persons in themselves from unequal environments is a way, if not of regarding them as equal, at least of moving recognisably in that direction; and is itself involved in equality of opportunity.

One might speculate about how far this movement of thought might go. The most conservative user of the notion of equality of opportunity is, if sincere, prepared to abstract the individual from some effects of his environment. We have seen that there is good reason to press this further, and to allow that the individuals whose opportunities are to be equal should be abstracted from more features of social and family background. Where should this stop? Should it even stop at the boundaries of heredity? Suppose it were discovered that when all curable environmental disadvantages had been dealt with, there was a residual genetic difference in brain constitution, for instance, which was correlated with differences in desired types of ability; but that the brain constitution could in fact be changed by an operation.[3] Suppose further that the wealthier classes could afford such an operation for their children, so that they always came out top of the educational system; would we then think that poorer children did not have equality of opportunity, because they had no opportunity to get rid of their genetic disadvantages?

Here we might think that our notion of personal identity itself was beginning to give way; we might well wonder *who were* the people whose advantages and disadvantages were being discussed in this way. But it would be wrong, I think, to try to solve this problem simply by saying that in the supposed circumstances our notion of personal identity would have collapsed in such a way that we could no longer speak of the individuals involved – in the end, we could still pick out the individuals by spatio-temporal criteria, if no more. Our objections to the system suggested in this fantasy must,

[3] A yet more radical situation – but one more likely to come about – would be that in which an individual's characteristics could be *pre-arranged* by interference with the genetic material. The dizzying consequences of this I shall not try to explore.

I think, be moral rather than metaphysical. They need not concern us here. What is interesting about the fantasy, perhaps, is that if one reached this state of affairs, the individuals would be regarded as in all respects equal in themselves – for in themselves they would be, as it were, pure subjects or bearers of predicates, everything else about them, including their genetic inheritance, being regarded as a fortuitous and changeable characteristic. In these circumstances, where everything about a person is controllable, equality of opportunity and absolute equality seem to coincide; and this itself illustrates something about the notion of equality of opportunity.

I said that we need not discuss here the moral objections to the kind of world suggested in this fantasy. There is, however, one such point that is relevant to the different aspects of equality that have been discussed in this paper as a whole. One objection that we should feel to the fantasy world is that far too much emphasis was being placed on achieving high ability; that the children were just being regarded as locations of abilities. I think we should still feel this even if everybody (with results hard to imagine) were treated in this way; when not everybody was so treated, the able would also be more successful than others, and those very concerned with producing the ability would probably also be over-concerned with success. The moral objections to the excessive concern with such aims are, interestingly, not unconnected with the ideal of equality itself; they are connected with equality in the sense discussed in the earlier sections of this paper, the equality of human beings despite their differences, and in particular with the complex of notions considered in the second section under the heading of 'respect'.

This conflict within the ideals of equality arises even without resort to the fantasy world. It exists today in the feeling that a thorough-going emphasis on equality of opportunity must destroy a certain sense of common humanity which is itself an ideal of equality.[4] The ideals that are felt to be in conflict with equality of opportunity are not necessarily other ideals of equality – there may be an independent appeal to the values of community life, or to the moral worth of a more integrated and less competitive society. Nevertheless, the idea of equality itself is often invoked in this connexion, and not, I think, inappropriately.

If the idea of equality ranges as widely as I have suggested, this type of conflict is bound to arise with it. It is an idea which, on the one hand, is invoked in connexion with the distribution of certain

[4] See, for example, Michael Young, *The Rise of the Meritocracy* (London: Thames and Hudson, 1958).

goods, some at least of which are bound to confer on their possessors some preferred status or prestige. On the other hand, the idea of equality of respect is one which urges us to give less consideration to those structures in which people enjoy status or prestige, and to consider people independently of those goods, on the distribution of which equality of opportunity precisely focuses our, and their, attention. There is perhaps nothing formally incompatible in these two applications of the idea of equality: one might hope for a society in which there existed both a fair, rational, and appropriate distribution of these goods, and no contempt, condescension, or lack of human communication between persons who were more and less successful recipients of the distribution. Yet in actual fact, there are deep psychological and social obstacles to the realisation of this hope; as things are, the competitiveness and considerations of prestige that surround the first application of equality certainly militate against the second. How far this situation is inevitable, and how far in an economically developed and dynamic society, in which certain skills and talents are necessarily at a premium, the obstacles to a wider realisation of equality might be overcome, I do not think that we know: these are in good part questions of psychology and sociology, to which we do not have the answers.

When one is faced with the spectacle of the various elements of the idea of equality pulling in these different directions, there is a strong temptation, if one does not abandon the idea altogether, to abandon some of its elements: to claim, for instance, that equality of opportunity is the only ideal that is at all practicable, and equality of respect a vague and perhaps nostalgic illusion; or, alternatively, that equality of respect is genuine equality, and equality of opportunity an inegalitarian betrayal of the ideal – all the more so if it were thoroughly pursued, as now it is not. To succumb to either of these simplifying formulae would, I think, be a mistake. Certainly, a highly rational and efficient application of the ideas of equal opportunity, unmitigated by the other considerations, could lead to a quite inhuman society (if it worked – which, granted a well-known desire of parents to secure a position for their children at least as good as their own, is unlikely). On the other hand, an ideal of equality of respect that made no contact with such things as the economic needs of society for certain skills, and human desire for some sorts of prestige, would be condemned to a futile Utopianism, and to having no rational effect on the distribution of goods, position, and power that would inevitably proceed. If, moreover, as I have suggested, it is not really known how far, by new forms of social structure and of education, these conflicting claims might be reconciled, it is all the more obvious that we should not throw one set of claims out of the window; but should rather seek, in each situation, the best way of eating and having as much cake as possible. It is an uncomfortable situation, but the discomfort is just that of genuine political thought. It is no greater with equality than it is with liberty, or any other noble and substantial political ideal.

15
Egoism and altruism

I shall be concerned with issues of egoism as against morality, and with the question whether there are any rational considerations by which an egoist who is resistant to moral claims could, under the unlikely assumption that he was prepared to listen, be persuaded to be less resistant to them. The discussion is all about antagonism between egoism and morality, and does not say anything, or imply much, about the proper place of egoistic concerns within morality. That is in many ways a more important subject, but I find it necessary to get clear about this one first.

I have placed the issue in terms of 'morality', but the title refers to *altruism*. I take altruism, in the sense I intend, to be a necessary feature of a morality. It follows that a principle to the effect that everyone ought exclusively to pursue his own interests – the principle of what is rather quaintly called 'ethical egoism' – would not constitute a morality or be a moral principle. There perhaps could be such a principle, and I shall refer to it occasionally, but it will, in my use of the terms, stand in contrast to morality. That remark is not meant to be much more than an announcement of terminology, and is not intended to be worth arguing about. However, I think there is a point in using the terminology in this way: it helps to emphasise what I take to be one basic and universal function of morality.

Since in this use, morality implies altruism, a correspondingly minimal interpretation is intended of 'altruism'. In particular, it is not to be taken, as the term very commonly is, to mean a disposition to strenuous and unsolicited benevolent interference. Rather, it refers to a general disposition to regard the interests of others, merely as such, as making some claim on one, and, in particular, as implying the possibility of limiting one's own projects. Two questions at once arise, especially when such a disposition is regarded as a necessary part of morality: how important is it, and how extensive does it have to be in application? The questions are, moreover, connected. But we can head off these questions, I think, for the present purpose, by assuming the plausible general principles that any morality will regulate the relations of an agent to various groups of persons of varying degrees of social remoteness from him; and that altruism is a disposition which is to some degree necessary in regulating his relations with the most extensive group to which the morality applies, including the most socially remote. This admits the possibility of a tribal morality – there may be human beings to which the morality does not apply at all. All this leaves numerous and interesting problems about how to apply such notions as 'social remoteness' in different sorts of society: but the assumptions I have mentioned seem to be at least clear and substantial enough to cover central cases. One last preliminary, an important one, is that the disposition of altruism, so introduced, neither necessarily implies nor necessarily excludes a tendency to have sympathetic or similar feelings. The course of this argument may provide reasons for moving in fact towards a more Hume-like interpretation of the disposition, but no answers are presupposed on that matter by the way in which it is introduced.

Egoism is contrasted with that disposition, and is to be taken for the purposes of the present discussion as the position of an amoralist who rejects, is uninterested in, or resists this aspect of moral considerations, and hence moral considerations; and is concerned solely with his own interests. Beyond that point, it is implicit in the method that I shall adopt that I cannot yet say much more about him: for my question is put in the form, how much can he be allowed of human life consistently with his rejection of altruism – where that means, of course, such that *he* is consistent in rejecting or being uninterested in altruism, and not just that a consistent account can be given of him. It is important, I think, to approach the question this way round: the arguments tend to occur in the wrong place if one first tries to determine in detail what is the territory of egoism, and then asks how it is related to altruism. Rather, one should first draw a line on the edge of altruism, and then ask how much territory that might leave for an egoist.

We shall reasonably be unimpressed by the egoist if the territory which he can consistently and rationally occupy is too constricted. Of course a man can be consistent by having no, or very few, thoughts; and that some dismal self-seeking brute can satisfy the egoist specification I shall take to be of little interest. The egoist will be more interesting vis-à-vis morality if as well as having a fair range of territory to operate in, he should be moreover moderately attractive, where that means moderately attractive to us. He might, at the limit, even come out as a rather splendid figure – though there are certainly limits (which I shall not try to discuss here) to the respects in which he can consistently regard himself as a splendid figure.

What I shall first do is to consider a set of arguments designed to show that in order to occupy any territory at all, or any minimally extensive territory, the egoist already commits himself to something or other supposedly involving altruism. The very first argument of all, however, comes even before that, and tries to rest everything on a fact of his existence, namely that he and his activities are variously parasitic on other people, and in particular on their altruism. 'Parasitic' is uniformly a term of abuse in philosophy, as regularly elsewhere, something which neglects the truth that hosts often need parasites as much as parasites need hosts. The point here, however, is simply that he could not do and be what he does and is unless others were otherwise. He operates in society, fulfilling his desires and projects involves society, and we can add that the very existence of his desires and projects is the product of society, not just causally but conceptually. And society implies a degree of minimal altruism in order to operate.

Various of the facts in this familiar structure could be disputed, but in the present context, there is no point in doing so, since even if it is all true, it is all irrelevant, since the egoist can agree to it without disturbance. We can distinguish between an *external* and an *internal* justification of altruism. If it is true that altruism is necessary for society, and society for human life, including that of an egoist, then externally that provides a justification of altruism: we can see, among other things, why any society has to bring it about that most of its members have to some degree altruistic dispositions. It shows that there cannot be too many exceptions. It provides no argument for one who is an exception, however, that he should cease to be so: it gets no internal hold on his position. For his being an exception does not collapse the structure, as is shown by the fact that he is actually an exception; so the only means of bringing the external argument to bear on him is by some such consideration as that if everyone were like him, he could not exist – that is to say, via an imagined universalisation. But an imagined universalisation will merely be of no interest to him. It is essentially a form of moral argument; a natural, though not inevitable, way of putting its force in such a case is to appeal to the idea that it is not fair for him to rest his egoism on others' altruistic shoulders. Such an argument could not possibly have any force with the egoist unless he had already given up being one.

A mere fact about the egoist's existence, then, or at least that fact, is not going to undo him before we even start. If we now turn to properties of the egoist's thought and practice, there are certain arguments which aim to show that even a minimal commitment to rationality on his part is going to qualify his egoism. We might see in these arguments a version of the basically Kantian enterprise of trying to elicit altruism from certain structural conditions on rational practical thought; as opposed to the basically Humean claim that it is not such conditions, but rather a certain desire or sentiment, that constitutes the vital step in the direction of altruism. I hope that the considerations that follow will both give a rather more determinate sense to that debate than it has sometimes possessed, and also suggest an answer on the Humean side.

It might be suggested, first, that there is a certain question which the egoist has to be able to ask if he is to be able to reflect rationally on his action at all, namely a deliberative practical question; that this has to be expressed in the form 'what ought I to do?' or some equivalent; and that that question already imports considerations of what he, and anyone else in the same circumstances, *ought* to do, and that imports a moral consideration. Thus the ability to ask any deliberative question at all, which is certainly a requirement on rationality, already lands one in morality. This exceedingly simple argument fails for at least three reasons. First, it is not true that *the* deliberative question necessarily takes the form 'what ought I to do?' or anything else which even looks as though it had some moral implication: 'what shall I do?' will do just as well, and natural expressions in other languages ('quid faciam?' 'que faire?') lack the misleading overtone. Second, even if 'ought' were inescapable, it would not necessarily import a morality, but at most the principle of the universal application of reasons, a different matter which I shall come back to later. Third, even if 'ought' were inescapable and imported a morality, it would not be 'morality' in the sense used here, namely that in which it implies altruism: at the very best, it would be in that more extensive sense in which 'ethical egoism' constitutes a morality. But any interest which that last observation might have is diminished by its being doubly – and it is doubly – contrary to fact. Altogether, the simple approach through the deliberative question is perhaps not very interesting, but it is as well to get it out of the way.

It is worth considering another type of 'inescapable question' argument, not now about a question which the egoist cannot avoid asking, but one which, it might be argued, he cannot avoid answering (at least to himself). If he is considering self-interested conduct harmful to others, the question might be put 'is it all right for him to do this?', and it might be said both that if he is rational he must have an answer to this question, and that either answer is damaging for his egoism; since if he says 'no', he is condemned out of his own mouth, while if he says 'yes', he commits himself to the view that it must be all right for others similarly placed to pursue hostile courses against him, which (it might be said) is to will or accept something contrary to his own interests.

I think that there is just one thing which the egoist would not be rational in saying, and that apart from that he has more than one consistent and rational way of coping with the question. What he would not be rational in saying is that it is all right for him, but not all right for others. For if that is to be taken as having serious content, it does irresistibly invite the question of what is special about him, and to that question he has no answer which is not either mad or involves him in taking off into some values other than egoistic ones. They may not themselves necessarily be moral or altruistic values – but their introduction even so will mean at least that he is not adequately articulating and defending his egoism, which is what he was supposed to be doing. To take a particular case, the question 'what is special about you?' might elicit such answers as:

1 I'm me
2 I'm Caligula
3 I'm called 'Caligula'
4 I'm the Emperor.

Of these, (4) represents not egoism, but autocracy; and that example does duty for many others which would invoke, if not a moral, at least a non-egoistic value, and are therefore beside the point. (3) lays his claim on an exceedingly insecure contingency and cannot possibly represent what he wants, all the more so since others might share this property (even if in this particular case that would be both improbable and dangerous). (2) escapes that difficulty, but leaves the question draughtily open, of what it is to be Caligula. The best candidate would seem to be some set of properties – though Caligula himself could not specify it – such that if they had not been co-instantiated, there would have been no such person as Caligula. But if that could be provided at all, then there would be questions, unwanted and unanswerable, about the relevant connexions between that set of properties and the special rights of Caligula. (1), finally, represents a point too tiny to rest any justification on at all; as an answer to 'what is special about you?' it certainly delivers too little. One might be disposed to claim that what is wrong with it is that anyone else could equally say *that*, but that would not be strictly accurate, since we can credit those words with just enough content to admit that if someone else uttered them, they would not be making the same statement. But it is a small quibble, since the egoist can scarcely be credited with having said what was special about him if the only sentence he could use to express it is the sort of sentence which on the lips of others would equally and inevitably make a true statement – even if it is not the same true statement.

So there seems to be reason for him not to say that it would be all right for him, but not for others. If giving a sincere answer, perhaps the best he could give would be that of saying that he does not use the notion expressed by 'all right' at all. It might be wondered whether he could just opt out of using the notion: a man can after all opt out of using all sorts of notions, and it will not stop their applying – a man's refusing to use the concept 'green' does not stop things being green, and similarly, it may be said, the question will still remain whether what he is doing is all right, even if he refuses to consider it. What that objection says is not altogether wrong, in the sense that it rightly makes the point that whether moral concepts apply to the egoist's projects is not just a function of whether the egoist wants them to. But it does not get us any further in arguing with him, since we knew already that he was declining to measure the world by moral notions by which others do measure it; what was needed was an argument to show that he gets into intellectual trouble in so refusing. That is not provided by the insistence that the 'all right' question does apply – it merely reiterates that he ought not to refuse.

However, as an alternative to opting out of 'all right', he could also coherently allow that it *was* all right for others also to embark on self-interested conduct, for instance against him. That would not be in a sense in which he was subscribing to a general principle under which it was thought to be a good thing that everyone should pursue their own interests. That would involve him in taking an impersonal point of view about whether it would be a good thing to happen, which he is not disposed to take; it might well involve him in giving reasons, which his egoism cannot conceivably involve him in giving, as to why that would be a good thing to happen; and it might even involve him in an evident defeat, of having to inhibit some of his own projects as possibly prejudicial to free-trade elsewhere, like a laisser-faire business-man confronted with the dilemma of anti-trust legislation. None of that can be his concern. But he can comprehensibly say 'it is all right for them to do those things', if he is taken to mean something like 'let them get on with it, if they want to: you are not going to find me moralising about it'. Which is not to say that he has permitted them to do it, or registered that it is permitted; just as a really permissive society would not so much be one in which those unpermitted things were permitted, as one in which they did not need to be permitted.

It may be said that even if we take 'all right' out of a structure in which it registers permission as contrasted with what is forbidden, nevertheless any sensible use of it must commit the egoist to something he cannot really want: he must be – as we put it in setting up the dilemma originally – 'willing or accepting' something contrary to his own interests. But in what senses can the egoist 'accept' or refuse to accept the hostile conduct of others? He can, of course, register that it is going to happen, and our man is doing that. And he can decide to oppose it or not oppose it; and the minimal use of 'all right' commits our man to nothing on that score – in the sense of 'accept' which can matter to him, he is not committed to accepting it. Still less, to willing it. The idea of the amoral man, if he says 'all right', willing the hostile conduct of others is certainly misplaced. One might be led to entertain it through the idea that 'all right' must embody some 'prescriptive' force, which has the effect, as it were, of telling them to do it. But this must be a mistake. The phrase we gave our man, 'let them get on with it', does not have the force of telling them to get on with it – or at least, not in any sense in which it will be contrary to his will if they do not. (A man who faced with assailants shouts 'Come and get me!' will not have had his will frustrated if they then run away.)

Let us now consider another tack for bringing down the egoist. He is allowed to be rational: he has, and reflectively considers, reasons for doing one thing rather than another. Thus *A* may want *X*, to get which it is necessary to take aggressive action against *B*; thus he recognises that want as a reason for acting in that way. But the notion of a reason is a universal notion, and if that want is a reason for *A* to act hostilely against *B* in those circumstances, then a similar want would be a reason in relevantly similar circumstances for *B* to act hostilely against *A*. Thus, it may be suggested, there is a reason for *B* to act hostilely against *A* in those circumstances; but *A* should be reluctant (the argument continues) to acknowledge this, because he must want to assert that there is reason (i.e. *A*'s interests) for *B* not to act hostilely against *A*. As these last formulations may have betrayed, there is some difficulty in rendering this line of argument even initially plausible. It rightly draws attention to the universality of reasons in the one sense in which that indeed obtains, namely that if *P* constitutes a reason for A to do X in certain circumstances, then *P* equally constitutes a reason for *B* to do X in similar circumstances (if we include relevant differences between A and *B* in the circumstances). This constitutes a certain symmetry of reasons. But it provides nothing at all in the way of a grounding for altruism. The hypothetical reasons that would obtain for *B* in the second, imagined, circumstance would yield altruistic conclusions only if they led to the conclusion with regard to that second situation, that A had reason to co-operate, or *B* had reason to desist. That, by the principle of symmetry, is on exactly the same footing as the proposal, with regard to the original situation, that *B* has reason to co-operate, or A reason to desist. There is no reason at all why A, the original egoist, should accept any of these conclusions: the argument certainly yields him no reason to desist, and he will not suppose that *B*, if he has any sense, has reason to co-operate.

If anything did make the argument plausible, it would be a shift from '*B* has reason to act hostilely' to something like 'there is reason in favour of *B*'s acting hostilely', where that latter might carry the implication, lacking in the former, that everyone who properly considers the matter would have reason to promote that outcome. The difference has been well characterised by Nagel[1] in his distinction between 'subjective' and 'objective' reasons, objective reasons being provided by a structure in which reasons are 'not just universal reasons in the sense that anyone can have them, but in addition reasons for anyone to promote what they apply to'. Nagel himself has argued that certain pressures of rationality tend to move one from the first level of reasons to the second, an idea which he supports by considerations drawn from the structure of self-interest itself. I shall not attempt to deal with Nagel's complex argument here; it is enough that Nagel himself does not claim demonstrative force for the move

[1] Thomas Nagel, *The Possibility of Altruism* (Oxford: Clarendon Press, 1970), p. 91. Nagel's book is well named: it is the possibility, rather than the necessity, of altruism that he is concerned with. Points at which, in a longer treatment, I should want to disagree with his argument are first, that his views about the integration of rational self-interested action over time precisely emphasise the difference, for an agent, between *his* prospects and *others'* prospects, and therefore tend to widen the egoistic gap which an analogy with prudence is later supposed to help us in crossing; and second, the eventual operation of impersonal or objective reasons as Nagel describes it incurs, unsurprisingly, the basic Kantian difficulty of its being obscure how the reasons one has for promoting a state of affairs, impersonally described, are related to the more primitive phenomenon of one's just wanting something. I hope to make these rather telegraphic comments more comprehensible on another occasion.

to impersonal reasons, and therefore even if Nagel were right, the egoist would not under pain of inconsistency have to move from the level of subjective reasons, which he certainly must acknowledge, to that of objective reasons, which would indeed land him in trouble.

It is somewhere around this point that Moore produced a multiple confusion on this subject, delivered in a characteristically emphatic manner: egoism, he said, asserted 'that *each* man's happiness is the sole good – that a number of different things are *each* the only good thing there is – an absolute contradiction'.[2] It is not easy to see why any version of egoism should be thought to have this consequence. So-called 'ethical egoism' might be taken as saying that the only good thing was the situation of each man's pursuing his own happiness. Our egoist, if he was ill-advised to use the language of goodness at all, would presumably say that the only good thing was his (the egoist's) own happiness: but it would not be very sensible of him to say this, since it naturally tends to imply the claim, at the level of objective reasons, that there is reason for everyone to pursue his (the egoist's) happiness, a claim which he has no grounds, but also no need, to make. Still less has any egoist the need to say that each man's happiness is severally the only good thing there is, an idiocy which it seems to have been left to Moore to ascribe to him.

Last in the catalogue of arguments designed to restrict or eliminate the egoist's territory, we can consider the claim that even if we can construct an agent without altruistic concerns and who nevertheless displays a measure of rationality, such a creature could not understand or have any insight into other human beings, grasp that they are in pain, and so forth, as ordinary persons, not entirely egoistic, can. That consideration, if true, could be applied in two slightly different ways. For one thing, it might be said that there is a purely cognitive task in which ordinary humans can succeed, but this creature would fail. Second, it might be recalled that we thought it would be more interesting if the egoist could be at least mildly attractive to us; and while no thorough-going egoist can be unqualifiedly attractive, the psychopath we seem to be left with if this objection is correct is unattractive to a revealingly extreme degree. This second line depends in some part on the first; for what would make our creation psychopathically repulsive would not be merely a high degree of selfishness, but an inhuman inability even to see the point or understand the source of human reactions, and that would be ultimately an aspect of his cognitive failings.

The claim that lack of altruism would imply such a cognitive

[2] *Principia Ethica* (Cambridge, 1903), p. 99.

failing is perhaps implicit in certain Wittgensteinian doctrines in the philosophy of mind, which claim that the understanding that someone is in pain involves a display of a wide range of characteristic human behaviour in pain situations, including sympathy and assistance. But if this is the claim, then it can at best only be taken as a principle generally true about society, and not exceptionless (like, and perhaps connected with, the points about the 'external' justification of altruism). For it is evidently untrue that no man can know that another is in pain unless he is disposed to help him. On the contrary, if he, and the situation, are sufficiently disagreeable, he may show that he knows that he is in pain precisely by not being disposed to help him. There are differences between cruelty, brutality, indifference, insensitivity, and psychopathic unawareness, and much would need to be said about them; but I see no reason to suppose that it would in any way support the idea that lack of altruism would necessarily indicate a purely cognitive failure.

In this area, there is a great deal to be said about what an egoist would be missing in terms of human contact, understanding, and so forth; and also, when that question is pressed, and when we go into exactly how extensive the territory is which by this time we seem to have conceded him, we will be faced with increasingly difficult questions about what exactly egoism is, and what satisfactions the egoist can at this sort of level consistently be allowed. I am going to approach one small aspect of those questions, by a different route, in the last part of this paper. But to complete the present part of the argument, I shall add three very brief remarks on the question of what he is missing. First, claims at this sort of level about what he is missing are likely to have an increasingly empirical character. Second, considerations designed to make him wake up to what he is missing are unlikely to take the form just of pointing out that he has unsatisfied desires, or that there are unrealised sources of pleasure – they will be more like arousing him or turning him round to a new idea of what might be worthwhile; they are therefore more like the things, if there are any, which would dispose him to altruism, and are likely not to be much like arguments. Third, and last, while it is no doubt true that the egoist as we have considered him would miss out on many familiar satisfactions, this point should not be pressed in too complacently a combative way by defenders of morality and altruism; for in the case of many human beings at least, the business of forming and sustaining the required moral dispositions itself involves the loss of many satisfactions, not merely in general (as almost all would agree), but also in those very areas of human contact which are supposedly specially lost to the egoist. Everywhere there is loss, and to suppose that those dispositions demanded on the one hand by the external justification, and on the other by the drives of the self, can be made unwastefully to coincide is always illusion, whether it be of Hegelian self-realisation, adjustment therapy, or the overcoming of alienation in the ultimate community.

Let us start again now in a different place. Kantians make the distinction between motivations which are emotional, grounded in desire, and particular, as against motivations which are universal, rational and of principle. The step to morality involves a discontinuous step to the latter. For Hume, there are desires of different degrees of generality, involving objects with different degrees of remoteness and independence from the subject: the slide towards morality is a slide along these continua. Connected with this is the point from which we started, that for Kant impersonal and intrapersonal altruism is grounded in the structure of practical reason; for Hume, it is grounded in a special sort of desire or sentiment. We have already seen some reasons for rejecting Kant – though, by the structure of the argument, which is negative and rejects various proposals in his support, our procedure has necessarily not been final or conclusive. Leaving that there, I shall now go on to try to give a definite sense to Hume's claims, and (I hope) give reason for thinking them correct.

The trouble with the egoist is not that it is *desires* that he expresses, nor that they are *his* desires – the trouble is that all his desires are for things *for him*. I shall adopt a device employed by Kenny,[3] of replacing the variety of 'want' expressions (such as 'I want to . . .', 'I want *x*', 'I want A to . . .', etc.) uniformly with the propositional formula 'I want that *p*', where '*p*' specifies the state of affairs which, if it came about, would satisfy the want. All the egoist's wants are either of the form 'I want that I . . .', where this is followed by something which specifies his getting something, entering into a desirable state, or whatever; or else, if they are not of that form, they depend on another desire which is of that form, in the sense that it is only because he has that latter desire that he has the former, and that if the latter went away or were satisfied in some other way, the former would go away. Thus an egoist might have a desire of which the natural propositional formulation was 'I want that Smith pay the money into the bank': this does not have 'I' in the propositional content. However, it will, in the egoist's

[3] *Action, Emotion and Will* (London: Routledge, 1963).

case, depend on some desire which does, as for instance a desire that he receive some money. I shall use the term 'I-desire' for a desire whose propositional content requires 'I' or related expressions ('my' etc.); and the term 'non-I desire' for one that does not. I shall speak of a *basically* non-I desire, to refer to a non-I desire which does not depend on an I-desire.

Just as there are non-I desires which depend on I-desires, so there are I-desires which depend on non-I desires. Thus a man might want to help someone, that is, want that he help them. That could be a through-and-through I-desire, in the sense that if *he* could not do the helping, then all desires he had relative to that situation would be cancelled. But equally, his desire to help that person may depend on, be a special application of, the desire that they be helped, which is a non-I desire. It is no part of my thesis that it is at all easy to tell an I-desire from a non-I desire. All I claim is that both sorts of desire are possible: questions about how frequent or how pure non-I desires are, are just as difficult as in fact they are.

It may be worth, quite briefly, getting rid of a couple of muddled philosophical arguments which might be used to support the view, to which some people are inordinately attached, that there cannot be such a thing as a non-I desire. I shall consider a couple of epistemological muddles. More prevalent and powerful than these, in fact, are age-old confusions about desire and pleasure, for instance the confusion between desiring the satisfaction of one's desire (which is a trivial derivative of having a desire), and desiring one's own satisfaction. These confusions have been exposed countless times, and there would be no interest in doing it again.

First, an argument about knowledge. It might be said that if I want that *p*, then I must want that I know that *p*, and hence that every desire must be an I-desire at least to that extent. But even if the principle were true, it would not show that all non-I desires were basically I-desires: my desire to know that *p* might itself depend on the desire that *p*. In any case, the principle seems mistaken, even in the liberal form (which would be the only defensible one) that if I want that *p*, then I must want that *at some time or other* I know that *p*. Imagine an old rationalist whose daughter wants to be a nun. He loves his daughter, and wants her to be what she wants to be. But he cannot bear the idea of her being a nun. Despairing of reconciling his basic wants, he just wants that she be a nun but he not know that she is.

Second, a related muddled argument about belief. I am, necessarily, not in a position to distinguish the two following states of affairs: that *p*, and that I believe that *p*. Hence I am not in a position to distinguish the desire that *p*, and the desire that I believe that *p*, since the satisfactions of those two just are the two indistinguishable items mentioned. Hence every desire that *p* is indistinguishable from a desire that I believe that *p*, and there are no really non-I desires. But the premisses of this argument are just, in the required sense, false. The first premiss is true only in this boring sense, that to the question '*p*?' and 'do you believe that *p*?' I cannot standardly return different answers. But consider now a proposition *p* whose truth-conditions lie in the future. Clearly I can give different answers to the questions 'will *p* be true?' and 'will you believe that *p* is true?'; the thesis correspondingly cannot hold that there is no distinction between the desire that *p* then, and the desire that I believe then that *p*. The best it can do is to say that one cannot distinguish between the desire that *p* then, and the desire that I believe now that *p* then. But I evidently can – apart from the question about me, one desire is about then and the other is about now.

Examples can also be found in which the two desires quite clearly come apart. This is a little hard, not because the two desires are not always distinct, but because three things very naturally go together – my wanting that *p*, my wanting to have some beliefs on the subject of whether *p*, and my wanting my beliefs to be true. These, taken together, produce the two desires in question. But there are cases in which the second of these three things is missing (as in the rationalist's daughter case). There are even cases in which the second is present but the third is missing – they are rare, because of our dislike of deliberately and consciously deceiving ourselves, but they are possible. Thus a man might be faced, by some manipulator, with the choice between the following: on the one hand, that *p* should be the case later but that he (the subject) should after a few minutes believe that not-*p*; on the other hand, that not-*p* should be the case later, but that he, after a few minutes, should believe that *p*. No conceptual manoeuvres could possibly persuade a man who wanted that *p* that he had to choose the latter alternative. If *p* involved someone else's welfare, this set-up could constitute something of a test for altruism.

The resistance to believing in non-I desires may in some people be due to the belief that they are necessarily altruistic. It may therefore help, and it is anyway important, to see that they are by no means all altruistic, or directed to others' welfare. Among possible non-I desires which are not, one might mention, first and nearest to altruism, a concern for the welfare of material objects, as one might want the sideboard to be kept polished. Next, there are aesthetic wants, as that a picture be better displayed, or a certain building revealed, or another building pulled down – people leave money for such things. It is a question notoriously discussed in the theory of aesthetic value, whether such a want, if clear-headed, would have to involve the want that somebody should see these things – but it certainly does not involve any want that the man himself should see them. Related, but not the same, would be some fanciful or cranky wants, as again eccentrics can seek to provide for in their wills: some madman, not believing in life after death and so not expecting to be a witness of it, might want a chimpanzees' tea party to be held in the cathedral, just because it would be such a striking event. Lastly, and most importantly, there is the inverse case of desire for another's welfare: sheer malice, the selfless desire that another be harmed, whether one comes to know about it, or has anything to do with it, or not. A cynic might suggest that this was the only purely non-I desire that existed.

It is of course possible that somebody should entertain one of these wants, particularly of the testamentary kind, in a rather confused state of mind; his vivid fantasy of the eventual outcome might run his non-I desire rather close to being the I-desire of wanting to be there to witness it.[5] But he can pull himself back from that, and still retain his desire; and it is important that the undoubted fact that men enjoy thinking about the realisation of a non-I desire, as of other desires, does not mean that what they really want is to think about its being realised. Rather more difficult, and not yet dealt with by the classification, is the case of desires for such things as posthumous fame, such as that of Herostratus, who, *avidus malae famae* as it is said, burned down the temple of Artemis at Ephesus to gain a niche in history.[6] Such desires pass the original test for being I-desires, but the sense in which 'I' has to occur in specifying the propositional content is peculiar – my desire is for a state of affairs in which I am mentioned, and my necessary occurrence in the propositional content is intensional. For the present purpose, there is no point in trying to do more with such cases – we can leave them on one side, and deal only with I-desires where my involvement in the desired state of affairs is straightforward, contemporaneous and extensional, and my desire is that I should later get, have, enjoy, witness etc. whatever it may be.

[5] For related issues, see 'Imagination and the self', pp. 39–40.

[6] It is a nice point in the theory of reference, whether he succeeded; the only identification we have of him, so far as I know, is just this.

Suppose that a man has a basically non-I desire, and that is – moreover – a desire for someone else's welfare: thus, it might be a desire that Mary be looked after. This is a desire to the effect that a certain state of affairs obtain, which we may label '*S*'. *S* does not contain the man nor does a specification of it essentially refer to him, or imply his existence or any relation of his to anything or anybody in S, for instance Mary: while some specifications of *S* might refer to him, for instance by specifying Mary as his Mary, the same state of affairs could equally be specified without making such a reference. Least of all does the specification of S, that which satisfies the desire, have to mention the desire itself.

This being so, S could obtain without our man existing at all, and this our man should be able to reflect on. We can invite him to consider two possibilities for a world without him, one in which S comes about and one in which it does not. So far as is compatible with that, the possibilities are maximally alike: it just comes down to a question whether his desire that S obtain is satisfied or not – which, since it is a non-I desire involved, is of course not the same question as whether in the projected circumstances he gets what he wants or not.[7]

It must follow from what we have already put in, that he prefers one of these possibilities to the other; the one, of course, that contains S. It is important to see what this kind of preference does *not* do. It does not yield any more complex or exigent level of reasons than do I-desires: this can be seen by considering other non-I desires which are not benevolent or other-regarding. They equally involve, as the testamentary examples illustrated, the picture of a world without the desirer, but they can be as arbitrary or weakly supported by reasons as one likes. Of course, a man must be able to say what it is about the two worlds, one with S and one without it, which makes the difference – but that is just to specify his desire, something he can be asked to do with any desire whatsoever. The non-I preference for a world containing S does not, moreover, yield any stronger *impersonal demands* than does an I-desire; a man's having this preference has no implication for his thinking that others ought to share it, nor does he suppose that others' having such preferences implies that he ought to share theirs. Nor does it imply that he thinks that it is impersonally a good thing that Mary should be looked after, in the sense that it would be reasonable for others to promote this end.

[7] For a relevant ambiguity in this notion, cf. 'The self and the future', pp. 48 *seq.*

However, what his preference, being of the benevolent kind it is, does import is the thought that it would be a good thing for Mary, or in Mary's interests, if *S* came about. Granted his desires, that thought (other things being equal) is adequate to motivate him to action. The feature of *S* which motivates him to action to promote *S* is not anything about him or his desires, neither of which even occur in its specification, but rather something about Mary. A consideration which does not refer to himself motivates him, because he has a certain desire. Similarly, the altruist is more generally motivated by thoughts to the effect that someone needs help or that someone's interests are involved, and he is motivated by those thoughts because he has a certain kind of disposition. He is motivated by the thought 'they need help', not by the thought 'they need help and I have an altruistic disposition'; similarly our man is motivated by the thought 'Mary needs help', not by the thought 'Mary needs help and I have a desire that she be helped.' The structure of our man's thoughts in these respects is in fact no different from the altruist's, nor are either his thoughts or his desires any more concerned with himself than are the altruist's.

What is defective with him vis-à-vis the altruist is rather that his non-I benevolent dispositions and desires are so restricted, both because their objects are (relative to their needs) randomly selected, and also because he has no sympathy for others who have non-I desires for persons in whom they are interested. It is possible that reflection on the character of his own non-I desires may help him to extend his sympathies in the required directions. But it is not necessarily true, psychologically, that that should be so; nor (a different point) is there any purely rational requirement on him, so far as I can see, that it should be so. No purely rational process can require a man to move from I-desires to non-I desires; nor from particular benevolent non-I desires to more general altruistic dispositions. What we can say, however, is that so far as the logical structure of these attitudes are concerned, there is a bigger difference involved in the first step than in the second. Between the second and third of these attitudes there is a basic similarity in the motivating thought.

These considerations, together with the negative results of the first part of this enquiry, should encourage the view that both in moral theory and also in moral psychology, it is not the Kantian leap from the particular and the affective to the rational and universal that makes all the difference; it is rather the Humean step – that is to say, the first Humean step – from the self to someone else.

Bibliography

A list of my philosophical articles published to date, including the items in this book. It leaves out book reviews, with the exception of items (7) and (25). Items printed in this volume are marked with an asterisk.

1 'Tertullian's Paradox' in Flew and MacIntyre eds., *New Essays in Philosophical Theology* (London: SCM Press, 1955).
2 *'Personal Identity and Individuation', PAS LVII (1956–7).
3 'Metaphysical Arguments' in Pears ed., *The Nature of Metaphysics* (London: Macmillan, 1957).
4 'Pleasure and Belief', *PASS* XXXIII (1959).
5 'Descartes', article in Urmson ed., *A Dictionary of Philosophy and Philosophers* (London: Hutchinson, 1960).
6 *'Personal Identity and Bodily Continuity – A reply', *Analysis* 21 (1960).
7 *'Mr Strawson on Individuals', *Philosophy* XXXVI (1961).
8 'The Individual Reason', *Listener*, 16 November 1961.
9 'Democracy and Ideology', *Political Quarterly* (1961).
10 *'The Idea of Equality' in Laslett and Runciman eds., *Politics, Philosophy and Society* II (Oxford: Blackwell, 1962).
11 'Aristotle on the Good: A formal Sketch', *Philosophical Quarterly* (1962).
12 'La Certitude du Cogito' in *Cahiers de Royaumont* IV (Paris: Editions Minuit, 1962)
13 'Freedom and the Will' (14) Postcript in Pears ed., *Freedom and the Will* (London: Macmillan, 1963).
15 *'Imperative Inference', *Analysis supplementary volume* (1963).
16 'Hume on Religion' in Pears ed., *David Hume* (London: Macmillan, 1963).
17 *'Ethical Consistency', PASS XXXIX (1965).
18 *'Morality and the Emotions', Inaugural Lecture, Bedford College, London, 1965; in *Morality and Moral Reasoning*, ed. Casey (London: Methuen, 1971).
19 *'Imagination and the Self', British Academy Annual Philosophical Lecture, 1966.
20 *'Consistency and Realism', *PASS* XL (1966).
21 'Descartes' (22) 'Hampshire S.N.' (23) 'Rationalism', articles in Edwards, ed. *The Encyclopedia of Philosophy* (New York: The Macmillan Company & The Free Press; London: Collier-Macmillan, 1967).
24 'The Certainty of the Cogito' in Doney ed., *Descartes, A Collection*

of Critical Essays (New York: Doubleday, 1967). Translation of (12).

25 *'Knowledge and Meaning in the Philosophy of Mind', *Philosophical Review* LXXVII (1968).

26 'Descartes' Ontological Argument: a Comment' (27) 'Existence-Assumptions in Practical Thinking' (reply to Körner) in Margolis ed., *Fact and Existence* (Oxford: Blackwell, 1969).

28 *'The Self and the Future', *Philosophical Review* LXXIX (1970).

29 *'Are Persons Bodies?' in Spicker ed., *The Philosophy of the Body* (Chicago: Quadrant Books, 1970).

30 'Genetics and Moral Responsibility' in *Morals and Medicine* (London: BBC Publications, 1970).

31 *'Deciding to Believe' in Kiefer and Munitz eds., *Language, Belief and Metaphysics* (Albany: State University of N.Y. Press, 1970).

32 'The Temporal Ordering of Perceptions and Reactions' (reply to O'Shaughnessy) in Sibley ed., *Perception: A Philosophical Symposium* (London: Methuen, 1971).

33 'Conversation on Moral Philosophy' in Magee ed., *Modern British Philosophy* (London: Secker and Warburg, 1971).

34 'Knowledge and Reasons' in *Entretiens de Helsinki* (I.I.P.) (The Hague: Martinus Nijhoff, 1972).

35 'The Analogy of City and Soul in Plato's Republic' in Mourelatos and other eds., *Exegesis and Argument: Studies in Greek Philosophy Presented to Gregory Vlastos, Phronesis supplementary volume* 1 (Assen: Van Gorcum, 1973).

36 *'The Makropulos Case: reflections on the tedium of immortality', first published in this volume (1973).

37 *'Egoism and altruism', first published in this volume (1973).

PAS: *Proceedings of the Aristotelian Society.*
PASS: Supplementary volumes to those *Proceedings.*